Praise for Jeff Madrick's

Seven Bad Ideas

"'Zombie ideas,' it's been said, are those that should have been killed by evidence, but refuse to die. Even more obdurate are the axioms of orthodox economics, upon which pernicious policies are erected. Mythbuster Madrick, in clear and compelling prose, demolishes seven of the biggest of these. May they (hopefully) rest in peace."

—Mike Wallace, Pulitzer Prize–winning historian and coauthor of *Gotham*

"Fascinating and provocative. . . . Madrick makes a strong, persuasively argued case, offering a refreshing take on the political and fiscal policies that have defined our era, and the questionable foundations on which they uncomfortably rest." —*PopMatters*

"A readable, useful economic text. Somewhere, John Maynard Keynes is smiling." —*Kirkus Reviews*

Jeff Madrick

Seven Bad Ideas

Jeff Madrick, a former economics columnist for *Harper's* and *The New York Times*, is a regular contributor to *The New York Review of Books* and the editor of *Challenge* magazine. He is visiting professor of humanities at The Cooper Union and director of the Bernard L. Schwartz Rediscovering Government Initiative at the Century Foundation. His books include *Age of Greed*, *The End of Affluence*, and *Taking America*. He has also written for *The Washington Post*, the *Los Angeles Times*, *Institutional Investor*, *The Nation*, *The American Prospect*, *The Boston Globe*, and *Newsday*. He lives in New York City.

www.jeffmadrick.com

@JeffMadrick

Also by Jeff Madrick

Seven Bad Ideas

Seven Bad Ideas

HOW MAINSTREAM ECONOMISTS HAVE
DAMAGED AMERICA AND THE WORLD

Jeff Madrick

VINTAGE BOOKS

A Division of Penguin Random House LLC

New York

FIRST VINTAGE BOOKS EDITION, AUGUST 2015

Copyright © 2014 by Jeff Madrick

All rights reserved. Published in the United States by Vintage Books,
a division of Penguin Random House LLC, New York, and distributed in
Canada by Random House of Canada, a division of Penguin Random House
Ltd., Toronto. Originally published in hardcover in the United States by
Alfred A. Knopf, a division of Penguin Random House LLC, New York, in 2014.

Vintage and colophon are registered trademarks of
Penguin Random House LLC.

The Library of Congress has cataloged the Knopf edition as follows:
Madrick, Jeffrey G.
Seven bad ideas : how mainstream economists have damaged America and
the world / Jeff Madrick.
pages   cm
1. United States—Economic conditions—2009–
2. United States—Economic policy—2009–   3. Economics—United States.
4. Financial crises—United States.   I. Title.
HC106.84.M336 2014   330.973—dc23   2014006237

Vintage Books Trade Paperback ISBN: 978-0-307-95072-7
eBook ISBN: 978-0-307-96119-8

Author photograph © Michael Lionstar
Book design by M. Kristen Bearse

www.vintagebooks.com

Printed in the United States of America
10   9   8   7   6   5   4   3   2   1

To economists who do their job well,
and to Kim

Contents

Seven Bad Ideas

Introduction: Damage

Economists' most fundamental ideas contributed centrally to the financial crisis of 2008 and the Great Recession that followed—the worst economic calamity since the Great Depression. These ideas are so embedded in a way of thinking about the economy that many of the economists who have embraced them for a generation now are unable to criticize themselves seriously and are unaware of how narrowly focused their views of a working economy have become. Over the past thirty years, their way of thinking has in fact time and again damaged America and the world—the damage outweighing what good has been accomplished—yet we continue to take economists terribly seriously. Their culpability has scarcely been cited. Why?

I am referring to orthodox economists here, by which I mean the large majority of Western-trained academics whose political leanings fall somewhere between the right and the center-left. They would, of course, balk at such a description of their politics; many of them claim they are objective and have no political predilections that affect their economic ideas. They are considered mainstream, and they often teach or were trained at the most prestigious universities, among them Princeton, MIT, Stanford, Harvard, and the more openly conservative University of Chicago, as well as the countless others with similar curricula. I will usually not use the word "orthodox" when referring to these economists, and when discussing an economist who clearly does not fit into this category, I will make that clear.

Almost no economist predicted the 2008 financial crisis and its wretched aftermath. Even when a handful of economists warned of dangers, only one or two anticipated how devastating the economic consequences would be. Quite the contrary, shortly before the 2008 mortgage market collapse, many of the most respected economists in academia claimed they had mastered the craft of controlling the economy. Robert Lucas, who is on the right politically, said in his 2003 presidential address to the American Economic Association that the "central problem of depression prevention has been solved." Olivier Blanchard, a respected left-of-center economist from MIT and the chief economist at the International Monetary Fund, proclaimed as late as 2008—the year of the crisis—that "the state of [macroeconomics] is good."

Macroeconomics is the study of the national income, or the gross domestic product, and how its growth can be assured. A recession is defined by a significant decline in GDP and a rise in unemployment, and minimizing the occurrence and duration of recessions is a key objective of macroeconomics. Economists thought they had figured out how to do this.

The failure to predict the 2008 crisis is not the only grave mistake economists made. Of far greater concern is that their ideas contributed to or justified much of the financial behavior that caused the crash and the deep recession that followed. These are the harmful ideas that gained credibility in the 1970s and reached the level of doctrine over the succeeding decades, doing harm along the way.

In the mid-2000s, Ben Bernanke, an admired Princeton professor, claimed that the economy had been maintaining an ideal temperature—not too hot and not too cold—since the early 1980s. National income grew fairly steadily, with little threat of either unstable GDP or unstable inflation, both of which characterized the painful 1970s. (Inflation, a sustained rise in prices, is usually measured as an annual rate of increase.) Recessions, if painful, were short, and recoveries were quick. Like many of his esteemed colleagues, Bernanke, who succeeded Alan Greenspan to become chairman of the Federal Reserve Board in 2006, called the period from the early 1980s to around 2005 the "Great Moderation." At the end of 2005, a year before his death, Milton Friedman, the political conservative who was the most influential American economist of the last quarter of the twentieth century, more than agreed. Just when the issuance of risky mortgages was reaching its height, he confidently told the journalist Charlie Rose, "The stability of the economy is greater than it has ever been in our history; we really are in remarkably good shape. It's amazing that people go around and write stories about how bad the economy is, how it's in trouble."

Friedman was the godfather of the newly prevailing economic theory, which amounted to a laissez-faire revolution among the orthodox, including the moderate left. Government's role in the economy, they said, should be far more limited. Some observers called this hands-off policy the laissez-faire experiment, but "experiment" implies an open-minded analysis of the costs and benefits of the new approach. It was quite the opposite, as we shall see—a closed case presided over by closed minds.

During the period in which Friedman and his colleagues across most of the political spectrum lauded themselves, the economy fared poorly. Until recently, this broad failure almost went unnoticed. Wages in the United States for those the government calls production and nonsupervisory workers—most workers—rose only 3 percent since 1979. These wages had been stagnating well before the crisis of 2008. By a slightly different measure, wages for the typical male worker were lower, after inflation, in the 2000s than they were in the early 1970s and, depending on how they are measured, the 1960s as well. Meanwhile, the top 1 percent earned roughly 20 percent of the national income, compared to 10 percent in 1970—a level of inequality not seen since the 1920s. African Americans consistently had unemployment rates twice as high as those of whites for thirty years. The lack of decent jobs contributed to a surge in the number of men in prison. In some states, prison costs were the second-highest expenditure after Medicaid.

Economic mobility had stalled, leaving the United States well down the list of rich nations when measuring the ability of its citizens to climb up from the bottom income ranks. Those under twenty-five found it harder to get a job in the 2000s, even before the crash, than in any prolonged period since World War II. The employment of teens hit post–World War II lows, falling especially sharply after 2000. Women still earned less than men with comparable experience and education. And most tragically, the richest nation in the world had the highest child poverty rate among all wealthy nations.

All the while, transportation infrastructure was crumbling. Public education remained highly unequal, and a nationally accessible pre-K system could not be established. The United States spent far more per person on health care than did any nation in the world, with mediocre results.

Not least, there were countless financial crises in the United States during the Great Moderation, laissez-faire renaissance, and rise of financial deregulation: in 1982, 1987, 1989, 1994, 1997–98, and 2000–1. These crises led to the loss of trillions of dollars of wealth in the country and around the world and to subpar economic growth or outright recession.

In sum, the growth of GDP per capita was significantly slower after 1980 in the United States than before it. Some claim new products such as the iPhone or multiple cable channels compensated for slow income growth, but there had been equivalent new products throughout America's economic history, from the automobile to the cinema, radio, television, and jet travel. Life spans lengthened, but this usually had more to do with reduced cigarette smoking and new cardiovascular drugs, often developed by government researchers, than with economic vitality.

In recent years, the nation has seemed vexed, frustrated, and often fatalistic about its prospects. The economic recovery since 2009 has not produced enough new jobs, and those created were mostly low paying. Typical household income in 2013 was no higher than it was in 1999. The unemployment rate eventually fell below 7 percent, but only because millions dropped out of the labor force and were no longer counted as unemployed. The percentage of people of working age with jobs had thus fallen to lows not seen in a generation. In sum, 14 to 15 percent of the labor force could not find full-time work. The poverty rate did not fall, as it did in most economic recoveries. The stark jobs situation of those under twenty-five, with a record unemployment rate of 18 percent, would likely reduce their opportunities for the rest of their lives, and too few in a place of power were defending them. At least the elderly had well-developed and experienced lobbying organizations to fight for their interests.

Until 2008, the economics profession remained mostly oblivious to these marked and painful failures. And then the Great

Moderation about which economists had become nearly ecstatic turned into a great jobs emergency.

Economists were indeed set back on their heels by the financial crisis of 2008 and by the depth of the recession and the levels of unemployment that followed. Though not well implemented, the aggressive financial rescue efforts of the government in 2008 nevertheless kept matters from getting far worse that year. Were it not for the social programs started in the New Deal of the 1930s and expanded in the 1960s, including Social Security, unemployment insurance, and Medicare, and those adopted later, including the earned income tax credit and food stamps—the great embrace of government, not its denigration—the nation would likely have entered a full-fledged depression by 2009. For all the criticism, President Obama's roughly $800 billion stimulus package of government spending and tax cuts was also a vital contributor to a softer landing for the economy in 2009. Non-laissez-faire economics saved the day.

One of the more reasonable of the orthodox economists, Olivier Blanchard wrote with colleagues "Rethinking Macroeconomic Policy," a short mea culpa published two years after he had proclaimed macroeconomics to be in such good shape. Although he supported temporary government stimulus to enable economies to recover, he had hardly changed his central views. "It is important to start by stating the obvious," he asserted, "namely, that the baby should not be thrown out with the bathwater. Most of the elements of the precrisis consensus, including the major conclusions from macroeconomic theory, still hold."

The key assumption of the new laissez-faire consensus was that it is the natural order of things that economies rise from recession almost automatically. In recessions, prices rise slowly or fall; likewise, wages stagnate or fall, and interest rates slide downward, setting the stage for more buying by consumers, more hiring by businesses, and more capital investment. It's an intoxicating idea. Economies rarely get too far out of balance, goes the thinking—they are far more likely to be stable than not at any given moment. Such economies require only modest government intervention, mostly to control inflation and relieve suffering as jobs are lost, or maybe just a little push from lower interest rates, but the fewer such government policies the better. Most of the time, government can only do harm. This was the new but deeply incorrect consensus.

In 2001, after the Clinton administration had left office, Lawrence Summers, a Harvard professor and Bill Clinton's third Treasury secretary, endorsed this new faith in free markets and opposition to government intervention as a victory of new ideas. By contrast, in the 1930s John Maynard Keynes had advocated aggressive government spending—outright budget deficits—to stop recessions and support vigorous recoveries. "The political debates take place within a universe that is shaped by the development of new ideas," Summers told an interviewer, attributing the change to good, fresh thinking, not merely the return of an old laissez-faire ideology in a more politically conservative time. "Of those new ideas, none is more important than the rediscovery of Adam Smith and the idea that a decentralized system relying on price signals collects information and provides much more insurance than any kind of centrally planned or directed type of system." Summers, a onetime Keynesian, had for the moment changed his tune, and in this he represented economists generally.

Economists basically discarded Keynesian policy and relied on a narrow version of monetary policy: the manipulation of interest rates by the Federal Reserve, the nation's central banking system. "We thought of monetary policy as having one target, inflation, and one instrument, the policy rate," conceded Blanchard. "So long as inflation was stable, the output gap [the difference between potential and actual GDP] was likely to be small and stable and monetary policy did its job." He noted that "old-style Keynesian stimulus," by which he meant more government spending, was now "secondary."

During this period, Clinton, the first Democratic president since 1981, chose to act on the advice of Summers and Robert Rubin, his second Treasury secretary and a former head of Goldman Sachs, and pay down the nation's debt before seriously raising public investment. The federal deficit was widely thought to deter growth, limiting the money available to private businesses to distribute the nation's savings. In Clinton's last year in office, the level of federal public investment as a proportion of GDP was lower than in Ronald Reagan's last year in office, especially for physical infrastructure and education spending. It was also substantially lower for research and development. The policy was part and parcel of the laissez-faire revolution.

Had economists been fully dedicated to their free-market views, they would also have been up in arms over the glaring lack of regulation of the new and deliberately opaque derivatives market on Wall Street. Based on securities that could be bought and traded with little down payment, these derivatives were at the heart of the financial crisis. If someone is selling a good or a security, competitors cannot offer it for less if they do not know the price asked. Yet the Clinton administration, following the new economic thinking, prevented regulators from setting federal standards of openness in this market.

The most damaging of the new financial derivatives were credit default swaps, a technical name for insurance sold by financial firms to protect investors against price declines of securities. The insurance to protect against losses on mortgage securities became especially popular as the housing boom progressed—particularly insurance for securities based on subprime mortgages. Because the prices of these insurance-like derivatives were traded secretly, however, there was not adequate competition to keep prices sensible. Economists should have rallied in opposition to the lack of rules, but I could find no research papers done on the phenomenon until it was too late. Some investors and professional traders bought the insurance at high prices, some sold at low prices. Moreover, there were no legal requirements to hold a reserve to ensure that someone selling insurance could pay off—as is done with traditional life and property insurance. When the value of mortgages collapsed as the housing bubble burst, those who sold such insurance—notably the insurance giant AIG—could not pay off, making the crisis far worse. Investors who thought they were protected against falling mortgage securities were now losing fortunes, forcing them to sell other securities to meet their liabilities. This drove the prices of other securities still lower, and market prices fell further in a vicious spiral.

Economists also said little when they should have proverbially shouted about the obvious conflicts between those who issued securities and the agencies they hired to rate the securities they sold. These agencies, Standard & Poor's and Moody's, were inclined to make their clients happy and gave their securities high ratings, even those based on subprime mortgages. Giving unjustifiably high ratings to the securities of clients who were paying for them seems, well, almost inevitable. After the collapse, the agencies sharply, and with at least temporary embarrassment, reduced their ratings for the large majority of securities they had previously given their highest ratings, the value of which had often fallen to zero.

"Get the incentives right" had become a cliché for economic reform, especially in poorer developing nations. But financial incentives were awry on Wall Street. Traders were paid lavishly when they were correct but were not penalized commensurately when they were wrong, thereby incentivizing them to take risks. Much of the profits earned on trading the new derivatives were kept secret from buyers and sellers so that customers could not seek a better deal elsewhere. It was said that the very high compensation of bankers and traders reflected their unusual talents and that high profits for financial institutions meant they were contributing ever more to the nation's prosperity. Economists were barely disturbed by such implausible nonsense. Meanwhile, by contrast, laws to set higher minimum wages, it was argued by many economists, would only distort labor markets and result in lost jobs.

Wall Street itself exhibited the characteristics of a monopoly. Commissions were fixed at abnormally high levels for most financial transactions, suggesting the lack of true competition. Fees earned by bankers on transactions were always high but did not fall as a percentage of the soaring value of financial assets, which under normal competitive conditions should likely have been the case. Blanchard, looking back, wrote: "We thought of financial regulation as mostly outside the macroeconomic policy framework." The silence of so many economists when even their most bedrock conservative principles were violated was disturbing. They had spoken up as a group before, sometimes vociferously, about the benefits of free trade, for example. Their current views on laissez-faire economics, including financial deregulation, were now markedly sympathetic to big business and Wall Street.

In the 1980s, 1990s, and 2000s, the prices of stocks, bonds, and housing rose to untenable levels on the watch of free-market economists who preached deregulation. During this period, over-speculation led to serious financial crises at home and abroad as free-market advocates successfully reduced controls on lending and investing around the world. A series of major financial crises affecting America began with a 1982 Mexican financing debacle involving U.S. banks and climaxed with the 2008 crisis. Mexico had borrowed significantly from U.S. banks in the 1970s and early 1980s, the careless banks essentially speculating on the future strength of the Mexican economy with loans to the government and for spurious industrial projects. With no guidelines from government or international institutions, the banks had recycled petrodollars through loans especially to Latin America; a favorite recipient was Mexico. When interest rates were pushed up sharply by Paul Volcker's Federal Reserve in order to stanch U.S. inflation, interest rates on Mexican debt also rose sharply. At the same time, a resulting worldwide recession undercut Mexico's oil exports. The nation declared that it could not pay its debts to American banks. The Fed and the International Monetary Fund, a world lending organization, helped bail out the banks.

Ensuing financial crises were variations on this theme. The investors in equity incurred huge losses because of overly opti-mistic speculative investments that initially earned a lot of money and then went bad, but banks were often bailed out. Economies typically slid into recessions when inflation rose and the prices of these financial assets fell. The 1982 recession in the United States, for example, was the worst since the Great Depression—until the recession of 2008. Despite wide-eyed assertions by well-schooled

economists that Americans were now enjoying the Great Moderation, the financial collapses and ensuing recessions had, as noted,
cost Americans trillions of dollars in lost wealth and jobs, diminished investment, and failed companies. The U.S. housing crash
that began in 2006, along with the accompanying collapse in stock
prices, reduced the wealth of Americans by roughly $8 trillion by
the time it hit bottom. This crash was also of course the result of
overspeculation fueled by borrowing—homebuyers and investors
in complex and hard-to-understand mortgage securities kept buying at ever-higher and less sensible prices. While average wealth
rose again in the years after the crash, the money essentially went
to the wealthy. Banks had been rescued, stock prices came back,
and the well-off held the large majority of stocks; housing prices
rebounded only partially. The high-technology stock plunge that
occurred in the early 2000s resulted in comparable losses for most
Americans. Most high-technology stocks did not recover. Many
economists insisted such speculation was necessary to encourage
risk taking.

Devastation from financial crises was worse overseas. The
Mexican crisis led to a widespread recession. Many South American countries also had large debts to U.S. and foreign banks, and
the recession resulted in falling demand for their oil, copper, and
other exports. The 1980s are generally known as the "lost decade"
in South America, with excessive borrowing from eager American banks typically laying the foundation for weakness. On average, GDP across South America did not rise at all in the 1980s.
During this period, Mexican wages, for example, fell by 25 to 30
percent. Asian nations, including Thailand, Indonesia, and Korea,
suffered severe recessions after a deep financial crisis in 1997 that
was stoked by fleeing capital in the new free market in international
finance. More than ten million people fell below the poverty line in

Malaysia, Korea, Indonesia, Thailand, and the Philippines between 1996 and 1998. Unemployment tripled in Korea and quadrupled in Thailand. There were innumerable corporate bankruptcies.

Many orthodox economists noted that poverty rates had fallen in the developing world. But the claims were misleading. Most of the poverty reduction was in China and, to a lesser extent, India, neither of which followed the free-market policies prescribed by the West.

In Europe, many nations had been struggling with slower growth since the 1990s. The property bubbles of the 2000s brought on by inordinate speculation had become their temporary salvation, only to burst badly, leaving them with piles of government and private debt. European economists urged austerity: higher taxes and cuts in social spending to reduce budget deficits, even at the expense of growth. A majority of Britain's most influential economists supported the Conservative Party's embrace of such policies in the face of economic weakness. These were the worst economic policy decisions made since early in the Great Depression. Granted, many American economists opposed such severe austerity in Europe, but these policies were driven by research done at prestigious American universities based on the assumption that economies were self-correcting. As a result of austerity economics, unemployment soared in the weaker economies of Spain, Portugal, Italy, and Greece, and recession overtook the entire Continent and Britain. In late 2013, the GDP of these nations remained below pre-2007 highs.

The free-market economics that had been in vogue were now failing badly. The old remedy advocated by John Maynard Keynes to cure recession—federal spending that would lead to a temporary budget deficit—had been accepted momentarily but was again soon disdained by many. Since the inflationary 1970s, a federal budget deficit was increasingly seen as the culprit, even among Democratic economists, and this view has been hard to shake completely even after the major recession. The thinking was that a deficit often, even usually, created too much demand for goods and services, thus pushing up prices. It created more demand than the wages and profits the economy itself was generating, requiring borrowing to do so. Once slack was taken up, it was believed, a deficit resulted in an overheated economy. Keynesians typically argued with the new free-market orthodoxy over whether full employment had been reached and whether the capacity of the economy was fully utilized. It was said that the debt financing that pushed up interest rates also left less room for businesses to borrow.

To call economists overconfident during the modern laissez-faire experiment understates their hubris. The susceptibility of economists to new fashions in thinking, their opportunistic catering to powerful interests, and their walking in lockstep with the rightward political drift of America are disturbing for a discipline that claims to be a science.

The philosopher Isaiah Berlin categorized writers who have one big idea as hedgehogs. The economist Dani Rodrik of the Institute for Advanced Study, borrowing the term, calls economists hedgehogs if they are overly devoted to a theory of self-adjusting economies and believe that the market can handle almost all products and services efficiently. Milton Friedman and his followers, including many leftist economists, certainly fit this bill. They were hedgehogs who feared government intervention.

Again borrowing from Berlin, Rodrik calls economists who entertain at least some doubts about how economies correct themselves foxes, who know many small things. Economic foxes usually want more regulation than do hedgehogs. They want to invest more in public goods. They want to protect workers more through higher unemployment insurance and other social programs.

Rodrik's foxes, though, are in fact usually hedgehogs, too. They are indeed a little more willing to resort to government policies. They mostly hold that when markets fail—in the production of social goods, such as education and roads, or in the creation of such so-called externalities as pollution, or in paying workers what they deserve—the government should step into the gap to correct these inadequacies. But this is a fundamentally ambiguous school of thought. "I want to point out a bias built into that theory," wrote the Columbia economist Richard Nelson. "By the way it is formulated, market failure carries a heavy normative load, to the effect that markets are preferred to other forms of governance unless they are basically flawed in some sense. . . . As one reflects on it, the argument that we need government because markets sometimes 'fail' seems rather strange, or at least incomplete. Can't one make a positive case for government, or families, for that matter, as a form that is appropriate, even needed, in its own right?"

One of the characteristics of laissez-faire that is so alluring to economists is the fact that it is a clean economics, unsullied by muddy details and exceptions. The new laissez-faire period started as an attempt to stabilize the high unemployment and inflation of the 1970s, and in some respects it succeeded. But then the theorists sought universal principles to be applied to almost every situation, scrubbing economics of the particularities of individual episodes and events. Paul Krugman, the *New York Times* columnist and Nobel laureate, once argued that economists had to deal more with "messy" details, but he was mostly referring to the more extremist conservative economists who wanted to prohibit any government intervention at all. The admonition applies to moderate orthodox economists as well, including those on the left.

In his mea culpa, Olivier Blanchard came to agree that economists' objectives had to be wider ranging than just low, stable inflation. He even agreed that the inflation rate should be higher than the commonly accepted target of 2 percent. But he only cast mild doubt on the central assumptions that enabled economists to form their ideas and on the misleading and damaging policies based upon them. He did not wonder about whether the profession itself had become too doctrinaire.

Economics needs more thoroughgoing foxes interested in the particulars. It needs economic sociologists, historians, and anthropologists rummaging through history and current events to see where theory applies and where it does not. To economists, however, sociology is dreaded. During the 2008 economic crisis, it was clear how little economists had investigated the risky structure of the Wall Street mortgage products, whose value amounted to hundreds of billions of dollars. Some economists—but not nearly enough—have used their tools constructively to explore such issues. Others—usually on the losing end of the policy battles of recent years—have admirably criticized the profession's ideological drift. But economists generally have not done the kind of real-world digging needed to make useful economic judgments. They haven't looked under the hood.

Economists could benefit from the advice that the novelist Henry James once gave students: "Any point of view is interesting that is a direct impression of life. You should consider life directly and closely." In economics, theory is not enough and is often patently wrong.

Here our focus is on the evolution of economic thinking and practice over the past thirty to forty years. I have organized the reigning theories into seven bad ideas. Some of these ideas started out as good ones but were eventually seriously misused. They were all intoxicatingly powerful and elegant, and they ultimately all did damage.

Chapter One

The Beautiful Idea: The Invisible Hand

Adam Smith's theory of the Invisible Hand is the founding idea of modern economics. It describes the process by which buyers and sellers come together without any government or other outside presence to agree on what Smith argued would be the ideal price for a good or service. This idea, powerful and alluring, has influenced all of economic theory ever since Smith introduced it. From this fountainhead emerged the other six ideas in this book. But the Invisible Hand has too easily turned heads—including, for a time, my own.

As a subject to study, national prosperity was fascinating to me as a college student and, later, as a young economics writer. Widespread prosperity is relatively new in human history. Those of us who grew up in the 1960s were especially lucky because it was a period in which the economy grew fast, wages rose at all income levels, and poverty levels were falling thanks to new government programs. The prosperity of that era, however, would not last.

I had a sense early on that prosperity shaped our confidence in our ability to control our destiny. Democracy was fostered by prosperity: prosperity gave people a sense of self-control and individual importance. I came to realize that these relationships were more complex than my early and often naive thinking suggested, but the social and philosophical consequences of prosperity were clearly robust and often underestimated.

Given its social, political, and personal impact, I wanted to know where this prosperity came from. Adam Smith essentially wanted to know the same thing. Of course, I and many like me had the advantage of two hundred more years' worth of often brilliant thinking and writing on the subject. Smith published his classic book *The Wealth of Nations* in 1776, and the great reduction in hunger, poor health, and economic insecurity—the early markers of prosperity—began roughly with the Industrial Revolution, which started in England in the late 1700s. Since then, the incomes of the major rich nations of Europe and North America have on average risen consistently, if cyclically. Average world GDP rose ever so slightly for two thousand years, and then, beginning in the late 1700s and early 1800s, it suddenly rose at a historically rapid rate. America's own development coincided with the Industrial Revolution, and the resulting prosperity determined how Americans thought about themselves and helps explain why the idea of America's exceptionalism took such hold in the public imagination and became a founding myth of the nation.

Material gain led to vast philosophical changes. Prosperity and a new sense of power prompted people to try to explain, rationalize, and reinforce their growing self-confidence. The idea of individualism—an emphasis on one's ability to control one's destiny and, in the view of some, one's responsibility to do so—took root. When oversimplified, however, individualism stood in contrast to the idea of community and helping others.

Continued material improvement was necessary to reinforce people's confidence and newfound beliefs. There were tragic exceptions—most notably slavery—but economic self-sufficiency became widespread in early agricultural America because of the availability of arable land. This self-sufficiency fueled Americans' sense that they could determine their own fates and had the right to vote for their own governments. Both the American and French revolutions occurred around the time that the Industrial Revolution was gathering steam.

The Enlightenment, the intellectual revolution of the late 1600s that emphasized the importance of individuals and their rights, preceded the Industrial Revolution. Feeding it were regions of prosperity spread across Europe and its colonies. The Netherlands was relatively wealthy throughout the 1600s, Spain before that, and parts of France and the Italian city-states before that. European historians routinely assert that the first industrial revolution occurred not in the 1700s in England but in the 1100s in Flanders with the development of water mills and other technologies to make cloth and refine grains, along with improvements in transportation and agricultural techniques. Thus, pockets of prosperity had already affected people's thinking and their sense of individual rights.

This first early round of prosperity did not take off the way the the second one did for a variety of complex reasons. Many if not most economic scholars argue that what delayed a broader revolution was a lack of new technologies and raw materials. I eventually found this widespread idea fundamentally narrow, however popular it remains. The slow expansion of prosperity probably had more to do with the relatively small size of markets for goods and services at that point in history. These markets became large and durable only a few hundred years later, enabling economies of scale—the reduction in production costs brought about by many more units being sold. "What really gave the impetus to industry and probably to innovation as well," wrote the pioneering economic historian

Fernand Braudel about the Industrial Revolution, "was the substantial enlargement of the domestic market." This was the cornerstone of Adam Smith's explanation of wealth, the concept of economies of scale as the source of rising productivity. Smith was fully aware that the advantage of more production could only be exploited if the markets were big enough, and he devoted an early chapter in *The Wealth of Nations* to it. The process of making pins he'd read about in Scotland was but a "trifling" industry, he said, but the pin factory turned out to be among the great metaphorical examples in all the social sciences, the economic principles applicable to almost every industry, even today.

Whatever the causes, beginning in the 1800s the ability of people to meet their basic needs more easily allowed for what we would now call self-empowerment. Though the road was rocky, robust democracy was not far off.

With a predilection for seeing political and social development in economic terms, I naturally turned even as an undergraduate to economics for the answers. The possibility that a single mechanism could explain economic advance was exciting. The idea gripped me as soon as I read my first economics textbook, as it clearly had countless others. I eventually got a master's degree in financial economics. The mechanism's workings depended on self-interest, but the outcome was the betterment of the community. Even as they tried to maximize their own benefits, consumers and producers worked together to reach a price at which buying and selling would balance in a way that was ideal. Consumers would get the most at the price they were willing to pay, and producers would sell the most at the highest price they could get. Consumers would not pay more for a product than it was worth, business would earn on each product what it was worth. Workers would get a fair wage, business a fair profit. Investors would pay a fair price for the amount of risk inherent in any security they bought.

The economy was propelled by self-interest, but self-interest works for the overall good. Most important, price signals were sent to encourage business to employ and produce more where their products were in most demand, and employ fewer and produce less when they weren't. If you sold all you made at a certain price, you could invest in order to make more, and hire more people while you were at it, to maximize profit, or raise the price. If consumers bought less as you raised the price, you cut production and maybe workers. Through the Invisible Hand, consumers registered their desires and business received signals about where to invest or disinvest. The economy thus grew. This theory swept aside many of the seeming complexities of economic incentives and fairness, allowed them to be reduced to a single economic mechanism.

The Invisible Hand became the foundation of modern laissez-faire economics. Free prices were the signals that determined production and investments. Therefore, any regulation of prices by government would distort the economy and diminish prosperity. I didn't ever believe government was totally absent from this mechanism, and neither, by the way, did Adam Smith. But what a lovely mechanism it was. Here were explicit, seemingly unambiguous answers to the mystery of prosperity. The Invisible Hand was, as said, the start of traditional economics—but, as we shall see, in a fundamental way economics hardly progressed beyond it.

I am still surprised at how little credit is given to economic prosperity as a cause of social and philosophical change. Thomas Jefferson enthusiastically cited Smith's *Wealth of Nations* as proof that individuals could make their own decisions without government help. But his was an ex post facto analysis: people were already making their own decisions.

The great economic thinkers from Smith on were trying to understand conditions that already existed. They were not creating a model of capitalism from whole cloth. The Invisible Hand as a wide-ranging guide to policy came later. (Smith directly applied it to free trade.) Smith wrote about an already prosperous Britain. Economists ever after, including Keynes, analyzed the world they knew (though Keynes and others did eventually imagine how to improve it, which was the ultimate goal).

When economic times are good, people are often more tolerant and open to change. When economic times are bad, they often are not. This is another reason to study economics. The painful and confusing economic conditions of the 1970s—the high inflation, unemployment, interest rates, and federal deficits—explain a lot about why Americans have become so distrustful of government. Many observers neglect this. In his book on Ronald Reagan, for example, the American historian Sean Wilentz claims that the president ushered in a new politically conservative age, but he hardly mentions the harsh economic conditions that set the stage for the tax cuts and deregulation that are Reagan's legacy. He mostly attributes the change to Reagan's talent for articulate leadership. But Reagan had been uttering the same kinds of ideological pronouncements since the early 1950s, and he usually failed to get his political way; it was the high inflation and then the 1982 financial crisis that created the conditions for the ascendance of his conservatism. In 1971, early in his second term as governor—and in part to enhance his conservative credentials as he contemplated a run for president—Reagan strongly pushed to amend California's constitution to cut the state income tax sharply and permanently. But the proposal, known as Proposition 1, was soundly defeated in early 1972. Californians, still progressive and feeling prosperous, did not support cutting their taxes at that point.

By 1978, after double-digit inflation, soaring unemployment, and a severe recession, all that changed. Californians overwhelmingly passed Proposition 13 to cut property taxes and bar any tax increase of any kind in the state unless it was passed by a two-thirds majority of the appropriate state or local legislature. Adverse economic conditions, not solely the power of ideas, made it possible. Howard Jarvis, whose huge personality also had a lot to do with the passage of Proposition 13, was a factor but not the major one. In 1978, the proposal by Representative Jack Kemp and Senator William Roth to cut the federal income tax sharply also gained wide support. The time had apparently come. Congress cut capital gains taxes significantly, too. Reagan, who had been trying to run for president since 1968 espousing the same views, only got the presidential nomination in 1980 after a decade of punishing economic conditions.

The stagnating wages and relatively high unemployment over the thirty years since Reagan took office have made economic hardship a characteristic of American life and are a major cause of the conservative antigovernment attitudes that have since prevailed in the nation—even, for the most part, during the Clinton presidency. Similarly, disappointing economic achievements have led to a resurgence of conservative policies and antigovernment attitudes overseas. Many attribute America's ideological turn to the concerted organization of corporate lobbyists and right-wing think tanks in America in the 1970s. But Britain adopted almost identical policies even sooner than the United States, motivated largely by the same difficult economic conditions.

On the other hand, prosperity hardly guarantees democracy and the protection of human rights. Russia became wealthy in the 1930s but was a dictatorship until the 1980s. After a decline following World War I, Germany reached full employment under Hitler, and its renaissance was mostly the result of public spending and rearmament in the 1930s. The rich oil kingdoms of the Middle East remain mostly autocratic.

A wealthy America has obviously not created economic equality for all its people, either, even with the progressive civil rights legislation of the 1960s. Today, the unemployment rate for African Americans remains much higher and their average life span lower than those of whites. Labor discrimination by race and gender is still widespread, despite considerable legislative gains. The inequality in public education is stark and hurts the poor the most. Until President Obama's health care reform, single poor people did not qualify for Medicaid under the federal program targeted at poor families, although some states made exceptions. And it is not yet clear whether most states will choose to implement Obamacare's expansion of Medicaid coverage. After a generation of stagnant wages, the landmark voting rights legislation of the 1960s has been partly overturned by the Supreme Court, with only modest public complaint. If the United States becomes even more politically divided, it will likely be because so few have benefited from its economic growth since the late 1970s.

If Eastern European democratic nations—or even some of the Western European states being punished with severe austerity programs as I write this—revert to totalitarianism, it will be because economies faltered, not because prosperity spread. If new Muslim movements are to stabilize, economic development will be required. Much Islamic rebellion grows out of poverty, though the leaders of these movements are often educated and middle class. Truly poor people have little strength for leading rebellions but much willingness to join them. Yet a detailed report by the Rand

Corporation on the "long war" with Islam does not mention economic development as a strategy for peace. Instead, it reduces the possible solutions to military effectiveness and containment of belligerents. These are more reasons to uncover the mysteries of economic growth.

Adam Smith could not have conceived of the Invisible Hand without observing the prosperity around him. But it is also clear that ideas, once formulated, take on a weight and influence of their own. Economic determinism—the concept that economic conditions are the main cause of historical change—seems a powerful way to make sense of how history unfolds. Improved economic conditions help explain why we are confident enough today to demand security, civil rights, and—a highly radical idea—"the pursuit of happiness." Who could have imagined happiness for an entire nation before the Industrial Revolution? Perhaps it had been possible in prosperous China hundreds of years ago, or for the privileged men of tiny ancient Athens, but certainly not in the West.

As I learned my economics and further explored the influence of the Invisible Hand, the power of ideas became clearer to me. Economic ideas have had enormous influence on economic conditions—and vice versa. Over the past thirty-five years, the ideas at the center of orthodox economics, we will see, did damage and laid the groundwork for the financial crisis of 2008 and the Great Recession that followed. The Invisible Hand, though alluring, is highly ambiguous—it does good and harm.

A beautiful idea can be described as one that explains a lot with a little. Such ideas are often simpler than previous explanations of a phenomenon. But they can be siren songs, and throughout history many such ideas have been found to be wrong: the Aristotelian belief that heavy items fall fastest to earth; the once-dominant idea that the veins and arteries are separate circulatory systems; the notion, which seemed undeniable to educated people at one time, that the earth is the center of the universe.

The Copernican idea that the sun, not the earth, is the center of the solar system is a classic example of the best kind of beautiful idea. It is elegant and simple and, most important, ultimately correct. But time was still needed to break the shackles of the older, mistaken beautiful ideas. Once accepted, such ideas are hard to shed. They become part of us and color how we think.

Physical observation alone did not pave the way to the Copernican idea, which took some time to gain acceptance. There were also cultural and philosophical changes that opened paths to such thinking. Our sense of our uniqueness as a species may have already been diminishing culturally and intellectually before Copernicus's astronomical theory took shape, making it possible to accept the radical notion that the earth was not the center of it all. History is more a circle than a line—a feedback loop rather than simple cause and effect. I'd argue that economists too often overlook that. Honest economists readily admit their oversimplifications; confused economists take them more literally.

The beautiful idea of the Invisible Hand enraptured economists as well as many political thinkers for more than two centuries. But it is not an idea with the power of, say, the Copernican discovery. It is more a loose metaphor for the way markets *may* work than an ironclad law. The Invisible Hand is believed by economists to demonstrate that markets where goods and services are freely exchanged will result in the greatest benefit to buyers and sellers alike, and as noted direct investment where it is most useful, enhancing the rate at which the economy can grow. All of this takes place without any outside government intervention.

Orthodox economists have made the Invisible Hand the basic foundation of their work. They grudgingly agree that sometimes government intrusion in the market is necessary. Usually, though, government efforts are seen as harmful. Most extraordinary, many economists claim that just as the market for cornflakes is self-adjusting, so, too, is an entire economy. Supply and demand automatically adjust to a "general equilibrium" that satisfies as many people as possible. In a recession, prices, wages, and interest rates will fall. More goods will be demanded, and production will rise again. Excessively rapid growth will result in higher prices, which dampen demand and will perhaps create a recession that lasts until the economy readjusts. A recession will only be temporary, as will excessive growth.

Unlike the Copernican revolution, however, the Invisible Hand is an assumption, not a scientifically based law. Its obvious limitations have not prevented its supreme influence. The alllure of the Invisible Hand is its elegance. The profound weakness is that it is not nearly as complete a model of markets as many economists insist it is. Its underlying assumptions—that people have material preferences that don't change, that they are rational decision makers, and that they have all the price and product information they need—are extreme. The Invisible Hand is thus a limited proposition, elegant but impure.

It especially draws theorists toward the laissez-faire model of governing, which holds that government intervention should be minimized. Indeed, the free market, not government, is accepted as the dominant organizing mechanism of society.

Smith used the term "Invisible Hand" just once in *The Wealth of Nations* and only once in his earlier work, *The Theory of Moral Sentiments*. The historian Emma Rothschild, in her book on Smith and the Marquis de Condorcet, two towering Enlightenment scholars, argues that Smith was more ironic than serious about the Invisible Hand, always assuming an active role for government in creating the rules and regulations of society and fully conscious of the need for compassion and community, which he outlined rather beautifully in *The Theory of Moral Sentiments*.

But Smith took the Invisible Hand very seriously, I'd argue, even as he assumed a large role for government. He was a complex thinker, breaking new ground in many areas, and too much time has been spent trying to make his abundant ideas consistent with one another. He could believe in limiting government in some ways but expanding it in others. Even though he explicitly mentioned the Invisible Hand only once in *The Wealth of Nations*, elsewhere in his masterpiece he addressed it at length.

Smith was formally a moral philosopher at the University of Edinburgh, and he had come to believe that individuals could often make their own decisions without help from a higher authority, a staple idea of the Enlightenment that was rapidly gaining cultural acceptance. A market undirected by government fit this philosophical disposition very well. Smith was determined to show that such self-oriented behavior on the part of individuals led to a common good. "Man has almost constant occasion for the help of his brethren," he famously wrote, "and it is in vain for him to expect it from their benevolence only. He will be more likely to prevail if he can interest their self-love." And then follows his most quoted line: "It is not from the benevolence of the butcher, the brewer, or the baker, that we expect our dinner, but from their regard to their own interest. We address ourselves, not to their humanity but to their self-love, and never talk to them of our own necessities but of their advantages."

Emma Rothschild, appropriately skeptical of the Invisible Hand, emphasizes its "loveliness." To many, she observes, it is "aesthetically delightful." Rothschild notes that for the Nobel laureate Kenneth Arrow and his highly regarded coauthor Frank Hahn the Invisible Hand was "poetic." Arrow and Hahn wrote that it is "surely the most important contribution of economic thought." Another Nobel laureate, James Tobin, called it "one of the great ideas of history and one of the most influential." The American conservative philosopher Robert Nozick is impressed by how it finds an "overall pattern or design" out of a seeming jumble of decisions.

Its simple elegance, as I've said, is part of the reason for its influence. Rebuttals of it tend to be intricate, but this does not make them wrong. A rare readable rebuttal of Smith's moral contentions can be found in *Adam's Fallacy,* a short book by the nonmainstream economist Duncan Foley. Others have built economic systems that give less credibility to the central proposition that economies are a collection of markets driven by the Invisible Hand and more to the influence of tradition, culture, power, war, and the development of the law, the banking system, and other institutions. Economic growth cannot, it turns out, be explained by the simple mechanism of the Invisible Hand, however key a role it played. These other less traditionally economic factors matter enormously. Foley is part of this tradition, as is the similarly nonmainstream Lance Taylor, whose *Maynard's Revenge* is a variation on the failures of Smith's theory. The Invisible Hand, however, overwhelmingly trumps all these insurrectionary ideas in the practice of economics today.

———

With the stakes so high, how could I not have wanted to understand the way economies create wealth? How could I not have embraced the Invisible Hand? Was there some set of conditions and choices that underlay prosperity, a set that could be maintained and enhanced? In short, was there a universal key to economic growth? Political decisions, the tides of history, scientific breakthroughs, the spread of literacy, the rise of rapid transportation—all these and more affect growth. But my college textbooks, even when they included sections on Keynesian government stimulus, by and large agreed that prosperity is mostly a consequence of the Invisible Hand—that is, a free market.

Adam Smith may not have been an economist per se, but to my mind he was an economic historian of his times. Better said, he was an economic sociologist. He wanted to understand the causes of the prosperity that existed in Scotland and the rest of Britain. History's leading theoretical innovators were trying to make sense of what they saw as surprising and robust economic advances since the 1700s. They noted how wealthy many individuals were becoming; how cities were growing; how agriculture was feeding more people; how new water mills and factories were producing goods more cheaply; how many new businesses were being started; how canals and, over time, railway lines were proliferating; and how technology was advancing rapidly. Neither they nor their greatest successors created economic edifices out of theory; instead, they created theory out of the concrete edifices they observed. Unlike, say, Newton's or Einstein's theories, which offered predictions based on immutable laws of nature (within defined limits, granted), economic theories did not predict the Industrial Revolution or the fabulous wealth of today's rich nations. John Maynard Keynes was a brilliant but mostly conventional economist until the devastating Great Depression; when the facts on the ground changed, he said, he had to change his ideas.

Adam Smith did not begin *The Wealth of Nations* with the Invisible Hand. The general cause of increasing wealth is productivity, he wrote in his first chapter, the growing quantity of goods and services that can be produced per hour of work. More income was produced per worker as productivity increased. The persistent increase in productivity, accumulating over years, decades, generations, and centuries, is the cause of the economic benefits we enjoy today. This was accomplished through what Smith called the "division of labor."

Smith started with the aforementioned pin factory, a classic example of rising productivity, both simple and highly illustrative. Smith may have called the manufacturing of pins "trifling," but the availability of cheap pins was important to the burgeoning textile industry. Smith explained that one man could make one pin a day, perhaps twenty. But when manufacturers learned to divide and specialize the work, productivity exploded. Smith reported that there were up to eighteen separate operations—"one man draws out the wire, another straights it, a third cuts it, a fourth points it"—and by dividing the labor, twenty men with specialized skills could now make an astonishing forty-eight thousand pins in a day. This huge multiplication of output was achieved even as the cost of labor remained low. Here, in a nutshell, was the miracle of modern wealth. But it was the Invisible Hand that directed business to make such investments as demand created opportunity; it was the guidance system, so to speak.

This primitive example of growing productivity is crystal clear. Smith went on to show how it characterized industry after industry. More than a century later, the division of labor became the basis of mass production, which made use of elaborate machines that, by and large, worked on the same principle of breaking tasks down to their simplest level. Henry Ford took this to the extreme, paring down the multiple tasks involved in building a car to a degree that no one had imagined possible.

When Ford started out, a car with an internal combustion engine typically cost around $5,000. He eventually got the price down to a few hundred dollars, having figured out a way to make so many more cars with little change in labor time or costs. There have been countless examples in industrial history of this reduction in price. By the end of the 1920s, about three-fifths of American families had a car—compared to a little over one-fifth a decade earlier—and a huge number owned washing machines, radios, and telephones. The increase in television ownership in the 1950s was even more explosive—and even with TVs being relatively more expensive, adjusted for inflation, than the computer would later be. But since the 1980s, the price of a personal computer has dropped substantially, and now about three-quarters of Americans own one.

Division of labor was the central principle, but other factors were exploited to increase productivity. New sources of power made a significant difference by reducing labor time: wind and water at first, well before Smith's day, then coal, oil, and, finally, the generators that produced the electricity (and, to a much lesser degree, nuclear fission) that powered the increasingly complex machines that produced more and more goods faster and faster with less and less labor. Another major factor was the rising speed of the transportation of raw materials, parts, and finished goods to producers and markets—first over the waterways, then by train, and soon on trucks and huge oceangoing vessels. The steam engine was key to these developments, but so were navigational techniques. Transportation costs were sharply reduced, which also radically enhanced the mobility of labor. Soon communication became faster, further boosting productivity. The telegraph was critical to American economic development in the mid-1800s, as was the telephone by the end of the century. Lower costs of parts made it possible to produce countless newly invented products over the decades.

The size of the market was every bit as critical as output—and maybe more so—and has usually been overlooked by contemporary economists. The division of labor and other productivity improvements could only be made if the market was large enough. Smith knew this, giving the third chapter of *The Wealth of Nations* the title "That the Division of Labor Is Limited by the Extent of the Market." What good would it be to make forty-eight thousand pins rather than two hundred if there was no need for those pins, even if the price dropped drastically? Markets had to expand beyond the village to the region, the nation, and the world. This was another reason that more efficient and low-cost transportation was so necessary to the advance of productivity.

The process that created the incentives to increase productivity and guide production and prices was itself driven by self-interest, Smith argued. He observed that it is merely a human "propensity" to want to barter and that the way to get what one wants is by giving others what they want.

How much to produce? At what price to sell? Is this really for the overall good? Shouldn't somebody decide? This is the process of the Invisible Hand. "By directing that industry in such a manner as its produce may be of the greatest value," Smith wrote, "he intends only his own gain, and he is in this, as in many other cases, led by an invisible hand to promote an end which was not part of his intention."

The fact that Smith used the term "Invisible Hand" only once in *The Wealth of Nations* has, as noted, misled some scholars into thinking that he did not really care about or even fully believe in it.

Yet the chapter in which he described it without explicitly mentioning it—"Of the Natural and Market Price of Commodities"—is the most important in the book. First of all, Smith assumed there was a "natural" price for every good, one ambiguously based on the long-term costs of producing the product. "When the quantity of any commodity which is brought to market falls short of the effectual demand," he wrote, "a competition will immediately begin [among those who want to buy it], and the market price will rise." In other words, as demand increases, the price rises until it reaches the point at which the entire quantity produced is consumed. If supply increases, the opposite occurs. As he wrote, "When the quantity brought to market exceeds the effectual demand . . . some part must be sold to those who are [only] willing to pay less, and the low price which they give for it must reduce the price of the whole." Thus, more people can own the product at the lower price.

Supply and demand shift to strike a balance at a specific price, which is called the equilibrium point. If there is too much of a commodity or, similarly, too much labor or land, the employer will cut jobs or wages or the landowner will reduce the price or amount of salable land until the wage or the price reaches its so-called natural level. If there is greater demand, the employer will hire more workers or the landowner will prepare more land for use. Natural price and effectual demand are ambiguous ideas, but they were key, if unexplained, assumptions for Smith. Later economists would spend a lot of time trying to make these ideas more explicit. But they essentially accepted the assumptions without ever to this day devising a complete explanation of how price and demand are determined. Price always gravitates to its natural level, Smith said, so that demand is fully met and the resources of a nation are fully used. Economists assume as much today.

Smith acknowledged potential obstructions to the ideal functioning of markets. Producers can try to keep secret a rise in demand, thus avoiding competition. Lack of widespread information about prices and the availability of goods is an inherent problem. Similarly, anyone with a monopoly can keep the market understocked or prices too high. A tariff to keep exports out keeps prices too high to satisfy effectual demand.

Smith did not fully explore some other problems. Simply said, he believed market participants must know what they want and what they are willing to pay. Barring such (rather formidable) obstacles, the process is automatic. Government will only hinder it with taxes, product standards, and price regulations.

In his chapter on natural and market price, then, is Smith's almost complete description of the Invisible Hand. So accepted and seemingly obvious is his theory that it is hard to believe that Smith did not conceive of the supply and demand curves that all first-year economics students learn. Alfred Marshall, the talented British economist, drew these about a century later.

In the chart below, Marshall's demand curve slopes downward.

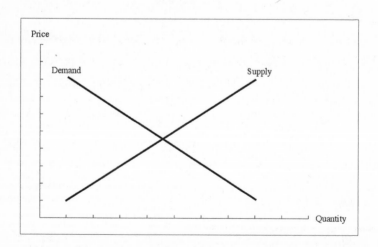

As the price (which is measured along the left-hand line) falls, the demand (measured along the bottom line) increases. As the price rises, businesses will want to sell more; thus, the supply curve rises. The lines cross at the price that maximizes the quantity demanded with the quantity sold—the equilibrium point. As I say, it is a beautiful idea.

In addition to the problems just cited, there is another major gap in the explanation of how the Invisible Hand functions. The main claim is that price sends a message to buyers and sellers on how they can adjust their consumption and production. But the countless buyers and sellers must communicate with each other, after all—in effect, bargain. This is no easy task.

Smith's proposal that there is a natural price for a product is sketchy, to say the least. There is no convincing explanation of where this natural price comes from. Smith presumed that there exists for goods and services a price known by custom and practice and that the price goes down and more people buy as new and cheaper supply comes on the market. Within this set of narrow possibilities, the Invisible Hand can spread the benefits of productivity and induce businesses to invest more, expand capacity, increase production, and reduce labor costs. They may also hire more workers and even raise wages.

A bookseller, for example, might sell a book for $19.95 and see how many takers he gets, thus testing the market. But what if a $14.99 price would attract many more buyers, resulting in a greater total profit for the bookseller? A competitor might then sell a similar book as cheaply, and so the experimentation that led to an equilibrium price would continue. Léon Walras, the influential French economist who in the late 1800s used mathematics to expand the Invisible Hand as a model for the entire economy, did not have an answer to how the process would work in real life, either. Walras presumed that there was an economy-wide "auctioneer" who gathered all prices of goods and sold them to those willing to pay. That assumption about the process by which the Invisible Hand matches buyers and sellers has not been improved upon by contemporary economists. How the equilibrium point is reached remains a mystery.

This central ambiguity matters a lot. Prices can in fact be shoved around by powerful forces: big business, strong unions, and ubiquitous monopolies, or at least oligopolies with market power. In financial markets, prices can be manipulated by collusion or secret trading or access to inside information. In labor markets, wages can be affected by the ability of businesses to fire workers without cause or by stern government policies that restrain growth and keep unemployment high.

Belief in the Invisible Hand allows economists to minimize these concerns. The battle against unions, for example, is driven by a claim that the Invisible Hand guides business and labor to set fair wages. Union organizers believe that they are not set fairly and that workers need collective bargaining to level the playing field. Alan Greenspan, as Federal Reserve chairman, believed that bargaining power mattered. High unemployment, he realized, could keep workers insecure and therefore less willing to bargain hard for their jobs, giving business more power over wages than the Invisible Hand would dictate. One measure of insecurity is the rate at which workers are willing to quit their jobs. If the quit rate is high, workers are secure and might ask for higher wages, putting pressure on business to raise prices and stimulating inflation; if the quit rate is low, workers don't have the security to bargain hard. (Of course, unions sometimes have too much power, too, driving wages too high.) Greenspan kept a close eye on this and seemed to encourage worker insecurity.

Faith in the Invisible Hand led to the once-general belief that a higher minimum wage results in lost jobs. It presumes that the wage paid reflects the worth of the workers and that any wage increase resulting from a minimum wage law represents an overpayment to workers, reduces profits, and also reduces the hiring of new workers. But in fact often the wage can be too low because of a business's power or generally restrictive government policies that keep unemployment high. In that case, a hike in the minimum wage would be healthy economically, restoring demand for goods and services, and would not cause jobs to be lost. At the turn of the nineteenth century, the American economist John Bates Clark made one of the first claims that, economy-wide, wages reflect the worth of labor. As we shall see, there is little serious empirical work to justify this conclusion, and recent studies—what I call dirty economics— have shown that increases in the minimum wage result in very few lost jobs, if any. Empirical analysis is at last changing economists' minds.

Another concern regarding the labor and other markets is often referred to as asymmetric information. The classic example is the used-car salesman who has more information about the car than the buyer has, much of which is kept secret. As Smith feared, a market cannot work under these circumstances. Buyers cannot make proper bids without knowing what they are buying. This concern extends to markets in health care, insurance, and mortgages— and arguably to most other markets as well. It is not only the poor subprime mortgage buyer, for example, who will make errors, but almost all homebuyers who enter into such transactions only two or three times in their lives. How can they possibly be knowledgeable and informed? Even sophisticated pension fund managers clearly did not have enough information about the complex mortgage securities fashioned by Wall Street to make sensible decisions in the years leading up to the 2008 crisis. Countless pension funds and individual investors and the Department of Justice have been suing major banks like JPMorgan Chase and Goldman Sachs over alleged deceptive practices, and in several cases multibillion-dollar settlements have been reached. One Goldman Sachs banker—if only one—has gone to jail for selling the complex products without informing his buyers. A pure interpretation of the Invisible Hand suggests such easy fraudulent behavior should not be possible.

The Invisible Hand also depends on market participants knowing and understanding their self-interest well and therefore making rational decisions about buying and selling products. Behavioral economics has uncovered many examples of buyers being unable to make such rational decisions, a factor economists once minimized. An obvious example is herd behavior in buying stocks, in which buyers are lured into paying high prices because so many others are. The opposite, also damaging, is irrational risk aversion, with investors refusing to buy even when the odds of gains are good. Another example is susceptibility to misleading advertising. Still another is fashion itself, evident in surges in demand for new products like the iPhone or traditional ones like an Hermès Birkin bag. One can argue that there is some satisfaction in being a part of fashion, of course, but not if it leads to buying bad products or stocks whose prices will inevitably fall precipitously.

The seeming power of the Invisible Hand, however, enables many economists to neglect or set aside these concerns. Milton

Friedman forcefully argued that competition will correct most wrongs. Fraudulent products or manipulated financial services will create opportunities for honest competitors, overpricing will create opportunities for sellers to reduce prices, and herd behavior leading to overspeculation will be counteracted by sellers who know better. There is no need for labor unions to offset the power of business, as John Kenneth Galbraith had claimed in his concept of "countervailing power"; unions will only keep wages too high by interfering with the Invisible Hand.

The Invisible Hand is a source of clean economics in a dirty world. Great castles can be built on the Invisible Hand, but a rising tide will wash them away. This is what happened in 2008.

Among the most important limitations of the Invisible Hand are economies of scale. The Invisible Hand presumes that it will eventually cost more to produce a good, not less. As the chart on page 38 shows, price should eventually rise as demand grows. The supply curve rises to meet the demand curve. But the greatest productivity increases in the Industrial Revolution were arrived at as the volume of sales increased; this is what enabled Henry Ford and others to cut prices. The more you make, the lower the unit cost. The supply curve could actually fall when more units were demanded at lower prices, and it often did. Economies of scale are a major component of wealth creation and of the history of economies. Smith's pin factory was a version of this.

The grandest leap of faith among economists, however, concerns more than how the Invisible Hand works in a single market. A general equilibrium was reached for all markets and the economy as a whole. This conclusion, arrived at by economists like Léon Walras, is remarkably convenient, but the assumptions required to make such a claim are extreme.

The many obstacles to the workings of the Invisible Hand amount to an overwhelming criticism. The Invisible Hand is an approximation, usually not applicable in the real world without significant modification. Dependence on it leads to major policy errors, most of them having to do with restraining government intervention. We assume away monopolies, business power, lack of access to information, the likelihood of financial bubbles, economies of scale.

The proof is in the pudding. Predictions about economies based on this generalized theory have often been proved wrong. The most important of these is that economies should be stable because they self-adjust to reach general equilibrium. Yet we have had countless deep recessions and financial bubbles and crashes since the start of the Industrial Revolution. The eighteenth century was rife with them, but so have been the past thirty years of the modern laissez-faire era. Simplistic, convenient belief in the Invisible Hand led to mindless financial deregulation beginning in the 1970s and an astonishingly misplaced faith—one that ignored asset bubbles and income inequality, among other things—that the Great Moderation would maximize prosperity. This is why the devout believer Milton Friedman could state in 2005 that the economy was stable; he couldn't imagine that it wasn't, and he never looked under the hood of Wall Street securities to see what was really going on.

If rightly read, Smith's theory proposes the opposite of laissez-faire political practice, suggesting that there is a need for a visible hand of government. It describes both why markets work and why they fail, as well as how much guidance from an outside force is needed to keep them on track. The Invisible Hand is a brilliant idealization of markets that shows how limited laissez-faire theory is in reality.

Chapter Two

Say's Law and Austerity Economics

The controversial austerity economics that dictated Western economic policy in the wake of the Great Recession of 2008 was based, usually unwittingly, on a two-hundred-year-old law attributed to Jean-Baptiste Say, a French economist of the early 1800s. Simply stated, Say's law holds that supply creates its own demand. If businesses make products, the wages paid to the workers employed will enable them to buy all that is produced. Similarly, if individuals and businesses save, all the savings will be allocated to capital investment. Finally, there will never be too many workers because their wages would fall until all are hired. Thus, any glut of goods, savings, or workers will be only temporary, and economies will adjust on their own to a more prosperous level.

John Maynard Keynes devoted his major work to showing why Say's law did not apply to a contemporary economy; to him, it had clearly failed, and the Great Depression was the result. Nonetheless, Say's law made a comeback after the Great Recession.

In the 1970s, orthodox economists began to believe again that the entire economy worked according to Smith's theory of the Invisible Hand. They drew "aggregate demand curves" to represent all the buying in the economy and "aggregate supply curves" to represent all the selling. They said that the market for every good and service will find its equilibrium point, where price balances supply and demand, and that during a recession, when prices and wages fall or stagnate and interest rates fall, consumers will start buying the lower-priced goods and businesses will hire and invest again. (They by and large indoctrinated first-year economics students with this view.)

This is an enormous assumption for economists to make, and it requires not merely the Invisible Hand to hold but that Say's law be true. Where does the money to buy excess goods come from if workers lose jobs when companies cut back in a recession? According to the predominant theory, as prices fall in a recession, people's savings become more valuable; they will be able to buy more with the same amount. The historian of economic thought Mark Blaug summarizes the proposition a little more technically: "If demand proves insufficient to sell all goods . . . prices must fall. The purchasing power of [cash savings] will rise. . . . The demand for commodities increases until the excess supply . . . is eliminated."

Moreover, it is said that a growing labor supply will create more jobs on its own. More workers should mean falling wages and so businesses will hire more. Say's law suggests, notes Duncan Foley, the author of *Adam's Fallacy,* that "in the aggregate there cannot be a chronic excess supply of labor." Thus, any serious unemployment is voluntary; people can find jobs if they want them.

Similarly, it is said, more savings will stimulate more investment because interest rates fall unless government must borrow the money to make up for a budget deficit. Budget deficits are therefore said to undermine growth by absorbing national savings and keeping interest rates up. Government budgets, then, must be balanced, even during recessions. This advice is especially prevalent today and was also given during the Great Depression of the 1930s.

As Say put it, the answer to any glut of goods, workers, or savings is simply to make more goods, thereby employing workers. Prices, wages, and interest rates will adjust to balance supply and demand.

Once again, government, in particular, is not needed. It can only do damage by creating inflation, keeping wages too high through regulation, or eating into savings by spending more on say, unemployment insurance or Social Security than taxes bring in. As long as prices and wages are flexible, government is out of the way, and budget deficits are reduced, writes Blaug, facetiously, "the system does tend to self-correcting equilibrium." In a free market, to sum up, there can be no lasting gluts of production, savings, or labor: this is the central proposition of what is today called neoclassical economics and the main idea driving current economic policy, and austerity economics, in particular.

A cursory look at the history of the 1800s raises pretty serious questions about this assumption of a self-adjusting economy. New methods of mass production resulted time and again in enormous overproduction of goods in the 1800s, and frequent recessions with high unemployment followed. "Could the capitalist system absorb the constant increases in productive capacity?" asks Blaug. The neoclassical answer is yes, so long as government's role is limited. As Keynes put it, Say's law conformed "with the needs and wishes of the business world of the day."

But the Great Depression threw a wrench into the "great assumption" that the economy would adjust itself. The secretary of the Treasury from 1921 to 1932, Andrew Mellon, demanded austerity as the economy collapsed. Falling prices would ultimately solve all problems. "Liquidate labor, liquidate stocks, liquidate farmers, liquidate real estate," Mellon advised President Herbert Hoover. "It will purge the rottenness out of the system. High costs of living and high living will come down. People will work harder, live a more moral life. Values will be adjusted, and enterprising people will pick up from less competent people." He advocated spending cuts to keep the federal budget balanced, and he opposed cuts in interest rates to pump up the money supply. Say's law justified such restraint. But the economy, rather than adjusting itself, kept on sinking. Keynes's recommendation for more government spending and lower interest rates to keep demand and capital spending strong was, as we know, ultimately successful.

Almost every economics textbook in the United States and much of Europe assumes even today that the basics of Say's law are mostly true, that the total economy is one big self-adjusting market. "The implicit view behind standard models is that markets and economies are inherently stable and that they only temporarily get off track," noted the coauthors of a critical analysis of the 2008 crash. "The majority of economists thus failed to warn policy makers about the threatening crisis."

So it was that during the 2008 crash the University of Chicago economist Casey Mulligan wrote with great authority in a *New York Times* column that the government should not bail out the banks because the recession would be mild. He believed that businesses would keep on investing, no matter the devastation in the financial markets. "It turns out that John McCain, who was widely mocked for saying that 'the fundamentals of our economy are strong,' was actually right," wrote Mulligan. "We're in a financial crisis, not an economic crisis. We're not entering a second Great Depression."

His thinking was based on Say's law, which dictates that if some banks fail, others will rush in to replace them. As long as businesses keep operating, production creates its own demand and—with rising profits and wages—its own savings, which banks will lend out. In spite of the chaos, Mulligan believed, the economy would simply bounce back on its own. Finance was entirely separate from the real economy.

"The current unemployment rate of 6.1 percent is not alarming," he wrote, "and we should reconsider whether it is worth it to spend $700 billion to bring it down to 5.9 percent." The unemployment rate, however, climbed to more than 10 percent, and though the government bailout, the 2008 Troubled Asset Relief Program, was not handled ideally, it was necessary to minimize further financial collapse. Almost no orthodox models of the economy included the possibility of fragility in the financial markets.

Say's law was probably originally shaped by what took place in ancient barter economies. In a barter economy, trade is made not in money but in goods. (Some have argued that there is a version of money and credit in barter economies, albeit minimal by modern standards.) Tools made in a foundry are traded for, say, a month's worth of milk. This explains one of Say's comments: "Products are paid for by products." Earlier, the French economist François Quesnay put it this way: "All that is bought is sold and all that is sold is bought."

But what happens in a modern economy if consumers save some of what they earn, perhaps because they feel insecure in a recession, and don't buy all the goods they are expected to? Like Karl Marx after them, the classical economists of the late 1700s and early 1800s, including Smith, Say, and David Ricardo, found it hard to imagine that consumers would not spend all of what they earned because at that time most people needed so much. Adam Smith believed in Say's law in the short run. If workers "sell" their labor, they will buy something with it, he said.

Lured by the magical Invisible Hand, Léon Walras and other neoclassical economists of the late 1800s made it seem likely, based on more complex math, that all markets could stabilize at an ideal general equilibrium. No one could be made better off without making someone else worse off: this was roughly the argument, now called Pareto optimality, first made by the Italian economist Vilfredo Pareto.

An elaborate mathematical theory published after World War II by the future Nobel laureates Kenneth Arrow and Gerard Debreu added to the economists' confidence in an ideal general equilibrium. Arrow and Debreu showed that Pareto optimality was possible. But ironically, the model also showed how very unlikely it would be to achieve. As they stressed, their model required extreme assumptions about free-market competition (complete information, no monopolies, rational decision makers). Arrow, in particular, made a point of noting that their "proof" was based on assumptions that did not hold up outside of the mathematical world they created. "Arrow devised his model," says Joseph Stiglitz, a student of Arrow's and a fellow Nobelist, "and then spent the rest of his career showing it was wrong."

At first, in fact, such models were actually used to predict how economies would be affected when more realistic assumptions were made. For example, how much does lack of competition in a marketplace reduce income? What happens to unemployment when wages do not fall in a weak economy because of union power or custom? Or vice versa, what happens if wages are kept too low, which is precisely what happened, I'd argue, in the past forty years.

To repeat an earlier point, virtually no one dealt adequately with the central mystery of how consumers and businesses in countless markets trade with each other in order to reach equilibrium prices. Equilibrium, it was basically assumed, simply happened. Everyone got a fair price almost automatically.

Duncan Foley called this general equilibrium model the "most abstract (and some might say ideological) branch of economic theory." The MIT-trained economics commentator Jonathan Schlefer wrote in *The Assumptions Economists Make:* "It promised that, if only markets were perfect, there need be no struggle among capitalists, workers, and landlords, but each of us would do as well as we possibly could." He declared that of the many utopias proposed by political thinkers, including Marx, general equilibrium was the "bravest of all."

Although John Maynard Keynes believed in Say's law as a young economist in the 1920s, it became obvious to him that it could not explain the Great Depression. Wages fell sharply in the early 1930s, but businesses did not rehire and the unemployment rate soared to 25 percent and stayed there. Attacking Say's law became the principal objective of his highly influential 1936 book, *The General Theory of Employment, Interest and Money.*

Money and finance were the main differences between modern economies and more primitive ones. And they undermined Say's law. Classical economists (Smith, Ricardo, John Stuart Mill) and neoclassical economists (Walras, Pareto) simply assumed that financial systems were efficient at their principal task, which was to facilitate the real economy of trade and exchange of goods. Contemporary economists across most of the political spectrum have adopted this view even in the modern world. Casey Mulligan made this assumption in his wrongheaded *Times* column. Even to this day, Olivier Blanchard admits, finance, in which speculation can be rife, could undermine Say's law, but it has no place at all in most contemporary macroeconomic models. Mark Blaug, again facetiously summarized Say's law and thinking like Mulligan's this way in 1978: "Depressions cannot be permanent because supply creates its own demand on a micro- and a macroeconomic level through automatic price and interest variations." The trouble was that the Great Depression, if not permanent, looked to be painfully persistent.

Keynes injected modern finance into the fairy tale of the self-adjusting economy. In a barter economy, a product is made and then soon "sold." In a money economy, a product can be made and then sold a long time later, and producers can borrow money to hold them over. As a result, there are often long lags between the making of a product and the receipt of revenue needed to pay wages and increase profits.

In a money economy, consumers can save part of their wages. Neoclassical economists argue that if consumers save, the money they put in the bank will be invested because interest rates will fall (or not rise as much as they otherwise would have). Banks lend the money to businesses. Consumers might also buy stocks and bonds. No income demand is lost in the process. But Keynes, as we see below, argued the lower rates often did not lead to more investment by business in deep recessions.

Keynes introduced psychology and uncertainty into economics, two very inconvenient concerns for orthodox economists. Keynes believed that business investment is not just affected by the supply of national savings but by the state of optimism. If consumer demand for goods is not strong, a business will have little incentive to invest, no matter how great its profits or how low interest rates are on bank loans. In other words, contrary to Say's law, savings will not automatically be invested.

In a money economy, the state of mind of consumers and businesspeople—their exuberance or, conversely, their lack of confidence—is important, according to Keynes. Consumers' expectations regarding inflation and job prospects affect their buying and savings decisions. In recessions, they often fear for their jobs, so they may choose to let the money in their bank accounts sit right there. Businesses are driven to invest not merely by rational analysis but by "animal spirits," as Keynes put it, and they can be restrained by excessive caution in recessions. Keynes focused on emotional and irrational decision making. The central critique of Keynes in the dominant conservative philosophy since the 1980s was that consumers and investors are highly rational.

In addition, Keynes believed that stock prices can distort economies. He did not believe the stock market was an objective meeting place for traders and investors but more like a newspaper contest in which people were asked to choose the most beautiful woman from among those pictured and could win a prize if they chose the woman most others did. The best strategy would be to try to guess who everyone else thought most beautiful, instead of picking personal favorites, noted Keynes. Similarly, stock prices were often dependent on fashion—on what everyone else thinks everyone else thinks about a company's value. Speculative bubbles are to be expected, and they in turn stimulate too much investment. In market declines—bear markets—subdued spirits often depress investment too much. In a recessionary environment, he concluded, contradicting Say's law, demand for goods, services, and capital investment will often be inadequate. This "paradox of thrift"—

too much savings—is what happened in the Great Depression and again after 2008 (and, to a lesser extent, in previous recessions). This represented a radical thrust against orthodox thinking. Economies did not automatically adjust from recession. There could indeed be persistently inadequate demand, even when wages, interest rates, and prices fell. This is impossible in a Say's law world. And all this could persist because an equilibrium—a balance between supply and demand—could be reached with high unemployment. The economist Stephen Marglin, one of the few liberals left on the Harvard faculty after the 1960s, notes how far-reaching were the implications of Keynes's *General Theory:*

> The major theoretical conclusion was that once undergoing a shock that moved it away from full employment, an economy might remain mired in depression indefinitely. The economy would reach an unemployment equilibrium, equilibrium in the sense of a position at which the forces moving the economy one way or the other are just balanced. A full-employment equilibrium might exist in the mind of God or his mainstream votaries, but no way exists to get from the here of unemployment to the there of full employment. Not only would the "self-correcting mechanism" of the market fail, but under certain circumstances, it might be impossible for monetary policy alone to move the economy to full employment.

This is a clear, concise summary of Keynesian thinking.

Keynes taught the world that government budget deficits were often necessary, the reverse of personal thrift. They created the demand that motivated business investment in a recessionary economy. Neoclassical economists argued that deficits reduced national savings and thereby, under Say's law, investment; economies were like families. But when it comes to financial health, governments are not at all like families. In hard times, a family saves to improve its future prospects; its savings do not affect the prospects of others. If most people in an economy save more, however, spending goes down, setting off a spiral of less spending, less investment, and less confidence. In a weak economy, this could lead to recession. Keynes showed how this could happen quite brilliantly.

Keynes believed in savings, but in the long run. A sudden increase in the budget deficit, as he proposed, can lead to economic growth and higher incomes. Over time, consumers with these higher incomes will be able to save more, and it is in the long run that the pool of savings matters. As the economist Brad DeLong notes, "It is important to say, loudly, that Say's Law is not true in theory, and it takes delicate and proper technocratic management to make it work in practice." He also points out that Say himself more or less eventually repudiated the proposition.

Contrary to the claims of some of his later critics, Keynes's thinking was not based on an economy of imperfect markets or market failures, where the Invisible Hand was undermined by unions, slow-falling wages, or monopolies that set high prices. Keynes actually believed in economic equilibrium. What made this believer in capitalism radical was his argument that a steady state of equilibrium could be reached, but often at a high level of unemployment and other unused resources. This was a blow to the heart of neo-classical economics, which argued that equilibrium was reached at an ideal state of economic prosperity.

The conventional example of Keynesian wisdom was the large increase in government spending during World War II, which was enough to lift the U.S. economy from the Great Depression. But it is not the only real-world example. Public spending in Germany in the 1930s is also an example of Keynesian success; the German economy flourished because of it. The sharp economic recovery in the United States beginning in 1933 is another earlier example, though it was undone by the adoption of austerity in 1937, as Frranklin D. Roosevelt, wrongly fearing a return of inflation, raised taxes and the Fed tightened money. In an example of so-called military Keynesianism, defense spending continued to be a boon to the U.S. economy in the 1950s and 1960s.

After a momentary resurgence in 2009 with the adoption of President Obama's often maligned $800 billion stimulus package of tax cuts and spending increases, Keynesian solutions, however, were rejected to a large degree in the United States and almost entirely in Europe. It turned out, and it is still not readily understood, that Say's law was too firmly entrenched in economists' thinking to be unloosed and Keynes was never fully accepted, even by the left-of-center economists from universities like MIT.

In retrospect, the triumph of Keynesianism among economists in the post–World War II era was a myth. Only modest portions of sanitized Keynesian thinking were widely adopted by U.S. academics in the 1950s and 1960s. In the Great Recession that followed the 2008 financial crisis, Keynesian principles were easy to reject.

American Keynesians after World War II were not purists. Led by MIT's Paul Samuelson, they did not accept the contention that high unemployment could persist, or even exist, in a state of equilibrium. To them, market imperfections warranted Keynesian stimulus, *but only temporarily.* The most important of these imperfections was the fact that wages and prices did not tend to fall, as the Invisible Hand would suggest. There was a strong tendency to maintain wages, even in a weak economy. Unions had a part in this, and so did businesses, which often exercised market power to resist price cuts. Neither wages nor prices always fell enough to allow the markets to correct, and therefore, Samuelson believed, unemployment remained high and consumption weak. The Invisible Hand was prevented from doing its work so government was needed to correct this market failure.

Said Samuelson:

> What I resisted in Keynes the most was the notion that there could be equilibrium unemployment.... The way I finally convinced myself was to just stop worrying about it. I asked myself: why do I want to refuse a paradigm that enables me to understand the Roosevelt upturn from 1933 to 1937? It's ... completely untrue that the New Deal didn't work until World War II came and bailed it out. Some of the highest rates of real increase in and highest levels of plant and equipment capital formation are in the period 1934 to 1937. I was content to assume that there was enough rigidity in relative prices and wages to make the Keynesian alternative to Walras operative.

The American version of Keynesianism held that once higher budget deficits were temporarily imposed to push down unemployment, the general equilibrium model of automatic self-adjustment would again take over, putting the economy back on a fast-growth track. Accurately called the neoclassical synthesis, the Samuelson revolution combined aspects of Keynesianism with conventional theory, including Say's law.

The American Keynesians were, however, at least more tolerant of inflation than their predecessors. They believed that somewhat more inflation led to reductions in unemployment because the economy could run more easily at full capacity; low average inflation could force some companies to cut back production because they couldn't raise prices at all. This relationship, known as the Phillips curve, after the New Zealand economist who first called attention to it, was the basis of policy for the American Keynesians.

Budget deficits, even if they caused a little inflation, were worth it because they created new jobs. But once the economy was back on track and full employment had been reached, it was imperative to balance the budget. In other words, the tolerance of these Keynesians for deficits and inflation was not unlimited. The leading economists in Lyndon Johnson's administration, for example, sought a tax increase in 1967 to pay for the Vietnam War and reduce the deficit when the unemployment rate had fallen below 4 percent. Johnson refused until it was too late. Inflation began its rise with LBJ and was further stoked in 1971 by Richard Nixon, who pursued aggressive economic policies to reduce unemployment in the hope of winning a second term the following year.

Milton Friedman's rebellion against Keynes was a fundamental return to pre-Depression economics but with even more allegiance to the self-adjusting economic model. The Great Depression was caused not by a failure of Say's law, he and his disciples argued, but rather by mistaken government interference. Friedman had claimed that a tightening of monetary policy—higher interest rates—by the Federal Reserve over a few months in 1931 pushed a moderate recession into a full-fledged depression. Some of Friedman's followers broadened this analysis, contending that FDR's new regulations gave unions too much power and the resulting higher wages caused the Depression. Others added that the Smoot-Hawley Tariff Act of 1930—whose advocates wanted to raise tariffs on imports to save American jobs that were being lost to manufacturers overseas—undermined free trade and contributed significantly to the Depression.

In the 1970s, Friedman's student Robert Lucas and his followers claimed that Keynes's theoretical dependence on the irrationality of consumers and investors was fundamentally wrongheaded. Consumers, businesses, and investors are, in general, highly rational and even prescient, claimed Lucas. They do not spend less because they fear that the economy will not improve, as Keynes insisted. In Lucas's rational expectations school of thought, it is unanticipated government interference that can fool people and lead to damaging consumer and business decisions.

Friedman at least acknowledged that the Federal Reserve could positively influence the economy in the short run by cutting interest rates and boosting the money supply. A rising supply of money would increase demand, he argued, not Keynesian government spending. But Lucas and his followers did not concede even the potential benefits of monetary policy.

Inflation was a particular concern of Friedman's. It is also among the most natural fears of those who believe in Say's law. Inflation complicates business decisions and makes markets work poorly, they argue. Say's law assumes there will be enough demand, so adding to it is inflationary.

Friedman insisted that the government could in no way push the unemployment rate below its "natural rate" (Friedman did not use this term, but his followers did) without creating ever-higher inflation. This is a classic Say's law proposition. Unemployment reaches its optimal low level on its own, as long as the Fed does not lower or raise interest rates too much. Friedman ultimately said the money supply—money being the sum of cash and demand deposits (checking accounts)—should grow at a fixed rate each year. He believed the Fed could follow such a fixed target, minimizing any discretion it might have. In explaining Friedman's view, the economist N. Gregory Mankiw warned, "Policymakers with discretion are tempted to inflate in order to reduce unemployment."

In the inflationary 1970s, Friedman's natural rate became integral to the thinking of American Keynesians as well. They came to believe that Keynesian policies—aggressive monetary policies that drove unemployment below the natural rate—caused persistent inflation and that the unemployment rate could be pushed down only so far. Because changing the levels of government spending often required congressional approval, a slow and clumsy process, even those economists who were not Friedmanites began to favor monetary policy as a more potent economic tool than fiscal policy. Friedman believed fiscal spending as stimulus was futile and preferred using interest rates to restrain or stimulate the economy. The emphasis was different but Keynes, too, believed that monetary policy could be useful.

As government policy was increasingly reduced to controlling interest rates to achieve low and stable inflation, Friedman and Lucas claimed victory in the rebellion against Keynes and the resurrection of Say's law. Although Lucas's rational expectations model was breathtaking in its extreme assumptions, its influence was vast, largely because it promised a utopia based on simple and easily quantifiable assumptions.

But Friedman and Lucas badly underestimated the depth of the 1982 recession. In the real world, their models failed much of the time. Lucas and his followers thought that sharply reducing inflation by raising rates, as Volcker did, would be seen by all-knowing consumers and investors as a sign that stability was to come. Spending and investment would fall only modestly and temporarily because rational consumers and investors saw the good times ahead. Volcker, far more traditional, did not believe that rational investors could look into the future and only wanted to stop inflation, which he considered destabilizing. He knew recession was a risk, though he underestimated its severity. Of course, the result was the worst recession to that point since the Great Depression.

Lucas's hubristic 2003 claim that the problem of depression prevention had been solved—made twenty years after he failed to anticipate the steep 1982 recession—is based on the same "rational expectations" model. There were new models still more extreme than the one Lucas had fashioned; known as real business cycle models, they held that only major changes in technology could affect the economy, as long as government stayed out of the way. The New Classicals, as those who ascribed to this theory were called, took the Invisible Hand to the extreme. Their models reflected, as had Lucas's and Friedman's, a general view that government was almost always the only problem economies faced. Although the authors of these models won a clutch of Nobel Prizes, none was able to forecast the devastating effects of the financial crisis of 2008.

One of the reasons Friedman's and Lucas's ideas influenced less extreme economists was that general equilibrium, if flawed as a theory, seemed like a close enough approximation of reality to suggest that free-market economies were essentially stable and that only very cautious intervention by government would ever be necessary. According to one economist, Friedman told him there was no point in studying the stability of general equilibrium (Friedman did not care much about the revolution of Walras and the others) because it was obvious the economy was stable. It had grown for two centuries, had it not? And while there had been bouts of unemployment, the economy always eventually returned to rapid rates of growth.

Friedman insensitively underemphasized the degree of suffering high unemployment created even in the medium term and the social instability faced by nations in depression. He and less radical economists also erred in thinking that the economy's seeming stability was the result largely of the signals sent by the

Invisible Hand. These economists habitually ignored other major sources of stability and growth we have discussed: new technologies with economies of scale; new sources of raw materials; social customs, such as the desire for homeownership, and the demands of families; a national faith in the importance of education; war spending; the growth of suburbs and exurbs in a contemporary version of manifest destiny; the recent culture of materialism; and institutions including marriage, schools and universities, and private property law that are stabilizers of personal and national life. Only a relative handful of contemporary economists have explored such "institutional" or "structural" factors, and often only in limited ways. Nineteenth- and early-twentieth-century economists had paid far more attention to broader institutional matters.

Another school of conservative thought developed that preserved some Keynesian principles but was highly influenced by the Friedman-Lucas revolution. The New Keynesians, who found homes at universities like Princeton, MIT, Harvard, and Berkeley, justified using interest rates to adjust economies in the short run but sought to minimize federal deficits. Though quasi-Keynesian disciples, they were mostly dedicated to the myth of the self-correcting economy. Although they occasionally favored temporary deficits when the economy weakened, they urged a quick return to a balanced budget. Unlike Lucas and his followers, they acknowledged that there were significant market failures—monopoly prices, inflexible wages, and lack of market information—that called for some government intervention. But these economists still gravitated to a Say's law world.

Judging by a 1992 article by one highly regarded New Keynesian, Harvard's Mankiw, some economists apparently had little idea that

Keynes believed unemployment could occur when the economy was in equilibrium. "On the right is the classical view of a well-functioning economy," he wrote. "On the left is the Keynesian view of an economy fraught with market failure." But to reemphasize, as Jonathan Schlefer observed, "The economic problems Keynes finds are not market imperfections, such as monopolistic firms or trade unions." Keynes considered economic problems to be "the problems of the human condition: we cannot predict the future."

Almost all textbooks today see it differently than Keynes did. "As prices fall [for the entire economy], the economy gradually recovers from recession," wrote Mankiw, a Republican adviser, in his first-year textbook. Olivier Blanchard and other economists nearer the political center did not discard most of the implications of Say's law. As the economist Peter Bofinger noted, Blanchard's textbook has by and large the same policy implications as Mankiw's. If a recession occurs or growth is slowed because of a reduced deficit, inflation will fall. As Blaug had said, the fall in inflation makes consumers' real assets worth more. Consequently, they can buy more without Keynesian stimulus. Having surveyed economics textbooks, Bofinger wrote: "After the standard presentation . . . a student must necessarily come to the conclusion that the macroeconomic sphere is in principle ruled by the same self-equilibrating forces as the microeconomic sphere. . . . Therefore, any interference of the government or the central bank must have the same destabilizing effects on the economy as government interventions [such as price regulation, tariffs, or subsidies] on markets for individual goods." After 2008, the self-correcting economic model only *seemed* to have made a major comeback; it had never really left.

The rebellion against Keynesianism even included a surge of support for new free-market interpretations of the Great Depression's causes. One of those causes was now said to be the New Deal itself, especially the legislative support for the formation of unions. If only government had stayed out of it! In March 2009, the supposedly nonpartisan Council on Foreign Relations dedicated a full-day conference to this point of view.

A fall in housing prices led to the start of the recession in 2007. The financial collapse that followed on Wall Street in the fall of 2008 resulted in the largest decline of incomes and most durable increases in unemployment since the 1930s. The nation's total income plunged more deeply than in any subsequent recession. Unemployment rose to nearly 10 percent in 2009, compared to nearly 11 percent in 1982, but it had fallen by only one percentage point two years later, while the unemployment rate in 1982 fell by two and a half percentage points in two years.

Keynesianism now made its momentary return. In 1980, Lucas said, with youthful certainty, "At research seminars, people don't take Keynesian theorizing seriously anymore; the audience starts to whisper and giggle to one another." In 2008, he said, "Well I guess everyone is a Keynesian in a foxhole, but I don't think we are there yet. Explicitly temporary tax cuts do nothing: people just bank them. Supply side tax cuts [cuts in the tax rate on income] are fine with me, but they take time to work and at some point we need the revenue to run the government. I feel the current situation requires a lender of last resort but not a fine tuner."

Lucas was still reprising the conservative arguments. Consumers were so farseeing that they knew a rise in deficits would eventually require a hike in taxes, so they saved rather than spent, undermining the idea of a Keynesian stimulus. Even if people continued to save rather than spend, the savings would flow right to investment. John Cochrane of the University of Chicago was a classic anti-Keynesian who digested Say's law as an eleventh commandment. "Keynesian fiscal stimulus advocates want money spent on consumption, not saved," he wrote. "They evaluate past stimulus programs by whether people who got stimulus money spent it on consumption goods rather than save it. But the economy overall does not care if you buy a car, or if you lend money to a company that buys a forklift." It was Say's law, of course—money saved leads to more investment and then consumption.

But Obama took office in early 2009, and the several economists of modest Keynesian bent on his staff urged fiscal stimulus. They included Summers, the former Treasury secretary, who had regained some Keynesian allegiance after years of praising Friedman and implementing financial deregulation; Austan Goolsbee, who taught at the University of Chicago; and Christina Romer of the University of California, Berkeley, a Great Depression scholar. Not one of these advisers was an anti-Keynesian ideologue per se.

There were lots of outspoken anti-Keynesians, though, and the Obama team had a hard time rounding up Republican economists to support the stimulus. For example, Mankiw, the self-proclaimed New Keynesian, openly criticized the idea of more government spending as a stimulus, advocating modest tax cuts at most. He argued that monetary policy—lower interest rates—could still do the job. Another influential economist, John Taylor of Stanford, who had advised both George W. Bush and his father, also argued against a stimulus. The outspoken Cochrane told a reporter in 2009 that Keynesianism is "not part of what anybody has taught graduate students since the 1960s. They [Keynesian ideas] are fairy tales that have been proved false. It is very comforting in times of stress to go back to the fairy tales we heard as children but it doesn't make them less false."

In Europe, economists were even more widely skeptical of a stimulus. The European Central Bank, which had dominated the Continent's policy for years and was ever fearful of a return of inflation, consistently kept interest rates relatively high. It was following in the tradition of Germany's central bank, whose economists typically discounted Keynes and emphasized the dangers of government deficits, believing them to cut into private savings and undermine the supreme importance of price stability.

The view of American and European economists that Keynesianism did not work stood in contrast to the preponderance of empirical research showing significant benefits from running government deficits in times of high unemployment and economic weakness. In a 2011 paper written after her tenure as chairwoman of the Council of Economic Advisers, Romer cited persuasive research studies to demonstrate that a dollar of government spending led to more than a dollar's increase in GDP. Keynes called this the multiplier. Increased spending in states where there were bumps in federal spending from military outlays or Social Security benefits resulted in still-greater increases in overall income.

In the face of such evidence and with the slow economic recovery, economists like Cochrane softened their view on fiscal stimulus by 2012, but they still insisted the research was ambiguous. Romer's paper, however, was a convincing layman's summary. In her defense of the Keynesian multiplier, she insisted that she was not philosophically a Keynesian but was merely reporting the empirical facts.

President Obama recognized the need for a substantial stimulus. Within a month of his taking office, Congress passed the American

Recovery and Reinvestment Act, a $787 billion (later calculated at $830 billion) package of spending increases and tax cuts, the equivalent of about 5 percent of the economy's value. It was a significant political achievement. Though some of his staff, including Romer and Summers, argued that a greater sum was needed, the president, still dedicated to "bipartisanship," would not spend political capital on support for a bigger package; moreover, he conceded to Republicans by including tax cuts as well as spending programs. Without a strong economic consensus, a larger stimulus defied his moderate sensibilities; even in an economy whose bottom was falling out, a stimulus of well more than $1 trillion was outsize by historical standards and may not have passed Congress. If the economy faltered, there was still the possibility that he could propose a second stimulus within a few months.

Despite myriad claims to the contrary, the stimulus unambiguously did its job. The sharp reduction in job losses that coincided almost precisely with the spending of the stimulus money is persuasive. Without the cash infusion, the economy would have kept shrinking and job losses would have risen rapidly. Probably three million jobs were created, though the unemployment rate stayed well above 9 percent until 2011 because so many more jobs than expected had been lost during the depths of the recession in 2008 and early 2009. Obama's economists had incorrectly promised that the unemployment rate would not exceed 8 percent. The Keynesian model was not wrong; they just badly underestimated how weak the economy was at the time they made their forecast. As many as eight hundred thousand jobs were being lost each month, and the administration did not have the current data to understand the implications.

This was a major political blunder. With unemployment rising to 10 percent, it was easy to convince the American people the stimulus was not working. Led by Cochrane, Taylor, and Mankiw, conservative economists grumbled loudly about mistaken Keynesian nonsense, and moderate economists hardly fought back. A notable exception was Alan Blinder, a former vice chairman of the Federal Reserve. He coauthored a research study, based on an economic model created by the private economist Mark Zandi, that argued the stimulus had clearly worked, creating millions of jobs. Other studies corroborated their findings. But President Obama chose not to trumpet his Recovery Act and its successes.

Say's Law and Deficit Mania

The obsession with government budget deficits since the crisis of 2008 and the subsequent recession illustrates the damage done by mistaken economic ideas. In the rich West, tens of millions of people lost jobs that could have been saved.

The deficit was caused by the collapsing economy, the tax cuts instituted by George W. Bush early in the 2000s, war spending, and the short-term stimulus. At the end of 2007, the debt was 30 percent of GDP. By 2008, under George W. Bush, it moved to about 38 percent, and by 2010 it was about 55 percent. That the deficit was obviously not caused by too much social spending didn't matter to policymakers in Washington or to some in the media—or, eventually, to Obama.

Those opposed to government spending relied on two arguments. One is that government, with only a few exceptions, adds nothing to economic growth or efficiency and interferes with the job-creating sectors of the private economy. The other is that deficits eat into savings under Say's law by crowding out private investment and pushing up interest rates. As Blinder wrote, "The tarring of the Recovery Act was the tarring of the name—and even the concept—of stimulus."

The focus on the dangers of social spending was a magician's misdirection, orchestrated by those opposed to Obama's policies. Eliminating deficits of course appeals to Americans' instinct for self-sufficiency, sacrifice, and discipline. Keynes fought off these instincts because they could be counterproductive.

Obama may not have known that he subscribed to Say's law or that it was a foundation for economists' attacking the deficit. But even though he supported his stimulus package, he was more the deficit hawk than he should have been. Five days *before* his 2009 inauguration, he called for a budget summit, and when it convened a month later, despite his sponsorship of the fiscal stimulus package, he raised cutting the deficit to a major priority. "So if we confront this crisis without also confronting the deficits that helped cause it," he said at the summit, "we risk sinking into another crisis down the road as our interest payments rise, our obligations come due, confidence in our economy erodes, and our children and our grandchildren are unable to pursue their dreams because they're saddled with our debts." The president apparently believed a high deficit was political poison.

In early 2010, Obama created the National Commission on Fiscal Responsibility and Reform, appointing two fiscal conservatives, Erskine Bowles, who had served as Clinton's chief of staff, and the former Republican senator Alan Simpson, to lead it. New forecasts of rising budget deficits were coming in from all sides, striking fear into a manipulated public and creating fodder for anti-Obama Republicans. Led by the billionaire investment banker Pete Peterson, a well-financed campaign by the Concord Coalition and the Committee for a Responsible Federal Budget had significant influence. The Bowles-Simpson commission called for federal spending to be no higher than 21 percent of GDP, the average since the 1970s. Alas, this average is insufficient for a country with an aging population and rising health care costs and in need of updated infrastructure and pre-K education. To achieve the 21 percent figure would require sharp cuts in social spending, including Social Security and Medicare. All this in service of the dubious proposition that the projected deficit had to be cut sooner rather than later.

President Obama did not accept the stringent recommendations of his own commission, which called for far more spending cuts than tax increases. Soon enough, though, full-fledged austerity economics—by which I mean the belief that reducing the budget deficit during periods of weak economic growth could foster prosperity—was imposed on the United States.

In November 2010, when the midterm elections were held, the unemployment rate stood at 9.6 percent. The Democrats lost control of the House as well as many seats in the Senate, though they retained a majority there. Obama would thus be checked by a recalcitrant Congress for the remainder of his first term and into his second.

Ultimately, in a showdown with Republicans over raising the debt ceiling, the president in 2011 agreed to an automatic sequestration of government funds to go into effect in early 2013. If Congress could not compromise on budget cuts and a reversal of George W. Bush's tax cuts, government spending would be automatically cut—sequestered—for all but a handful of major social programs. Tax increases on those who made more than $450,000 were passed, but demands for social spending cuts resulted in a deadlock and sequestration began. The resulting spending cuts, including for the Defense Department, ate significantly into economic growth, especially in 2013. The deficit was being reduced by Congress, which, according to Say's law, should have led to more investment. It didn't.

Obama's opponents mostly drew attention to the long-term deficit, which by the 2020s would rise rapidly as the costs of Medicare and Medicaid soared. But the ten-year budget deficit was well under control; according to the forecast of the bipartisan Congressional Budget Office, it was expected to average only 1.5 percent of GDP, far lower than its high of 10 percent during the Great Recession. Through the end of 2013, however, Congress retained the sequester, needlessly slowing economic growth.

The media focused on the politics of the budget debate, but economic ideas had a central role in the outcome. Believers in Say's law predominated. Notable economists did research that supported the anti-Keynesian contention that cutting deficits in times of economic downturns, known as contractionary expansion, could be an effective policy. The most prominent research was led by Alberto Alesina of Harvard University, where conservative economists—that is, those skeptical of government intervention—had displaced much of the formerly pro-government liberal faculty of the 1960s. "This is Alesina's hour," declared *Bloomberg Businessweek* in 2010. "In April in Madrid, he told the European Union's economic and finance ministers that 'large, credible, and decisive' spending cuts to reduce budget deficits have frequently been followed by economic growth." Cut deficits, went Alesina's argument, and you will restore the business confidence to invest fully the excess savings; spending cuts were more effective than tax increases in reducing deficits.

Alesina's research was poor. Most important, his analyses, which started in the early 1990s, didn't distinguish the economic conditions under which austerity policies were adopted. Essentially, Alesina's optimistic conclusions about austerity expansions applied only when economies were already strengthening or their currencies were falling in value sufficient to spur exports—conditions not applicable to either the United States or most of Europe.

Nonetheless, the Tea Party used Alesina's research to support its demand for spending cuts. European leaders put great store in the research as well. In early 2010 austerity economics prevailed in Europe. The Eurozone demanded government spending cuts and higher taxes in debt-ridden Spain, Portugal, Italy, and Greece as a precondition for aid. Across Europe, recession soon followed, unemployment soared, and the risks of social unrest rose. In spite of this, there was the belief that Say's law would eventually work.

In the fall of 2010, economists at the International Monetary Fund, including Olivier Blanchard, discredited Alesina's main paper with their own research—which properly adjusted for the economic context in which austerity was undertaken. In almost no case did such austerity work if an economy was weak. In 2012, a second paper from the IMF dealt an even more severe blow to Alesina's findings. The European Central Bank at last decided it would guarantee certain private government securities, acting much more like the U.S. Federal Reserve. It was the first crack in the ideological dam.

In early 2010, a paper more influential than Alesina's by two other Harvard economists unfortunately lent credibility and gravity to the austerity argument. Carmen Reinhart and Kenneth Rogoff, riding high on the success of their book *This Time Is Different,* published a historical study of a variety of nations in which debt was at one time or another high as a proportion of GDP. As debt levels reached 90 percent of GDP, they found, economic growth slowed sharply on average. If government health care spending kept rising rapidly into the 2020s, America's debt-to-GDP levels could approach and even exceed this level.

The 90 percent threshold caught on like wildfire. *The Washington Post* editorialized that "debt-to-GDP could keep rising—and stick dangerously near the 90 percent mark that economists regard as a threat to sustainable economic growth." Representative Paul Ryan, who proposed a budget with draconian social spending cuts, referred to it as "conclusive." Reinhart and Rogoff were the favorite economists of Britain's chancellor of the exchequer, George Osborne, who imposed strict austerity to get debt down in the United Kingdom, causing a recession in the process.

No one could duplicate Reinhart and Rogoff's results, however. When they made their data available, belatedly, to Thomas Herndon, a graduate student at the University of Massachusetts Amherst, he found fundamental arithmetic, sampling, and computer flaws in their analysis. Herndon, with his faculty advisers Michael Ash and Robert Pollin, wrote that historical statistics showed there was no debt level that suddenly produced a sharp drop in rates of growth. Reinhart and Rogoff insisted there was some reduction in rates of growth at the 90 percent level, but even the most sympathetic interpretation of the facts showed it was a minor decline.

It was never clear from their paper, in fact, whether rising debt caused a slowdown in the growth of GDP or whether a slowdown in the growth of GDP caused the rising debt-to-GDP ratio, a point raised by some economists even before Herndon's analysis. There is persuasive evidence that the cause was slowing growth. Many policymakers and some economists emphasized only the conclusions they liked.

A school of Keynesians led vociferously by Paul Krugman in his *New York Times* column and the *Financial Times* columnist Martin Wolf called for fiscal stimulus. Ben Bernanke had been doing the heavy lifting to support the economy by cutting interest rates to nearly zero and implementing a new plan, known as quantitative easing, to buy mortgage and other securities to keep long-term rates down as well. The rates could only go so low, however. As the Fed cut its target interest rate to zero, Gauti B. Eggertsson, a Fed staff economist, argued that fiscal stimulus was needed. Eventually, Bernanke, a follower of Milton Friedman in these matters and skeptical of fiscal policy, agreed that fiscal expansion was necessary. Reinhart and Rogoff also supported sharp doses of temporary fiscal stimulus in the United States in 2009.

Several economists, including N. Gregory Mankiw and John Taylor, presented the case for austerity in strong if misleading terms. Taylor pointed to an example in which tax rebates produced no rise in consumption. His economic argument was highly misleading. Christina Romer noted that consumption had been falling at the time. The tax rebates stopped the fall, which was the test of whether the Keynesian policy worked, not whether consumption increased.

Britain provided one of the clearest examples of the failure of austerity economics. Immediately upon taking office in early 2010, Prime Minister David Cameron, a Conservative, announced a package of spending cuts and a sharp increase in the national value-added tax. The objective was to cut the large budget deficit that had resulted from the recent recession, as economists like Alesina recommended, even though the economy was weak. Britain had one advantage over nations like Spain and Greece: it could reduce the value of its currency to encourage exports; the currencies of

Greece, Spain, Italy, Portugal, and all members of the Eurozone were fixed to the euro and could not be devalued. With pompous confidence, Chancellor Osborne forecast that Britain would soon reduce its deficit as a proportion of GDP.

Twenty prominent British economists, half a dozen of them from the prestigious London School of Economics, wrote a letter in strong support of the Conservative program. The *Financial Times* ran an editorial in favor of it (even as the paper's leading economics columnist, Martin Wolf, severely criticized it). Say's law seemed to be alive and well in London.

The British deficit only grew, however. Britain announced that the policy to cut the near-term deficit would not be reversed. Not only did the chancellor predict that the budget deficit would fall as a percentage of GDP, he also predicted a healthy rise in exports because interest rates would now fall due to a diminishing budget deficit, meaning less demand for the pound. A lower pound would stimulate exports, also helping growth. Most important, following Say's law, business confidence would be restored and capital investment would again flow liberally.

None of this occurred. By early 2013, Britain's budget deficit as a percentage of GDP (excluding interest rates) was one of the highest in Europe. Its account deficit, a measure of export weakness, was the same as it was in 2008. Capital investment grew at half the forecasted rate. GDP was well below its 2009 high. In the summer of 2012, nine of the twenty respected economists who had signed the pro-austerity letter publicly changed their minds and urged a change in course. The *New Statesman* found that most of them had been markedly overoptimistic about the impact of the country's austerity measures. The economists' turnabout had no influence on the Cameron government.

The seventeen nations that had adopted the euro were similarly confused, and their leaders did even more damage. As Greece, Spain, Portugal, Ireland, Italy, and other nations faced government debt crises amid soaring budget deficits—more the result of the bursting of property bubbles than profligate governments—the European ministers did not reach for fiscal stimulus as they should have. Those controlling the Eurozone, notably Germany, imposed serious austerity—mostly tax hikes and sharp social spending cuts—on the struggling nations in return for bailout money. To the Germans, as Martin Wolf observed, "economics is a branch of moral philosophy. . . . it's immoral to promote growth by increasing fiscal deficits." The German policymakers in turn had a slew of prestigious and influential economists who supported such ideas, many from American universities.

The Germans distorted the sources of their own economic success. Austerity drove the Eurozone into recession in 2011, but unemployment in Germany remained low because the government had been suppressing wage growth to stay competitive internationally. The low wages kept down export prices, thus increasing trade deficits in other Eurozone nations. German banks had been major lenders to these nations, benefiting from earlier confidence in the single-currency alliance. Now Germany refused to help stimulate the Eurozone through more aggressive government spending, even though it was the only nation economically healthy enough to do so. The head of the German central bank, Jens Weidmann, was a purist. He had been trained to believe that raising savings through reduced deficits was the path to growth. Say's law had no more enthusiastic advocate. He worried that Keynesian policies would breed inflation. European policies made America's sequestration look modest by comparison.

Austerity has a strong appeal. Martin Wolf's comments about moral ideology in Germany suggest an important conclusion: the growing deficits were proof to the public of irresponsibility, and that required sacrifice. The British media generally supported austerity, *The Guardian* being a notable exception. In the United States, Jack Lew, the head of the Office of Management and Budget and future Treasury secretary, compared the benefits of government thrift to family thrift when introducing the annual budget. Obama also irresponsibly made a similar comparison. The analogy, as noted, is completely inappropriate.

In July 2013, the president finally told *The New York Times* that it was time to abandon austerity economics in the United States. He'd been arguing against the arbitrary spending cuts of sequestration since early that year. But much of the damage had been done, not least by Obama himself. Journalistic reports claimed it was his economics team that floated the idea of sequestration in the budget compromise with the Republicans.

An example of such myopia and political posturing was exhibited once again by Britain's George Osborne in 2013, when the British economy had begun to turn up slightly. After years of failure, the chancellor now declared that his policies were right. So did the prime minister of Spain, which also experienced a slight uptick in economic growth. But in England, GDP was still well below its precrisis high, and in Spain unemployment hovered around 25 percent—depressionary levels.

Robert Solow, a colleague of Paul Samuelson's and a moderate Keynesian, could not imagine how economics had become so purist. In 2008, the Nobel laureate wrote a short, relevant comment about the severely conservative macroeconomics and the highly quantitative school of thought embraced by the New Classicals.

> There has always been a purist streak in economics that wants everything to follow neatly from greed, rationality, and equilibrium, with no ifs, ands, or buts. Most of us have felt that tug. Here is a theory that gives you just that, and this time "everything" means everything: macro not micro. The theory is neat, learnable, not terribly difficult, but just technical enough to feel like "science." Moreover, it is practically guaranteed to give laissez-faire-type advice, which happens to fit nicely with the general turn to the political right that began in the 1970s.

This statement summarizes the arc of economic practice since the 1970s—and includes more orthodox economists than the New Classicals. Say's law was the central assumption of those who supported austerity, but it was not an empirically justified postulate. It defied serious proof. History has shown time and again how damaging the idea has been.

Austerity economics has driven much of the West into recession and may hold the United States back for decades. Dedication to the ideas that underlie such economic policies is keeping the country from investing adequately in itself to compete in a global economy and from creating social policies that include all Americans and promise them a life of dignity. Bad ideas cost jobs and may ultimately cause political instability.

Chapter Three

Government's Limited Social Role: Friedman's Folly

In today's orthodox economic theory, government is mostly a bystander. Even politically liberal economists generally argue that government must only correct what they define as market failures. These obligations can be significant, such as investing in infrastructure, regulating monopolies, establishing unemployment insurance, creating a public retirement system, or setting limits on pollution. But there is no scientific, unambiguous way to measure a market failure. To the contrary, the underlying assumption is that markets rarely fail. Economists have no viable theory of government's place in the economy, except as a filler of occasional gaps in free markets.

You would assume that political scientists view the economy as essential to the political decision-making process they analyze and that sociologists think the economy plays a major role in social systems. Similarly, you would also imagine that all economists acknowledge how critical government is to human rights and social justice. But you'd be wrong. Milton Friedman, the profession's most rigorous defender of markets, believed that a free market without government interference provides, but for a few exceptions, all the governance and all the protection of liberty a nation needs. In economic theory, there is no true sense of government's central role in a nation's economy and in every aspect of its citizens' lives. I call this Friedman's Folly.

It is important to make clear that Friedman's contention is not a mere extension of Smith's Invisible Hand. Smith believed that the Invisible Hand worked, but he could not imagine that a free market was almost all a nation needed to govern itself and maintain its social policies. The philosophical discourse about the purposes of government was vigorous in Smith's time. But it is much less so now. Modern economics has not made a positive case, in Richard Nelson's words, for what government must and can do. Government, after all, is society; it is all of us getting together. The economy is not. But prevailing orthodox economics would have us believe, following Friedman at least to a degree, and with only a little exaggeration, that it is. Today's economics could not even serve as a guide to the many factors that contributed to economic growth in the two and a half centuries of America's history. The prevailing theories of growth are limited, abstract, and badly misleading.

It is not that economists don't think about government's part in growth or social justice. But since the 1970s, they have been unable to escape the strong ideological tendency toward limiting its duties to the mere protection of free markets. The latest thinking among economists on this subject is that government "institutions" are important. The idea is appropriated from institutional economists, the leftist and less orthodox economists who have long argued that institutions affect economic outcomes as much as or more than do markets themselves, but the new version is different. The power of corporations over their workers is an example of leftist concerns, as are cultural and religious traditions and attitudes.

Nonorthodox economists believe that government investment in infrastructure, education, research and development, and health care is at least as important as private capital investment and creates the necessary conditions for business to thrive and for a just and optimistic society. This investment is not required simply because markets fail. Institutional economists recognize the need for equalizing education, but also for persistent regulation of markets, which, in their view, are rarely if ever perfect and do not reach even an approximation of the Invisible Hand. Some believe federal budget deficits must always be maintained because there is a tendency for demand to be inadequate in a free-market economy. They welcome, within limits, labor unions and regulations on minimum wage and maximum hours. Many think health care is a right of citizenship. Some argue that government must go beyond the hard-to-define ideal of equal opportunity for all and provide cash assistance to a large proportion of the population to ensure a dignified life for all. Some recognize that government research has been visionary, creating opportunities for entrepreneurs that would not have existed otherwise. They also, of course, recognize that people cannot be allowed to steal, that private property must be respected. And they allow for the need for national defense.

As an example, over the past forty years, wages and salaries have stagnated in the United States, with those in the bottom half of the income distribution experiencing very modest gains or losing ground. Since the 1970s, Social Security, unemployment insurance, food stamps, the earned income tax credit, and other forms of government assistance have provided more than half the income of these people, and a very high proportion of all the income in the lowest 25 percent. This suggests more than a mere market failure; it suggests a chronic problem with free markets that requires persistent government response.

The allegedly new way of thinking among orthodox economists calls attention to the need for adequate institutions to support economic development, but this thinking amounts to nothing more than a pseudoreform of conventional free-market theory. It is largely a restatement of the market failure school of economics in updated language. Leading new thinkers in the field are Harvard's Daron Acemoglu and James Robinson, who claim in their book *Why Nations Fail* to have found a holy grail: the beginning of the chain of events that leads to economic growth. They implicitly discount geographical explanations of why some nations have grown rich, including those provocatively advanced by the anthropologist Jared Diamond in *Guns, Germs, and Steel,* and minimize attention to labor unions and government social programs.

Instead, Acemoglu and Robinson essentially hypothesize that the institutions needed and developed by rich nations are those that allow laissez-faire markets to work. These include a guarantee of property rights and contracts, efficient banking, and minimal regulations for business formation. When it comes to public services, government must provide a level playing field for "business transactions," whatever that means. "Economic institutions," they argue, "must feature secure private property, an unbiased system of law, and a provision of public services that provides a level playing field in which people can exchange and contract; it also must permit the entry of new businesses and allow people to choose their careers." As I say, it is all about enabling markets to work.

But the devil is in the details. What institutions are they referring to? Labor unions are mentioned merely five times in a five-hundred-page book on needed institutions and are never seriously praised as critical to a market economy. The minimum wage is mentioned twice. The protection of infant industries through tariffs is not mentioned at all, though such beneficial tariffs were levied on manufacturing imports throughout most of America's history.

The authors sound gracious notes about the inclusion of all people in the economy and the necessity of state intervention to accomplish this. "Inclusive economic institutions [a source of growth] require secure property rights and economic opportunities not just for the elite but for a broad cross-section of society. . . . Inclusive economic institutions need and use the state." Where we need hard thinking, we get such ambiguities and platitudes about economic opportunities for all, but few explicit suggestions. How do we include a broad cross section of people? The authors seldom go beyond Friedman's libertarian framework and do not nearly achieve the nuance of the Austro-Hungarian political scientist Karl Polanyi, whose landmark book *The Great Transformation*, published in 1944, had as its theme that government and the economy are inseparable. Acemoglu and Robinson never offer a true blueprint. While they scorn some kinds of elites, they say too little about the elites who might suppress regulation, social programs, public investment, fair wages, labor unions, and true pluralism in the West.

Another major flaw in their thinking is a failure to carefully address causality. Which came first, institutions or economic development? The authors contend that the statistical evidence they offer supports the notion that institutions were first, but it is unconvincing. In fact, economic development itself has historically led to the creation of needed institutions—banking, public education, social programs like Social Security. Some critics claim Acemoglu and Robinson have not proved their point, statistically or historically.

A key criterion of the authors' successful institutions is that they are inclusive, as noted, leaning more toward egalitarian than elite societies. But they stack the deck by mostly citing severely dysfunctional nations like North Korea as examples of nations with bad noninclusive institutions and consequently poor-performing economies. They compare North Korea to South Korea, where institutions are constructive, but they pay only lip service to how South Korea aggressively used government to educate its people and subsidize its industries and how it delayed the full adoption of free, unregulated markets until it had a wealthy economy and mature industries. These policies do not fit readily into the authors' categories of needed institutions. In their thinking, as I noted, free markets are primary.

Milton Friedman set the new economic template for limited government. I emphasize his influence because his views, even when too extreme for most, have somehow become pervasive. His simplicity of thought and articulateness are what make his writing so attractive. His 1962 book, *Capitalism and Freedom* (edited by his economist wife, Rose), a compilation of talks he gave beginning in the mid-1950s, is compelling. It presents a clear dichotomy: the government is mostly bad, and the markets are mostly good. The Invisible Hand, coupled with Say's law, provides almost all the governance we need.

Friedman didn't have much use for the complexities of general equilibrium theory, the work of the neoclassical economists led by Léon Walras. He assumed that market-wide equilibriums were arrived at automatically, and he saw little need to discover and explain the process by which they were reached—an irresponsible characteristic of almost all orthodox economists. It was obvious to him that markets were efficient and that whatever damaging instability there was in the contemporary economy, such as the Great

Depression, was the result of government intervention. Not only did Friedman insist that an exchange of goods and services undisturbed by government controls or taxes led to an ideal and fair distribution, he also argued that it led to personal freedom, his highest goal. This moral point was the central theme of *Capitalism and Freedom* and, arguably, of his economic theories in general.

He wrote about this clearly, as usual: "It is widely believed that politics and economics are separate and largely unconnected; that individual freedom is a political problem and material welfare an economic problem; and that any kind of political arrangements can be combined with any kind of economic arrangements." This, he argued, is not true: "The kind of economic organization that provides economic freedom directly, namely, competitive capitalism, also promotes political freedom because it separates economic power from political power and in this way enables the one to offset the other."

Here is his characterization of how a market works efficiently:

> The possibility of co-ordination through voluntary co-operation rests on the elementary—yet frequently denied—proposition that both parties to an economic transaction benefit from it, *provided the transaction is bi-laterally voluntary and informed.* Exchange can therefore bring about co-ordination without coercion. A working model of a society organized through voluntary exchange is a *free private enterprise exchange economy*—what we have been calling competitive capitalism.

Note that his caveats—voluntary and informed—are difficult conditions to fulfill. This did not stop Friedman or most other economists. One quotation from Acemoglu and Robinson above seems directly from Friedman. To repeat, they write that public services must provide "a level playing field in which people can exchange and contract." Many textbooks make the same assertion. The hard part—how to define a level playing field—is mostly left unresolved. A level playing field might require equal power between workers and employers; equal access to quality education; excellent child care for all; minimal childhood poverty; multiple free parks and cultural institutions; income and health care supplements for people who do not have the material means to enjoy a decent life.

The Friedman doctrine has most damaged America by undermining the meaning of citizenship and community. According to Friedman, government is needed for little else than protecting private property, assuring the existence of competition (as if this were easily done), and investing in a few "neighborhood goods" like local roads, primary education, and modest programs for the very poor. His failure to define what we may owe each other beyond the Invisible Hand is Friedman's Folly, and it has had a deep and almost unconscious influence over economists. Friedman viewed collective decision making as the greatest danger. Give people what they need and then let them make their own way. A better view of the purpose of government is that it provide a dignified life for all. And what is government but collective decision making, after all?

Friedman had little sense of the historical importance of collective action, especially that undertaken through formal governance of some kind. As he wrote,

> The great advances of civilization, whether in architecture or painting, in science or literature, in industry or agriculture, have never come from centralized government. Columbus did not set out to seek a new route to China in response to a majority directive of a parliament, though he was partly financed by an absolute monarch. Newton and Leibnitz; Einstein and Bohr; Shakespeare, Mil-

ton, and Pasternak; Whitney, McCormick, Edison, and Ford; Jane
Addams, Florence Nightingale, and Albert Schweitzer; no one of
these opened new frontiers in human knowledge and understanding, in literature, in technical possibilities, or in the relief of human
misery in response to governmental directives.

This is, to say the least, a distorted recitation of these contributions. Consider the state-sponsored art of Periclean Athens or how
Renaissance artists were commissioned by princes or the church
(a central government if ever there was one) and how they often
worked in large guilds—basically apprenticeship trade unions. The
pope demanded that Michelangelo paint the ceiling of the Sistine
Chapel against the great man's wishes. The Medici rulers of Florence were passionate patrons of the arts. Jumping ahead a half mil-
lennium, think of all the fine works created in the Depression that
were financed by federal subsidies.

Government was also critical to the funding and encouragement
of countless educational and scientific achievements. Virtually all
the intellectuals mentioned by Friedman were educated at public
institutions, and many held professorships at public universities.
Newton was a member of the faculty at Cambridge University;
Leibniz was employed by Leipzig University; Einstein was hired by
an institute in Princeton, New Jersey, that enjoyed large tax deduc-
tions. The United States started subsidizing technical research at
universities in the 1800s, giving rise to schools like MIT and the
University of California, Berkeley. Army chemists discovered the
best ways to purify water in the early 1900s. Robert Oppenheimer
led the atomic bomb project, a directive of government, only a few
years before Friedman wrote these phrases. After World War II,
government-financed research and development produced many
wonders, from the computer chip to the Internet. Almost all the

science behind Apple's products was paid for by the government. The National Institutes of Health supports research that has led to numerous breakthroughs. By one count, 75 percent of major new molecules were discovered by the NIH in the post–World War II era. Government, not business, may be the great innovator.

Nevertheless, Friedman's suggestions in *Capitalism and Free-dom* are now broadly supported, often by Democratic economists. Friedman was opposed to Social Security, and today there are widespread calls to privatize it. The Clinton administration entertained such proposals, and President Obama had at times made compromises to reduce hard-won retirement benefits. Friedman vehemently criticized government subsidies of industries; such industrial policies eventually became taboo. He favored a version of charter schools, which are operated privately but receive government support. He denounced minimum wage laws, and the minimum wage has been raised so infrequently in the past thirty years that it has fallen significantly once adjusted for inflation. He opposed progressive income taxes (tax rates that rise with higher incomes), and now the country's tax system is much less progressive than it was in the 1970s. He deplored labor unions, to which 35 percent of American workers belonged at the time he was writing; less than 10 percent of the workforce is unionized today. He argued against regulation of prices, product quality, financial speculation, and ethnic and racial discrimination in labor markets. There is a direct line from Friedman to the weakening of federal antitrust laws, product and worker safety laws, and environmental requirements and, ultimately, to the financial deregulation that was central to the 2008 crisis.

Since the rise of Friedmanite theory, the expansion of federal programs that involve direct cash outlays rather than tax credits has been limited, resulting in inadequate social policy. For example, cash disbursements to families with preschool children, a common practice in Europe, Mexico, and South America, are resisted in the United States. Conditions could be attached to such outlays, including mandatory counseling for parents and medical and dental care for children. Under the new orthodoxy, such programs are unlikely to be funded, yet America has the highest childhood poverty rate in the rich world. Instead, we rely on a too-meager child tax credit, which provides a modest return of taxes to parents for each child. The earned income tax credit, another reduction of taxes for those making low wages, could be extended upward to include middle-class workers and downward to include more cash outlays for those who do not earn enough to benefit significantly from tax credits. Such programs may not see the light of day under current thinking, although President Obama did propose an expansion of this tax credit.

Given the politically conservative ideology he adopted after marrying the already conservative Rose, the influence of her conservative brother Aaron, who helped him get a position at the University of Chicago, where he was a faculty member, and the moderate conservatism of the school's economics department at that point, Friedman was more than a little receptive to the laissez-faire orientation of neoclassical economics.

In a 1995 interview, Friedman said he wanted to be a "zero-government libertarian" but didn't think such anarchism could work. Unsurprisingly, Friedman had a view of America's rise in the nineteenth century that was mythological. The conservative historian Angus Burgin quoted him as saying: "The closest approach that the United States has had to true free enterprise capitalism was in the nineteenth century. Anybody was free to put up an enterprise, anybody was free to come to this country: it was a period when the motto on the Statue of Liberty meant what it said. It was a period in which the ordinary man experienced the greatest rise in his standard of life that was probably ever experienced in a comparable period in any country at any time."

Friedman's uninformed romanticizing of history is the equivalent of Ronald Reagan's wishful movie-made thinking, his wholehearted belief in the unique rugged individualism of America. Friedman campaigned for Reagan, who, his intimates claimed, had read *Capitalism and Freedom*. But Friedman was not as wedded to Reagan's fantasies of the rugged individual as he was to the idea that self-interest made the free market work. Friedman believed that human nature was flawed and that the Invisible Hand brilliantly channeled man's inherent selfishness. For Reagan, laissez-faire had more to do with unleashing the individual's energies. He considered Americans not selfish but brave, not flawed but supremely talented. He rarely if ever talked about self-interest.

Friedman's contention that the nineteenth century saw the most rapid rise in the standard of living is astonishingly inaccurate for an economist, and a statistician at that. The standard of living of Americans rose far faster in the twentieth century, as the government became larger and intruded more into personal lives, and it was the first time that a true middle-class majority was created. Wages grew at about 1 percent a year on average (there were big ups and downs) in the 1800s, but at 2 percent a year in the 1900s, when government spending as a proportion of the economy was larger and increasing rapidly. One dollar growing at 1 percent a year over one hundred years would come to $2.70. In other words, the average worker's standard of living rose by 2.7 times over the course of the nineteenth century. One dollar growing at 2 percent a year would come to $7.20; the average worker's standard of living rose by 7.2 times in the twentieth century.

There is a clear-cut natural example of how bigger government affected and enhanced growth in America in the twentieth century. Two mainstream economists, Nancy L. Stokey of the University of Chicago and Sergio Rebelo of the University of Rochester, then Northwestern, studied the effect the rising income tax rate had had on growth since its implementation in 1913. The authors, no left-wing economists, could not escape the obvious conclusion: "This large rise in income tax rates produced no noticeable effect on the average growth rate of the economy."

The political scientist Lane Kenworthy approached the subject in a different way. He calculated government revenues in America as a proportion of GDP and compared them to economic growth rates. In the early 1900s, federal, state, and local government revenues as a percentage of GDP were about 10 percent; by the 1990s they leveled out at about 37 percent. Yet economic growth continued at very close to the same rates, with a few wiggles here and there, over the entire period—even during the Great Depression. GDP per capita continued to grow at about 1.2 percent a year as government got bigger.

Sweden and Norway also experienced rapid growth in the size of government over these years, to around 60 percent of GDP. Yet their rates of economic growth did not slow down, either. Sweden had a hiccup in the early 1990s and cut back social spending. To some economists, this was an indication that Keynesianism was failing. But Sweden's government revenues, as Kenworthy noted, had risen to 65 percent of GDP. At 60 percent, they did just fine. The United States is a long way from there.

Friedman's casual mythmaking shows how faith-based his economics truly were. His number one nemesis was government intervention, and he naturally targeted John Maynard Keynes.

Ironically, Friedman made a major philosophical claim that he based his thinking on empirical observation. This caused a rift between him and other conservatives, especially those in Europe. In one of his best-known short pieces, he argued that the assumptions of an economic model need not be justified; a model's usefulness depends solely on how well it predicts economic outcomes. He asserted most famously that the growth of the money supply determines the growth of GDP. It really doesn't matter how the money lever works; all that matters is that changes in the money supply have predicted changes in GDP in the past and, he presumed, will do so in the future.

Yet despite Friedman's claims of objectivity, there is little empirical research cited in *Capitalism and Freedom* to support his grandiose conclusions. It is a polemic, not a work of substantiated economics. There are mostly assertions based on how free markets *may* work according to the Invisible Hand, not on how they do work.

As we have seen, when the economy went badly wrong, Friedman blamed it on government error. The Great Depression was caused not by financial excesses and lack of demand for goods and services, he argued, but by the Fed's incorrect policies. Federal and local housing subsidies were the cause of juvenile delinquency, a growing concern in the 1950s and 1960s. He held public power projects, foreign aid, and urban redevelopment programs responsible for a wide range of problems.

He believed that education should be supported by government, but only to a point. It would be better to give out stipends and allow people to choose, forcing schools to compete. Competition would, of course, result in a better supply of schooling. This was the forerunner of the modern voucher plan. But is there enough money to give everyone an adequate stipend? The wealthy will be able to afford the better schools. A voucher program creates further advantages for those with above-average incomes.

Friedman was appalled that Americans are forced to pay a tax into the Social Security system to guarantee themselves at least a minimal retirement annuity. It is a violation of freedom, he asserted, conveniently ignoring the high levels of poverty that had existed among the elderly before the system matured—upward of 30 percent. Social Security is one of the country's greatest success stories. Elderly poverty rates are now around 10 percent; they would be 44 percent without it.

Progressive income taxes, welfare programs, and other forms of government intrusion lead to more, not less, inequality, Friedman argued. Writing in the 1950s and early 1960s, he claimed that countries with bigger government had more inequality. France more than Britain, he noted, and Britain more than the United States. Alas, today the United States has more inequality than Britain, and Britain more than France. Inequality is generally highest among the rich nations where government is smallest.

"Which if any of the great 'reforms' of the past decades has achieved its objectives?" Friedman asked in the last chapter of *Capitalism and Freedom*. He then proceeded to list the "exceptions," those government ventures that had clearly succeeded: the highways built in the 1950s; the school system, with all its admitted defects; the antitrust laws, which he conceded did foster competition; public health programs that limited infectious diseases; assistance measures that relieved suffering, by which he meant welfare; and the maintenance of law and order. To any objective observer, these are more than a little impressive.

"If a balance be struck, there can be little doubt that the record [of government] is dismal," he nevertheless concluded. This same line of nonempirical thinking, dependent on such a literal, uncritical view of the Invisible Hand, subsequently influenced other economists. Why is it misleading to believe so deeply in this market mechanism? Consider Friedman's views on the market for labor and the minimum wage.

It will surprise no one that he was utterly opposed to the minimum wage, "the effects of which are precisely the opposite of those intended," he declared. "Insofar as minimum wage laws have any effect at all, their effect is clearly to increase poverty."

The analysis is narrow Adam Smith. If the price of a product is raised, fewer will buy it. If a higher minimum wage is set by law, business will hire fewer workers. The key assumption is that workers get what they deserve—in economists' terms, that they are paid what they contribute to the economy. That shouldn't be tinkered with. Adam Smith's economics did not go that far; neither did Walras's. A couple of decades later, John Bates Clark attempted to develop a theory to demonstrate that wages reflect worker contributions. It remains only a theory.

Friedman treated this theory as simple fact. For a system of voluntary cooperation based on free exchange to work, workers must be paid what they are worth. But what if minimum wage laws actually raise wages to their right level, compensating for businesses' power over workers? The possibility did not enter his mind.

As two researchers recently wrote,

Derived from the assumption of individual maximization behavior and competitive markets, the hypothesis that production factors [workers, capital investment in the form of machines, for example] are paid their marginal products [what they contribute to a company's output] is one of the main ingredients of neo-classical economics. If one were to determine the share of contributions to theoretical or applied economics making these assumptions, one would come to the conclusion that there are few assumptions that are more widespread than the one that production factors are employed up to the point where their remuneration equals their marginal product.

Reading Friedman or many contemporary economists, however, one would have no idea that there is a controversy over a theory that claims that wages properly reward workers for their contribution. One would certainly have no idea how extreme the assumptions behind the theory are or how economists have developed so little empirical data to prove the point.

In a piece she wrote for *The New York Times* criticizing an increase in the minimum wage, Christina Romer, the former Obama adviser and considered by many to be a political liberal, implicitly made this same oversimplified assumption that workers usually get what they deserve. This is an example of Friedman's broad influence. Unions, with favorable laws, pushed wages up, perhaps to their appropriate and efficient level. Wages may have been too low to support adequate demand. It is a hard argument for most economists to swallow.

Recently, economists have been using case studies to explore the effects of increasing the minimum wage; the more reliable studies find, at most, small losses of jobs. Even studies using other methodologies find only modest job losses. A higher minimum wage, though, may raise demand in localities that support growth and the creation of new jobs.

Perhaps most eye-opening are Friedman's claims that a free market will minimize discrimination in employment. He argued that businesses will want to be as efficient and competitive as possible and will therefore hire the best person, regardless of color, gender, or religion. Friedman opposed civil rights laws vigorously. Such laws violate inherent freedoms, he said. Friedman explicitly supported the right of a grocer to refuse to hire a black man if the grocer believed doing so would discourage customers from shopping at his store. So strongly did Friedman feel about this freedom that he retreated to the absurd. After firmly avowing his opposition to discrimination, he wrote: "The appropriate recourse of those of us who believe that a particular criterion such as color is irrelevant is to persuade our fellows to be of like mind, not to use the coercive power of the state to force them to act in accordance with our principles."

Laissez-faire assertions based on the Invisible Hand do not explain the rise of wealth and social equality in the United States or other rich nations. History turns out to be much more complex than these models suggest.

Simply stated, there was no laissez-faire economy in early America. There were countless regulations on the sale of commodities and other products. Friedman wrote that anyone could come to the New World, but it was not so. Labor was not free; a large number of workers came to the United States as indentured servants, who had to win or buy their freedom.

The principal source of individual independence was not the economy itself, and not the Invisible Hand, but the widespread ownership of America's abundant land in the first half of the 1800s. Orthodox economists acknowledge the advantages of natural resource endowment but also see dependence on it as a liability that gives undue advantage to those monopolists who often control it. In America, the availability of land was often controlled and protected by the government and was not readily open to a free, manipulable market. After the Revolution, the colonies essentially confiscated the holdings of the huge land barons—the heirs to the British system. Thomas Jefferson was a leader in ending British practices that created mighty land monopolies, including entails, which prevented lands from being broken up, and primogeniture, which passed land on to only the eldest male heir. When the Constitution was adopted, the new states donated their land holdings to the federal government. Over time, regulations were created that made land cheaper and far more widely available than in Europe. Scholars estimate that almost two-thirds of Americans owned land around 1800, an astonishing proportion.

In the early 1800s, domestic and international trade grew rapidly. The nation needed roads, but there was resistance to the federal financing of them. State governments issued bonds for new canals. Jefferson's own party produced leaders like DeWitt Clinton, who financed New York's Erie Canal. Massachusetts, Pennsylvania, Maryland, and other states quickly followed in building their own canals. These government-financed canals made possible an early American boom.

Alexander Hamilton, often at odds with Jefferson and today a hero of the right, advocated a strong central government that could borrow money. He also proposed aiding industries through government financing—industrial policy—and supported a tariff. James Madison, Jefferson's ally and an author of *The Federalist Papers,* signed America's first tariff into law. States like New York raised money through bond offerings to invest in companies.

Government defense contracts for firearms in the mid-nineteenth century underwrote the development of the means to mass-produce them. This system by which large military contracts, not the market, made possible capital investment in production techniques became the envy of Europe. It was a major technological and managerial advance.

By the 1820s, America was committing itself to free public education for children, perhaps the nation's greatest achievement before the Civil War. The record shows that by 1850, the United States was spending more per child than any other nation except Prussia. School attendance as a proportion of school-age children was as high as in France and Germany, the European leaders. Primary education was paid for by property taxes on rich and poor alike; it was the nation's first system for redistributing income. A wave of high schools were built later in the century, as demand for better-educated workers grew. In addition to aiding economic growth, widespread education strengthened public discourse and democracy itself.

Railroads were by and large subsidized or actually built by governments throughout the rich world of the 1800s. The United States subsidized the development of its railroads through massive donations of land; by one estimate, these donations accounted for half of the capital. Outright spending by the federal government came to only 3 or 4 percent of GDP, but had the donated land been figured in at a reasonably estimated price, the size of government would have been understood correctly to be much larger. Before the Civil War, railroads provided a major stimulant to growth not only by increasing the speed and lowering the cost of transportation but by increasing the demand for processed iron and steel. After the Civil War, the amount of new track laid was astounding.

Government was exclusively responsible for sanitation in the late 1800s and early 1900s, something often overlooked by economists.

Clean water made the growth of cities possible, and cities in turn were major sources of growth, their dense populations providing demand for goods and labor in new and less costly ways. Government also led urban health campaigns, including inoculations that helped prevent persistent outbreaks of disease.

Classical economists from Smith on were supporters of free trade, eventually succeeding in getting Britain to abolish major protectionist regulations like the Corn Laws. This may well have aided in the growth of the nation that dominated worldwide manufacturing for so long. But the United States almost always had high tariffs—which were anathema to Friedman—minimizing them for only a brief period between 1860 and 1880. Although economists debate the matter, on balance tariffs protected the new manufacturing industries in the North, developed in competition with those in Britain and the rest of the Old World. With tariffs, American manufacturing grew rapidly into the twentieth century. Even those skeptical of tariffs, such as the economist Douglas A. Irwin of Dartmouth, concede that they often helped developing industries even if they at times penalized domestic consumers by raising prices of manufactured goods.

As industrialization swept the nation after the Civil War, change was radical. Cities boomed thanks to the health improvements financed and managed by state and local governments. The first progressive political movement resulted in laws to protect people from the dangers of factory work and long hours. Early in the twentieth century, the Federal Reserve was created to stabilize currencies; the large toll taken by repeated financial crises and recessions had shown the need for a lender of last resort and a guarantor of the dollar's value. Antitrust laws were passed to break up powerful monopolies.

American views on government intervention shifted several times in these years. The Progressive movement, which started in the 1890s, began to reform the abuses of unfettered markets, supplanting the antifederal attitudes that prevailed after the Civil War. Some scholars still defend these periods of antigovernment ideology, echoing Friedman's claims that social injustice would have eventually been reformed by the market itself. It is a difficult argument to accept.

The 1920s saw a return of laissez-faire ideals. It was a decade of fast growth led by a consumer revolution in cars, electricity, cinema, and radio. But overspeculation in the stock market and an unsupportable housing boom soon overcame the economy. The Great Crash of 1929 and the Great Depression followed.

During the New Deal, Roosevelt's Securities and Exchange Commission required disclosure of information for public deals. The government hired workers for construction and cultural programs. Social Security, unemployment insurance, and deposit insurance for banks were created. The new work of Keynes justified government budget deficits to restore growth, and, indeed, GDP came back strongly between 1933 and 1937. But Roosevelt, fearing the return of inflation and rising budget deficits, reversed course in 1937 and raised taxes, and the Federal Reserve raised interest rates. The economy plunged into a new recession. Spending for World War II eventually brought the country back to prosperity and cut unemployment, which had once reached 25 percent, to minimal levels.

After World War II, the interstate highway system was built; the National Institutes of Health was expanded to subsidize medical research; the Defense Department devoted enormous sums not only to building weapons but to research and development that had myriad civilian uses, especially in high technology; college attendance was subsidized; and Social Security was expanded, enabling millions of senior citizens to climb out of poverty.

In this period, income rose across the spectrum, and its distribution was less unequal than ever. The gap between the high and low ends of the income spectrum narrowed substantially. Milton Friedman casually said that lower inequality in America was due to its smaller government. But the narrowing of the income distribution was caused by the almost nonexistent unemployment rate during World War II, which was a consequence not of free markets but of war production and the resulting rapid economic growth—and in part the new acceptance of Keynesian policies.

The income distribution remained narrow in the 1960s and throughout most of the 1970s, when Keynesian policies were in vogue. In these years, the nation subsidized college education further and created Medicare and Medicaid. Johnson's War on Poverty helped reduce poverty rates from 22 percent in the early 1960s to 11 percent in the 1970s. The economy grew rapidly, until inflation—at first due to spending on the Vietnam War, but later to a variety of issues—began to rise dramatically.

In the first two hundred and fifty years of America's history, the Visible Hand of government was as evident as the Invisible Hand of markets. Pure and simple, there was no economy without government, and a growing and active one at that. Economists like Mariana Mazzucato argue that technological advance was now more a product of government investment than of private financing. Ignoring history was a requirement if one was to believe in Friedmanite economics, however. By the 2000s, almost no major university economics department in the nation required a course in the history of economic thought. The presumption was that the new models explained all. History was apparently irrelevant.

———

In the 1970s, America seemed particularly ready to go through one of its pendulum swings toward conservative policies. For a variety of complex reasons—including the pain of inflation and high rates of unemployment, new budget deficits, the lasting sacrifices of the Vietnam War, and the help social programs provided for people of color—government became the ready scapegoat for America's problems. Crop failures, the Arab oil price hikes, and the end of price controls all contributed to soaring inflation in the 1970s. But it was Friedman's ideas about the causes of inflation—low interest rates (and therefore rapid money growth) and big government—that seeped into economic theory and then overwhelmed it. What resulted was not exactly a return to pre-Depression economics, as some seem to think, but a new brand of even purer neoclassical economics that emphasized sharply reduced government intervention. Many economists deluded themselves into thinking that it was new facts that demanded new theories—that economics, like all sciences, had to change, and change naturally meant progress. As always, some constructive developments occurred, but for the most part it was a swing in ideology, not a well-developed theory, that influenced economic policy.

Most destructive, the new thinking placed citizenship and community in the background. It was vital that people work for themselves. Collective action was passé. Following their own self-interest, people would form not merely a prosperous economy but an ideal society. They were consumers, and maximizing their material gratification through the Invisible Hand was what governed America. When Reagan took office, he cut the staff of various regulatory agencies, including the Environmental Protection Agency, the Food and Drug Administration, and the Federal Communications Commission. He emasculated the antitrust authorities. He busted the air traffic controllers' union, which helped lead to rapid deunionization of the nation. And he cut taxes sharply. By 1982, as he stated in the preface to a new edition of the 1962 *Capitalism and Freedom,* Friedman believed the world had swung his way, just as he'd predicted it would.

No one would contend that government is always efficient. In highlighting its deficiencies, Friedman benefited from the work of colleagues James Buchanan and George Stigler. Buchanan asserted that government workers operated in their own self-interest, just as everyone else did, and this led to a tendency for more government than was needed. Stigler argued that regulators were captured by those they were regulating, thus turning government into an accomplice to finance, pharmaceutical companies, the defense industry, and big oil. Big business got tax breaks and was given a pass on monopolistic practices. The habitual cost overruns of defense contractors were rarely punished. In the 1990s and 2000s, it was obvious that financial regulators, many of whom went on to jobs on Wall Street, failed to stop a crisis.

But who would argue that business was optimally efficient in those years? Detroit was beaten up by Japanese competitors, as were electronics firms. Better industrial machinery and consumer appliances were made overseas. Speculative bubbles on Wall Street led to fiascoes. Many economists refused to imagine that government could work as well as business. But it often did. Social Security and Medicare, for example, are highly efficient. The National Institutes of Health is a national treasure. Government R&D has been vital to the nation's innovation.

———

Friedman's declaration of victory is ironic. Economic performance did not improve as his ideas gained dominance and the power of government receded. By every measure, the economic improvement in the 1950s and 1960s was superior to the improvement from 1980 onward when Friedman-type economics began to prevail. One reason for the poor performance was that Friedman's influence had extended far into the Democratic Party. Jimmy Carter deregulated the airline and trucking industries. With enthusiasm, he also began to deregulate finance by eliminating caps on the interest rates banks could pay. Financial regulations were watered down significantly during the Clinton administration, and necessary new ones were never undertaken. Clinton refused to regulate derivatives, the heart of the 2008 crisis. He ended the last major Glass-Steagall restriction on mergers with insurance giants, enabling Citicorp and Travelers Group to combine to become the largest financial concern in the nation. The sheer size of financial institutions then allowed them to borrow and invest aggressively, contributing significantly to the riskiness of finance and the ensuing crisis.

There were other regulatory derelictions—of both omission and commission—under Clinton. Corporations were not forced to put on their books as expenses the compensation paid to executives through stock options. Investor lawsuits were newly limited. Only after years of pressure did the Clinton SEC stop analysts from selectively giving out their recommendations to privileged groups of clients. Corruption in the form of accounting scandals, under-the-table payments to sell securities, and hiding debt obligations was rampant in the Clinton years and led to the enormous bankruptcies of Enron and WorldCom. Clinton's aforementioned refusal to regulate derivatives was the most irresponsible of his deregulatory acts.

George W. Bush extended the deregulatory movement, with the

SEC allowing investment firms to borrow much more. The leading deregulator was Alan Greenspan, however, who swallowed the purist arguments for the Invisible Hand whole, his ideology largely originating from his intimate relationship with the libertarian Ayn Rand but reinforced by Friedman. When confronted with evidence of fraud in the mortgage market in 2004, Greenspan looked the other way, apparently assuming the beauty of market competition—the Invisible Hand—would prevent it from becoming excessive.

The Fed dismissed the possibility of a serious bubble in the housing and securities markets, and its examiners failed to uncover the risky securities. These issues did not interest Greenspan, who believed, like Friedman, that competition would keep investors from making too many bad bets. If someone bought at too high a price, someone else would profit from the bad decision and sell. Government would only make matters worse.

The most important error in financial regulation was tolerance for low capital requirements, the proportion of deposits and assets banks must keep in reserve. The influence of Friedman and thinkers like him was paramount in this instance. Banks can basically regulate themselves, so give them freedom to borrow. Antiregulatory sentiment made the passage and implementation of the postcrisis regulatory bill, the Dodd-Frank Act, difficult. As of late 2013, there was still no agreement on higher capital requirements for financial firms, perhaps the single most effective way to control excesses.

Friedman's criticism of federal welfare programs also had increasing influence in these years. Clinton's far-reaching 1996 welfare reform limited payments and required recipients to find jobs. Even his Wall Street–oriented Treasury secretary, Robert Rubin, opposed the Clinton welfare reform. By the recession of 2008, the reform manifested the weakness its detractors had long anticipated. In the first years the law was in effect, when the economy was booming, the number of people on welfare fell dramatically, but by the mid-2000s recipients were kicked out of the program even though many could not find jobs. One measure of failure was that child poverty rose as parents fell below the poverty line.

Lawrence Summers's actions embodied the great shift in economics toward Friedman's ideas. In an interview in 2001, when Summers was flush with a sense of victory after the Clinton boom, he proclaimed his admiration for Friedman. "In many ways Milton Friedman was a devil figure in my youth, [in a] Keynesian household of economists," he told PBS. "I grew to see the issue as more nuanced as I was in school and ultimately have come to have enormous respect for Friedman's views on a range of questions. That's a respect that is born of the power of his arguments as one considers them more and more deeply."

Noting that government's role was too great in the past, Summers went on to say that new ideas were "born of the lessons of the experience of the success of decentralization in a place like Silicon Valley and of the failures of centralization in places like Central Europe and Russia." He saw the success of many high-technology firms as an example of a healthy decentralization away from Washington's influence and control. He asserted that old-fashioned "command-and-control" corporations like IBM and General Motors needed to be "drastically restructured" to spread authority and decision-making freedom throughout the ranks. For him, centralization was epitomized by the defunct planning ministries of the developing world and by Japan, where government control of industry had proved a "complete failure."

Summers heralded a new world of less government authority, but his historical summary, like Friedman's, was close to preposterous. Were GM and IBM now considered failures even though they had been so successful for half a century? Was Toyota a failure, too? Didn't the countless corporate miracles of the 1950s develop much as Silicon Valley had in later years? Consider Xerox, Johnson & Johnson, Schlumberger, Merck, Hewlett-Packard—all of these developed in the pre-Friedman era, when faith in government was high.

Today, in the so-called age of innovation, we increasingly think that government is in the way and private enterprise does the heavy lifting. This, too, is mostly myth. "When government was smaller, innovation was easier," proclaimed *The Economist* recently. "Industrialists could introduce new processes or change a product's design without a man from the ministry claiming some regulation had been broken. . . . Officialdom tends to write far more rules than are necessary for the public good."

In the interview in which Summers so effusively praised Friedman, he said, "There is something about this epoch in history that really puts a premium on incentives, on decentralization, on allowing small economic energy to bubble up rather than [taking] a more top-down, more directed approach, that may have been a more fruitful approach in earlier years."

In an environment so skeptical of government's purpose, there was an uproar over the 2011 bankruptcy of the federally financed solar panel company Solyndra. The Chinese government invested so heavily in cheaper panels that Solyndra could not compete. It became emblematic of Washington's inability to pick industrial winners. Of course, venture capitalists, who are often credited with knowing which companies to back, were also big investors in Solyndra, and they initially took a bath. Less noticed was how Obama's team backed many other renewable energy projects, only a few of which went bankrupt.

Mariana Mazzucato persuasively found that the conventional

wisdom that entrepreneurs, not government, are the great source of innovation is wrong. As she wrote, "Not only has government funded the riskiest research, whether applied or basic, but it has indeed often been the source of the most radical, path-breaking types of innovation."

Summers and others point frequently to the development of Silicon Valley as an example of private innovation at its best— innovation based on the "bubbling up" of great ideas rather than top-down dictates. But empirical research shows that it was military contracts that enabled the Silicon Valley firms to sprout, spread, and then innovate.

Similarly, Mazzucato noted, though we think of Apple as an innovative leader in pure technology, it has been able to exploit research done by various government-sponsored programs around the world. One eye-popping breakthrough was made by two European scientists at the U.S. Department of Energy's Argonne National Laboratory; when they won a Nobel Prize in 2007, the Royal Swedish Academy of Sciences announced that their work had led directly to the iPod. Other government-dependent break-throughs involved Apple's display screens, the touch screen of the iPhone and iPad, and silicon-related advances.

Seventy-seven of the eighty-eight most important innovations ranked by R&D magazine in 2011 were solely or partly funded by federal research according to Mazzucato. And most of those funds were made available in the early stages of development, before commercial possibilities were obvious.

The number of major innovations from Fortune 500 companies fell from forty-four a year in the 1970s to nine in the 2000s. Those from government have risen from eighteen in the 1970s to forty-nine in the 2000s. An e-mail Lawrence Summers wrote to President

Obama declaring government a "crappy" venture capitalist seems to have been mostly wrong. And as I write this, the United States is rapidly cutting its R&D spending.

Friedman's claim that taxes cause market distortions has proved highly influential. High tax rates, he said, reduce labor effort and investment incentives. Reagan cut income taxes sharply even though doing so drove deficits much higher than his economists, counting on the supply-side miracle, had forecast. The supply-siders argued that lower tax rates would so incentivize workers and investors that tax revenues would increase. But it's not likely Reagan really cared whether tax revenues increased. He wanted to starve the beast, which meant that government spending would have to be cut over time to reduce budget deficits. As Friedman wrote in *The Wall Street Journal,* "Under those circumstances, how can we ever cut government down to size? I believe there is one and only one way: the way parents control spendthrift children, cutting their allowance. For government, that means cutting taxes."

America was and continues to be nearly the lowest-taxed rich country in the world. Proposals to balance the budget in 2012 and 2013, even those by Democrats, usually suggested more cuts in spending than increases in tax rates. This was an ideological bias, developed over thirty years, but not one based on fact or trustworthy evidence. The budget balancers were predisposed to reduce the size of government, again reflecting a belief in the primacy of laissez-faire policies, and to avoid tax increases. But the best empirical data, for all the attempts of Friedman's followers to show otherwise, have not supported the case that lower taxes or smaller government leads to more rapid growth. The economist

Peter Lindert, in his book *Growing Public,* explains how government spending as a percentage of GDP has no measurable effect on GDP growth rates. Growth depends on where and how the money is spent and how it is raised. In *Taxing Ourselves,* the economists Joel Slemrod and Jon Bakija illustrate that there is no explicit relationship between higher tax rates and lower growth.

The danger of government was at the core of Friedman's thinking. Smaller government became the default position of well-trained, less ideological economists in his wake. Government policies were guilty until proved innocent. None of the University of Chicago professors Friedman called mentors were as radical as he was. Friedman argued famously that a business had only one responsibility: to make a profit for its shareholders. Frank Knight was the preeminent economist at Chicago during Friedman's early years there, but Knight, to take but one example of his disagreements with Friedman, argued that the pursuit of profits "must be sometimes seasoned with mercy." Knight wrote that a system completely focused on self-interest would raise moral problems.

America has not adopted an explicit economic growth strategy since the 1970s; it has instead adopted an economic policy of allowing markets to work efficiently. This would be enough, it was thought. The conservative economist Tyler Cowen wrote a brief book called *The Great Stagnation,* which made the *New York Times* best-seller list in 2011. According to Cowen, America's postwar prosperity is mostly reducible to plentiful natural resources in the early years, technological advances, and a more educated public.

While many criticized Cowen's book, his basic points were consistent with accepted contemporary growth theory, which attributed economic growth to greater savings and technological advances. Initial endowments of natural resources also mattered. Savings improved rates of growth, but returns on investment diminished over time. At that point, an economy could only grow if there were technological advances. Later, the development of human capital—education—was added as a major source of growth.

The model was then thought complete. But the simplified emphasis on technological advances, the neglect of whether consumer demand was adequate, and the minimization of government's role led to a highly misleading history of American prosperity. Consider the post–World War II era. Cowen is right to note the importance of natural resources. But it's important to review the real-world details. The price of petroleum, the most important natural resource at that time, increasingly inported from Arab oil producers, was kept artificially low by diplomatic machinations and the power of the United States and Western oil companies. Oil consumption tripled in the 1950s and 1960s, yet prices fell sharply because of government, not the free market. The market for oil was never free and unregulated. The U.S. government made the difference.

Cowen is also right to emphasize technological advances. But the development of useful technologies and their interactions are complex and often difficult to pinpoint. Economists treat them as one big batch of advances. One major source of research in these years, especially concerning the Internet, as is now widely known, was the Defense Department. In the 1980s, Sematech, the government-subsidized consortium of microprocessor and semiconductor manufacturers, including the giant Intel, enabled America to regain its lead in microprocessors over Japan.

Meanwhile, Cowen scoffs at Keynesian fiscal policies, as a good conservative would, but he ignores the fact that the economy in the postwar period neared full employment in good part because of high levels of defense spending. The Cold War and the growing political power of defense companies—Eisenhower's military-industrial complex—kept defense spending at 12 percent of GDP in the 1950s and 10 percent in the 1960s. (As I write this, military spending, even during a major war, is only around 5 percent of GDP.) Those decades also saw the building of the interstate highways, stimulating the fabulous growth of the suburbs, and the continuation of the GI Bill and other forms of college tuition subsidies, all of which contributed to growth. In other words, government spending added a lot.

Cowen also ignored the contribution of high and growing wages, supported by unions, to the demand for goods and services that kept growth at a high, full-employment pace. There is no room for the strength and persistence of consumer demand in the orthodox growth model developed by Robert Solow and Trevor Swan.

In the postwar years, union representation was strong. The agreements reached with the Detroit automakers, in particular, resulted in high wages. Unions can push wages too high, but the union-induced wages of those years were initially a key to growth. Detroit influenced wage demands by other unions and in non-union companies, even for salaried white-collar workers. Union bargaining rights were the work of government.

The increase in world trade was another source of growth. Here was the most basic argument of the classical economists led by Adam Smith: that tariffs, quotas, and other inhibitions to free world markets diminish wealth. After World War II, major trade agreements reduced such tariffs in the rich world. But the growth was made possible by dependence on the U.S. dollar as the basic means of payment, a dollar whose value was basically fixed over these years, and by a fairly flexible interpretation of trade rules. Friedman and his followers argued for these currencies to be set floating in a free market. They were set free in the first half of the 1970s and almost all economists across the political spectrum still support floating currencies. As for the flexible free-trade environment, economists today generally believe in tighter rules for manipulating trade than existed in the twenty-five years after World War II. Worldwide trading rules are not now working as well.

Cowen's narrow model of growth, fashioned by an intelligent, well-meaning economist, reflects the ideology of most economists. It mostly follows the contours of the Invisible Hand. Government has little serious role in these models. And contemporary theory, as I've said, would not have laid out the path to American development that the nation had actually taken so successfully.

Keynes and Friedman were very different kinds of thinkers. Wrote Keynes in the 1920s: "The fiercest contests and the most deeply felt divisions of opinion are likely to be waged in the coming years not round technical questions, where the arguments on either side are mainly economic, but round those which, for want of better words, may be called psychological or, perhaps, moral." Friedman argued that if people knew the facts, they would agree. His was a narrow view of life, and of history. But he said that his economics was moral, safeguarding freedom. The two most influential economists thought in moral terms.

Friedman believed the old-fashioned liberal like himself—he'd be called a conservative by Americans today—"conceives of men as imperfect beings." Social organization must prevent "bad" people from doing damage as much as it should allow "good" people to do good. In the philosopher Isaiah Berlin's classic terms, Friedman was talking about negative freedom. In a complex world, however, Berlin's positive freedom in a world of widespread disadvantage is more important. Government creates freedom when it enables people to get a good education and a good job, have good health, retain dignity. In the words of the philosopher and Nobelist economist Amartya Sen, it is being sure people have the capabilities to live full lives.

Not only was Friedman's denial of government's importance wrongheaded, but his ideal world never existed. Without government, there would be no serious economic competition, no capable workforce, far fewer innovations, inadequate transportation for commerce. The elderly would be poor, the unemployed would suffer badly, and social cohesion, not to mention democracy, would be threatened. Friedman's supporters have only weak counterarguments, mostly that individual Americans would take more responsibility for themselves. But we know of the far crueler world before progressive reform. A nation that operates as if free markets are adequate governance is a nation headed toward decline and tragedy. America abjured government for forty years. During this period in which Friedman's ideas gained ascendance, the economic record was mostly one of failure.

Economists across the spectrum were influenced by the extremist Friedman, I'd argue, because he always defended himself by being consistent with the beautiful idea of the Invisible Hand. By the time the financial crisis of 2008 hit, Americans did not feel themselves part of a great national enterprise, a democracy of opportunity and social justice. They were busy reinventing a modern materialistic individualism, unaware of and apparently not caring how lacking they were in community. The failure to sense an obligation to each other is the worst consequence of Friedman's Folly. There have been intelligent critics of his economic ideas, but economists in general are Friedman's handmaidens.

Government's role in American history did not follow contemporary economic theory. Today's ideas didn't build canals, provide clean water, send adolescents to high school, protect workers from abuse. Today's left-of-center thinkers seem content with their market failure doctrine. Because of Friedman and others, economics tells us too little about the value of government. Government is an afterthought in economic thinking today, as is citizenship. A robust and balanced exploration of the possibilities of government policies can be resumed, but it will be hindered by economists unless they unshackle themselves from their undue faith in free markets.

Chapter Four

Low Inflation Is All That Matters

Inflation targeting by central bankers has probably been the clearest example of the damaging oversimplification of orthodox economics. Starting with New Zealand in 1990, about two dozen nations around the world, rich countries as well as developing ones, have adopted a version of the approach. It involves using interest rates to maintain the rise in consumer prices at a specified, stable level. The most commonly accepted target is an inflation rate of 2 percent a year—that is, consumer prices on average rise by 2 percent. Prices of some products may rise faster, others more slowly.

Some nations adopted a specific, inviolable inflation target, which is formal inflation targeting. Others adopted informal, more flexible targets, but targets just the same. The United States was among the latter.

The purpose of inflation targeting, according to its advocates, is to keep the rate of inflation low and stable because higher inflation distorts market pricing. Slightly rising inflation can also breed still-higher inflation, it is feared. The expectation of higher inflation leads people to buy more in anticipation that prices will rise later, driving prices ever higher. As workers demand wage increases to cover rising prices of goods and services, businesses raise prices further to maintain profit margins. Such uncertainty about prices makes business and consumer decisions more difficult. Some say the greatest danger is that inflation left unchecked will suddenly soar to uncontrollable heights, as it did in the 1970s.

There is no doubt runaway inflation is dangerous. But the basic concern of inflation targeting is not to avoid very fast increases in inflation. Rather, it is to keep the rate of inflation low and unchanging. In fact, the only U.S. economic policy of importance since the 1980s has been the effort to keep inflation at the low rate of roughly 2 percent. "Inflation targeting is the new orthodoxy of mainstream macroeconomic thought," concluded the economists Gerald Epstein and A. Erinç Yeldan.

One of the leading advocates of this approach, Ben Bernanke, coauthored the landmark *Inflation Targeting* in 1999, several years before he became Fed chairman. The authors' opening sentence is an affirmation of a new age of limited government intervention: "At the end of the twentieth century, with communism largely gone and with state-dominated strategies being replaced everywhere by market-oriented reforms, there is a consensus that prosperity and economic growth are created primarily by private enterprise and free markets." Focusing on inflation targeting alone fits this ideological assertion ideally.

The authors acknowledge other duties of government, including investment in infrastructure. In terms of public policy, however, inflation targeting is almost all that matters to them. If inflation is low, free markets and unfettered business will result in the best economy possible; economies will run as efficiently as possible and will therefore grow as rapidly as possible. "[A] reason for setting price stability as the primary goal of monetary policy," they say, "is a growing belief among economists and central bankers that low inflation helps to promote economic efficiency and growth in the long run." Such a claim relies on an almost complete faith in the self-adjusting properties of economies—general equilibrium theory. Stable, low inflation enables market participants to anticipate prices, costs, and interest rates. By reducing uncertainty, rational decisions regarding future costs and sales can be made. In other words, higher inflation would disrupt the efficiency of the Invisible Hand.

More than a little ironically, the authors admit that "obtaining direct empirical confirmation of a link between inflation and the overall economic performance of the economy is very difficult." In other words, their theories rely not on empirical investigation but on faith in the Invisible Hand and the theory of general equilibrium that follows from it. They contend that low inflation will remove the most important obstacle to the working of laissez-faire economics and the maximization of growth and investment, but they cannot prove it.

Even if focusing almost solely on maintaining low, stable inflation made complete sense, why such a low rate of inflation? Persuasive studies find that only annual rates of inflation into the double digits affect economic growth. Moderate levels of inflation of well more than 2 percent show little appreciable damage. Some economists make a strong case that an inflation target closer to 3 percent would have been more beneficial to the United States. Few paid attention to this research, which seemed like a radical notion, a mere one percentage point rise in the target.

As far back as 1988, Alan Greenspan told Congress that the rate of inflation should be low enough that "households and businesses in making their saving and investment decisions can safely ignore the possibility of sustained, generalized price increases or decreases." In 1996, he told his Federal Open Market Committee, the group of Federal Reserve governors and regional bank presidents who set monetary policy, that the rate should be close to zero. But Greenspan settled for a 2 percent target because the inflation data collected by the Bureau of Labor Statistics overstated, he thought, the rate by a percentage point or more. The informal target of 2 percent annual inflation, as measured by the consumer price index, was therefore really closer to zero already.

A central bank like the Federal Reserve adjusts interest rates to target its inflation rate. Raising interest rates should slow the economy, reducing demand for goods and services, restraining wage increases, and keeping inflation at moderate levels. Some believe raising rates can also be used to reduce the growth rate of the money supply, which a few economists, following the lead of Milton Friedman, still think is a key factor affecting inflation and the pace of growth of the economy. This idea has been largely abandoned, partly because the ups and downs of the money supply are also caused by business activity. When banks make loans, they do so by putting the funds in checking accounts (demand deposits), which are the main component of money in modern countries. If business is so strong that companies want more loans, and if banks have the funds, the money supply will go up. The growth of the money supply is thus as much a result as it is a cause of business activity (which economists refer to as being endogenous). In particular, the Fed focuses on controlling the so-called federal funds rate, which is the rate banks charge each other for short-term loans. This directly affects the interest rate banks will charge for loans and, as a consequence, the interest rates on other securities.

Friedman's old saw that inflation is always a money phenomenon is still sometimes repeated. In a late 2013 piece, Bernanke himself restated it. But this should no longer confuse observers. Its meaning is now more metaphorical than literal. Even Germany's conservative central bank, the Bundesbank, which has watched changes in money closely, finds that any relationship between measures of the money supply and inflation is tentative.

The Fed has also begun to adopt announcements about its future inflation objectives as a form of policy. If market participants know the level of inflation the Fed wants, they are likely to remain confident inflation will not go much higher. Again, this is a way of removing concerns about inflation from consumption and investment decisions.

But the main problem with inflation targeting—and a low target at that—is that it has resulted in the Fed's neglecting its other congressional mandate. The Humphrey-Hawkins bill of 1978 required that the Fed both restrain inflation *and* maintain low unemployment. Though Greenspan and Bernanke would deny it, the Fed has not abided by this second mandate since Paul Volcker's reign. If unemployment is too low, the bargaining power of workers will increase and they will demand larger increases in their wages. If wages rise rapidly, it is thought, business will in turn raise prices. Greenspan and Bernanke would argue that if the economy is working efficiently because of low, controlled inflation, employment will automatically reach its best level possible anyway, as will the average wage. Again, this is a leap of faith in pure theory; there is no empirical case that a 2 percent rate of inflation is the right one, and recent history suggests it has been too low.

In fact, inflation targeting has become almost synonymous with subduing the growth of jobs and wages to keep inflation low. Over thirty years of inflation targeting, wages have stagnated, inequality has risen to levels not seen since the 1920s, and the unemployment rate has been high on average except for the few years of the late-

1990s boom, which was partly created by Wall Street speculation in high-technology stocks.

We can get a sense of how unnecessarily high unemployment has been since 1980 by comparing the actual unemployment rate to the Congressional Budget Office's estimate of the "natural" rate. If the unemployment rate is pushed by the Fed below the natural rate, theory has it, inflation will keep rising. But as the economist John Schmitt calculates, in two-thirds of the years between 1979 and 2012 the unemployment rate was kept above—often well above—the CBO's estimated natural rate. These are the years in which wages generally stagnated. Judging by these persuasive numbers, both economic growth and job creation were well short of what they could have been.

Greenspan did not hide his goal of making workers feel insecure. In this respect, he was more a Marxist than a neoclassical economist. Marx similarly argued that capitalists preferred unemployment so they could control the frightened army of the unemployed. "The rate of pay increase was markedly less than historical relationships which labor market conditions would have predicted," Greenspan proudly told Congress in 1997. "Atypical restraint on compensation increases has been evident for a few years now and appears to be mainly the consequence of greater worker insecurity."

In a speech two years later, he pointed out that a survey given in 1981 found that only 12 percent of workers feared losing their jobs; in 1999, even with the unemployment rate down to roughly 4 percent, the same survey found 37 percent concerned about job losses. Workers' backbones had been softened by two decades of high unemployment and poor wage growth, he was proud to report. Greenspan was focused almost solely on inflation, and

keeping it low was accompanied by higher than necessary unemployment rates.

Some economists enjoy telling the story of the scientific development of their thinking and of how inflation targeting was merely
part of the evolution toward better economics. But inflation targeting cannot be divorced from its historical place and time. It was
very much a reflexive reaction, not a scientific one, to the rapid
inflation and tumultuous economy of the 1970s. When inflation
reached double digits, Jimmy Carter appointed Paul Volcker, a
Democratic banker, to the chairmanship of the Fed.

Carter was by and large a fiscal conservative, and Volcker seemed
willing to fight inflation more aggressively than his Democratic
predecessors had. Carter did not know how willing he would turn
out to be. Volcker took over in 1979, and within a couple of years
he drove the key policy rate, the federal funds rate, to nearly 19
percent to slow the economy. Reduced demand for investment and
consumer goods and services finally cut into the inflation rate, but
at a steep price. The recession he caused was the deepest the country had experienced since the Great Depression, pushing unemployment to 10 percent. When Alan Greenspan succeeded Volcker
in 1987, he openly declared low inflation his primary goal, not
least because Volcker was widely revered for his tough stand and
his willingness to drive the nation into recession in order to battle
rising prices.

The high and punishing inflation created in the 1970s continues
to influence economic theory and policy to this day. It was the equal
and opposite reaction to what happened after the Great Depression
of the 1930s, when U.S. unemployment reached 25 percent. In the

wake of that painful depression, reducing unemployment dominated policy theory for a generation. But by the mid-1970s, public
opinion surveys found that people were more worried about inflation than their jobs. Orthodox economics donned a cape of intellectual rigidity, but in truth economists were highly influenced by
public sentiment and the economic environment of the moment. It
was not the facts so much as the fears that changed.

Low inflation was also especially congenial to those that made
loans. High inflation reduced the value of loans because they were
paid back in less valuable dollars. Low inflation kept the creditors
happy. It enabled them to lend more, culminating in the debacle of
subprime mortgages (mortgages sold to people with poor credit).
Once again, many economists seemed to be on the side of the rich
and powerful.

If Bernanke, the Princeton professor, ever believed the unemployment rate had been persistently too high over the period of the
Great Moderation, which he profusely lauded, he never said so. He
probably took comfort from the Clinton boom's low unemployment rates, which momentarily dropped below 4 percent without
generating inflation. He may well have credited the boom itself
to low inflation. But what he should have learned was that it was
possible the unemployment rate could have been lower and job
growth higher over much of the 1980s, 1990s, and early 2000s—the
period of the Great Moderation.

In the late 1990s and through the 2000s, the narrow focus on targeting consumer price inflation also blinded Greenspan and many
other economists to the housing bubble. Because of low inflation,
the rapid rise in household debt also perturbed few. Bernanke,
who took over the Fed in 2006, believed that financial speculation
in housing was not a concern as long as consumer price inflation

was low. If housing prices were actually too high, it would stimulate too much consumer spending and therefore higher consumer price inflation. If there was a lid on inflation, the consumer bubble would be avoided indirectly by subduing the economy to dampen spending. Stock prices and housing prices would fall, or rise more slowly.

Greenspan had been badly wounded by a temporary flirtation with a bubble-popping strategy. Following the advice of Yale's Robert Shiller, who believed stocks were in bubble territory in the 1990s, Greenspan warned of "irrational exuberance" in the markets in a December 1996 speech. The anticipation that the Fed would raise interest rates led stock markets around the world to fall sharply. Believing he'd made a bad mistake, Greenspan backed off. In fact, in his 1996 speech he had questioned whether it was possible to anticipate a bubble: "How do we know when irrational exuberance has unduly escalated asset values, which then become subject to unexpected and prolonged contractions as they have in Japan over the past decade?" In later years, he argued that the rise in interest rates necessary to pop such bubbles would do considerable damage to the economy.

Greenspan had other tools at his disposal, however. Some were traditional Fed weapons, such as raising reserve requirements for banks and stiffening margin requirements on how much investors could borrow to buy stocks. He could also have increased capital requirements for financial institutions, limiting their capacity to borrow; attacked widespread fraud in the issuance of mortgages; and demanded more examination and transparency of newer exotic instruments, notably financial derivatives and the mortgage securities known as collateralized debt obligations. He used none of these tools. He thought them government intrusions in the market and believed that the Invisible Hand would subdue these excesses.

As long as inflation was around 2 percent, all was right with the world, and certainly interest rates were not too low. Adopted to reduce the chances of high inflation, inflation targeting also had the opposite effect when inflation was low: it could result in policies that supported financial speculation.

Bernanke also apparently misread the causes of moderately falling unemployment rates in the first half of the 2000s, believing that contained inflation made the economy strong through efficiency. But intense housing speculation, not growing wages, drove demand in general; consumers spent based on their rising wealth and easy access to home equity loans. The number of home equity loans soared in 2006 and 2007. Unemployment hovered around 5 percent, but it wasn't because many new jobs were being created. In the first half of the 2000s, the rate of job creation was the slowest of any economic recovery since World War II, and many people were left looking for work or dropped out of the workforce altogether. The percentage of the working-age population that had jobs remained well below the 1990s highs. Noting that, on balance, the rate of economic growth did not improve in the Great Moderation, the economist Andrew Glyn observed: "Less volatility does not guarantee dynamism." That simple fact was lost on many, if not most, economists. Not only was there little economic dynamism during the Great Moderation, but there was also much less true economic stability than realized.

The inflation surge of the 1970s was critical to the new focus on inflation targeting. Inflation had generally remained low in the 1950s and 1960s, even as the economy and wages grew rapidly. Many attribute the onset of a more rapid rise in prices to the Vietnam War, which President Johnson at first refused to finance with

a tax hike. A tax hike was passed, but not until 1968, and as inflation increased, the Federal Reserve raised rates, throwing the U.S.
economy into a recession in 1969. This did not slow the rate of
inflation as much as economists had anticipated. Something new
was going on, it seemed. Inflation had crept into the economy at a
higher permanent level than in the past.

In 1971, President Nixon imposed controls on prices and wages,
which did stanch inflation. The trouble was that when these controls were lifted in the following years, many prices rose especially
rapidly, as if the lid had suddenly been taken off a boiling kettle.
Nixon, seeking a second term, had increased government spending
in 1971 and 1972, almost ensuring an explosion of prices when the
caps were removed. Meanwhile, the Federal Reserve, run by Nixon's
friend Arthur Burns, cut interest rates, which many interpreted as
an effort to help the president get reelected.

Severe crop failures caused the price of food products to jump
dramatically. And Arab countries raised oil prices three times
in the wake of the Yom Kippur War and then again by another
33 percent in 1974. Average consumer price inflation reached nearly
12.5 percent in 1974. Then, between 1973 and 1975, the economy
fell into its deepest post–World War II recession yet. Unemployment climbed from a low of 3 percent in the 1960s to 8.5 percent
in 1975. Mortgage rates rose to over 7 percent, compared to 4 and
5 percent in the 1960s. The prime rate for business loans hit
10 percent in 1974.

Milton Friedman's prominence soared. His claim that inflation
was caused by a growing money supply was now widely accepted.
In his view, the Federal Reserve, which kept interest rates too low
(and let the money supply grow too rapidly), was the biggest culprit, followed by the White House and Congress, which drove

the federal budget into the red. The increased borrowing by the Treasury put more pressure on the Fed to buy securities to keep rates low.

Apparently, blaming government seemed right to the public— or, more to the point, gave them a focus for their anxieties. The economist Alan Blinder showed credibly that, contrary to Friedman's assertions, the rising money supply could not have accounted for the rapid rise in inflation. According to his calculations, the end of Nixon's price controls, the crop failures, and the increase in oil prices were far more important in creating the inflationary surge. But in the heated focus on inflation, Blinder was generally ignored. Neither Republicans nor Democrats were patient enough to wait out the effects of these factors by raising interest rates only gradually. Volcker, unsympathetic to those who demanded a more measured approach, undertook his shock therapy.

Oil and food inflation did eventually subside. But then oil prices were raised again in 1979, and there was another crop failure. Consumer inflation momentarily rose to 15 percent, and mortgage rates to 12 percent. In this environment, which came to be known as stagflation, Americans were willing to accept a recession to stop inflation cold. But they could not know how harsh it would be. By the end of 1981, the economy had almost started to free-fall into steep recession under the high interest rates, and Volcker suddenly cut them in the summer of 1982. Ultimately, GDP fell more sharply than under Nixon and Ford, and the unemployment rate rose to 11 percent in late 1982. Stock prices dropped to their lowest levels in a dozen years, and capital investment collapsed.

Inflation, however, was subdued. To many, this was the key victory. Reagan never faltered in supporting Volcker's harsh policies

because he knew reducing inflation was a priority with the elec-
torate. But he also made good on his promise to cut income taxes
sharply, producing a mammoth budget deficit; this policy was contradictory. Nevertheless, consumer inflation fell below 4 percent in
1983, a remarkably rapid fall; the back of inflation had been broken, despite the Reagan tax cuts and rising federal deficit.

The American people, so punished by rising prices, lost jobs,
and high interest rates on credit cards and mortgages, seemed to
breathe a sigh of relief. They could not be blamed for wanting to
avoid a return to these circumstances.

"It's morning again in America," Reagan declared. It was no
such thing. His using tax cuts to help stimulate the economy was,
ironically, a Keynesian proposition. Keynes argued that a stimu-
lative deficit could be achieved through either more government
spending or a temporary tax cut. But Keynes didn't argue that tax
cuts permanently increased growth by raising incentives to work or
invest, as many of his opponents did. Reagan's tax cuts were excessive, and even after a tax increase—one eventually borne more by
the middle class than the well-off—America was left with a deficit
larger than Jimmy Carter's as a percent of GDP even toward the
end of Reagan's presidency. In fact, Volcker had hesitated mistak-
enly to cut rates faster probably because of the Reagan deficits. But
the policies had the people's support.

Inflation targeting was not the only result of the fear of a return of
high inflation. Next came the irrational focus on the budget deficit,
which was widely considered inflationary. In the 1970s, the United
States had produced its first significant deficits, though, as a percentage of GDP, they were small compared to the deficits under

Reagan. Nevertheless, such deficits, aided by Friedmanite economics, were long after associated with inflation in the public's mind. "Tax-and-spend" Democrats were mocked. Reduced social spending made America a far harsher place than it had been in the 1960s.

The people were more easily swayed by the rhetoric of free markets and the fear of government spending. Serious economists resorted to Say's law to explain why deficits were harmful. Friedman and right-wingers like Reagan led economists and politicians in pulling off this sleight of hand. They turned the fear of and the suffering caused by inflation into an argument against government programs altogether. In his final debate with Jimmy Carter before the fateful 1980 presidential election, Reagan said, "We don't have inflation because the people are living too well, we have inflation because the government is living too well." His popularity ratings, not that much higher than Carter's at the time, immediately went up. This was the same misdirection used after the financial crisis of 2008, when a soaring federal deficit aroused fears about government social spending.

The painful and panicky economic climate of the 1970s was the main cause of antigovernment attitudes in the United States. But many have also correctly blamed the animosity toward Lyndon Johnson over the Vietnam War and his bold social programs for the ideological turn toward conservatism. In 1964, Johnson used spurious information about North Vietnamese attacks in the Gulf of Tonkin to win approval of a resolution to use military force in Vietnam without a declaration of war. The Vietnam War dragged on tragically, of course. Johnson's commendable domestic legislation—including the Voting Rights Act, the Civil Rights Act, and the War on Poverty, which launched Medicare and Medicaid—ignited racial animosity because some saw these social programs as handouts to Americans of color. Moreover, war spending deprived Johnson of the money to make his Great Society work, according to his widely respected biographer, Robert Caro.

Johnson was followed by the dislikable Richard Nixon. The Watergate break-in led to his resignation, but he also failed to bring the Vietnam War to the quick end he had promised. This, along with his secret bombing of Cambodia, seemed like dissembling to many. Although he won reelection by a wide margin over the antiwar Democratic idealist George McGovern, he was never truly popular, and he hardly inspired confidence in government.

In recent years, there has been a growing literature on the concerted organization of the right and business interests into a powerful lobbying and public relations force in the 1970s. The Heritage Foundation, the American Enterprise Institute, and the Cato Institute all gained influence in these years through research that justified cuts in taxes and regulations. Many progressives believe people were being duped by these well-financed think tanks and their right-wing theories. But the rise of think tanks cannot explain the similarly harsh economic policies adopted in England, France, Germany, and other European nations.

Right-wing lobbyists and LBJ's unpopularity diverted blame from where much of it belonged: the economics profession. Many economists boarded the conservative antigovernment train, offering academically respectable cover to the harsh economic policies embraced by both Republican and Democratic administrations. The ideas behind them were formally developed by economists at a variety of academic institutions. Most rich nations suffered a sharp rise in unemployment and inflation in the mid-1970s resulting from the increase in oil prices, and they adopted similar economic policies based on Friedmanite principles.

Germany adopted a tight monetary policy throughout the 1970s to fight inflation, keeping interest rates high to suppress demand. It successfully held inflation down, but at the cost of slow growth and rising unemployment.

Under Margaret Thatcher, Britain began to tighten its monetary and fiscal policies in the late 1970s, before the United States did. Rising interest rates increased the value of the pound and made buying British debt—gilts—attractive, further pushing up the pound's value. But in the process, British exports fell as the price of goods sent overseas rose, sending much of British manufacturing into oblivion.

By 1983, even the French Socialist François Mitterrand, noted Andrew Glyn, "introduced a tougher, more market-oriented programme than anything else considered by the previous center-right administration." Its goal was to reduce inflation, and it succeeded in doing so, cutting the rate almost to the level of Germany's. But the unemployment rate rose to 10 percent. In the early 1990s, when the famously liberal Swedish government adopted harsh austerity policies to contain inflation and raised taxes, the country's unemployment rate rose to 9 percent, stunning by Swedish standards.

Sweden's cutbacks may have been justified in a nation with an enormous government presence. But in general, high levels of unemployment permanently infected the rich world beginning in the 1980s. Rarely did advocates of right-wing economics adequately warn of the cost in lost jobs of their policies. To the contrary, Friedman and his disciple Robert Lucas insisted any 1982 recession would be moderate at worst.

In America, Friedmanite economics provided useful cover to

avoid having to tell the people the truth. In the early 1980s, Paul Volcker claimed he was merely trying to control the money supply, not to send interest rates soaring to cause a recession—the decisive, old-fashioned way to get inflation down. A young Paul Krugman questioned him on this at a conference, suggesting that focusing on the money supply was a "stealth tactic." Volcker unconvincingly denied it. In fact, it was hard to imagine that Volcker believed he even had the power to act on Friedman's naive advice that the Fed should simply control the money supply. Carter's chief economist, Charles Schultze, pointed out that it was much easier to tell the people you were going to control the money supply than to say you would push up interest rates to unprecedented levels.

One of Margaret Thatcher's actions was to privatize state-owned companies. The contribution of these companies fell from 10 percent of GDP in 1979 to 6 percent in 2004. Britain sold off parts or all of British Telecom, British Airways, British Steel, and its water and electric companies. The sale produced substantial revenue and reduced the deficit, but the British government also gave up the profits that once flowed into the Treasury.

The overriding objective, though, was to tame inflation. According to right-wing politicians and scholars, privately owned and therefore more efficient companies would keep prices lower. But by and large, these companies did not become significantly more productive once privatized, noted Glyn, though they cut wages and jobs, which improved profits. And their employees had to work longer hours.

America had relatively few state-owned companies, so it did not resort to much privatization. But it did deregulate across the board. Reagan weakened one regulatory agency after another. Thatcher did, too. She swallowed Friedman's moral arguments whole, which reinforced her own ideological views. "Milton Friedman revived the economics of liberty when it had been all but forgotten," she wrote on his death in 2006. "He was an intellectual freedom fighter. Never was there a less dismal practitioner of a dismal science. I shall greatly miss my old friend's lucid wisdom and mordant humour."

The economies of rich nations may have needed adjustment after the rapid growth of the post–World War II years. The share of GDP that went to wages rose to unsustainable heights by the 1970s, for example. Corporate profits, meanwhile, were low. And the world trading system was expanding, with imports introducing low-cost labor to domestic markets in the United States and Europe.

But the changes led by Thatcher and Reagan and supported by many prominent economists went wrong. They did not restimulate economic dynamism in the United States and Britain over the long run. For the most part, both countries performed poorly in ensuing years, the self-congratulations of politicians notwithstanding. Until the speculative boom of the late 1990s, neither reproduced the low unemployment rates of the 1950s and 1960s. Disguising much of this poor performance was the big bull market in stocks—one in the 1990s, which ended in a severe crash, and one in the 2000s, again ending in a severe crash. A major cause of the problems of high unemployment and runaway asset speculation was the single-minded devotion to low price inflation.

Inflation targeting is quite simply one of the least theoretically substantiated policies of contemporary times: there is no empirically justified way to know what the right inflation rate is.

It is hard to escape the conclusion that the reason that inflation targeting caught on with orthodox economists had more to do with the economic history of the 1970s than with economic science. Some feared that almost any increase in inflation ran the risk of its soaring toward double-digit rates, as it had in that decade. Others believed that a predictable Federal Reserve policy was most important to maintain stability. Greenspan insisted that the Fed should have discretionary authority over policy, not set an explicit target. But some economists argued that it should adopt an explicit rule to set interest rates so that uncertainty about future Fed policy could be minimized. The rule some advised setting, devised by the economist John Taylor, seemed almost as subjective as purely discretionary policy, yet Taylor argued that inflation would have been controlled had it been adopted in the 1970s.

To summarize, the case against such a dogmatic adherence to inflation targeting is clear—especially when the target rate is so low. The ravaging inflation of the 1970s and early 1980s was indeed brought down, but at great cost. More patience would have accomplished the same goal with far less pain. Once inflation had fallen, the persistent pressure to keep it very low had harmful consequences, the most important of which was unnecessarily high unemployment.

Arguably of greatest concern is that wages have risen much less rapidly than productivity since the early 1990s. In a general equilibrium model, wages should keep up with the improvement in output per hour of work. Instead, the gains have gone to business. Over the era of the Great Moderation, the share of profits to business from GDP grew rapidly and the share of wages fell. It was getting hard to maintain with a straight face that workers got what they deserved—that they were rewarded according to their product, in economists' terms. Economists largely blamed such problems not on a tight monetary policy or the failure to raise the minimum wage but on unequal education in a time of technologically demanding jobs. Soon enough, however, many college graduates were not being paid adequately, either. Education was not the single or even the most significant cause.

In early 2013, some members of the Fed—including its vice chairwoman, Janet Yellen, who would succeed the retiring Bernanke in early 2014—began to call for more focus on poor employment conditions. Bernanke, the committed inflation targeter, now also seemed to agree. He was the principal rescuer of the American economy in 2008 and 2009, sharply cutting interest rates, providing guarantees for financial markets, supporting bank bailouts, and eventually buying long-term securities to keep rates down during a slow economic recovery—a strategy know as quantitative easing. He fought off those who thought such policies would lead to higher inflation. An intelligent man was forced by real-world events to unchain himself from the accepted theory and academic cant he propounded as a Princeton professor and do the right thing. He rejected the irrational fears of inflation, at least for the time being.

Questioning the Natural Rate of Unemployment

Milton Friedman's theoretical assertions regarding the natural rate of unemployment were a central justification of inflation targeting. He attacked the Keynesian principle that the nation could reduce unemployment in the long run with a modest increase in inflation. Friedman argued instead that letting inflation rise some by running an economy hotter—that is, pumping up demand—would only temporarily reduce unemployment. Either rational workers, realizing that higher inflation was eating into the wage increases, would stop working or businesses would cut back production, and also employment, because their profit margins were reduced.

Friedman's argument gave inflation targeters more ammunition. If the unemployment rate was pushed below its natural level, they claimed, inflation would just keep rising, with no improvement in unemployment. This natural rate theory has remained embedded in economic thinking. As Bernanke and his coauthors stated in *Inflation Targeting*, "Contrary to what was believed thirty years ago, it appears that the benefits of expansionary policies (such as lower unemployment) are largely transitory, whereas the costs of expansionary policies (primarily the inefficiencies associated with higher inflation) tend to be permanent."

But no matter how popular it continues to be with economists on both the left and right, natural rate theory does not hold up as readily as claimed. For one thing, economists concede they don't know what the rate actually is. It is a moving target. Even leftist economists argued the natural unemployment rate was 6 percent in the 1990s. But the unemployment rate fell below 4 percent in the late 1990s, and inflation did not rise at all.

It is not merely that economists cannot calculate the natural rate of unemployment. The theory itself is questionable, another example of the conservative orthodoxy's dependence on ultrarationality. It requires that workers can recognize how future inflation will undermine their pay increases. By Friedman's thinking, these workers won't seek jobs, then, or will seek ever-higher wages, pushing inflation up. The Nobelist George Akerlof successfully challenged this.

There are other criticisms. Higher wages could actually lower inflation by raising productivity. Higher wages raise demand, which can, under many circumstances, increase business efficiency. More can be made at a lower unit cost—a version of Adam Smith's pin factory. If output goes up, workers can often be given raises without reducing a business's profit margins, thus reducing pressure to raise prices. Two Dutch economists, Servaas Storm and C. W. M. Naastepad, have done pioneering work on this issue.

Two basic facts remain clear. First, most economists badly misestimated the natural rate. The experience of the late 1990s, when the unemployment rate fell below 4 percent without inflationary effects, should be deeply embarrassing to the profession. Second, putting aside the question of the existence of the natural rate, the unemployment rate tolerated by Fed policymakers has been damagingly higher than the CBO estimate of it since the late 1970s. Over this period, income inequality has risen rapidly as wages have stagnated.

The lessons for the future? Low inflation does not guarantee optimal employment or a stable economy. The task of policymakers is complex and requires adopting multiple objectives. Different inflation targets are necessary under different circumstances. Rising wages should be seen as possibly stimulating productivity growth and therefore as good for inflation and incomes. Empirical research is critical. No one could truly justify a 2 percent inflation target. Seldom did ideology so easily trump economic responsibility.

Chapter Five

There Are No Speculative Bubbles

What started out in the 1950s and 1960s as useful and innovative economic arguments developed by economists at the University of Chicago and MIT about how prices of stocks, bonds, and other securities are established in financial markets devolved into a destructive set of ideas known as the efficient markets theory. EMT was originally well thought out, with serious statistical evidence to support its argument that financial markets can be rational. Now its accepted economic assertions would befuddle any casual observer of financial markets, and the more extreme of these assertions have done harm.

Here are some of its ultimate conclusions: at almost any point in time, stock prices fairly accurately reflect the future value of companies; there are few serious speculative bubbles for any kind of financial instrument, including stocks, bonds, currencies, and derivatives, and trying to control them does more harm than good; the only objective of executives should be to maximize the value of their companies' stock; enormous compensation for CEOs, which has risen from sixty times average wages in 1970 to over three hundred times in recent years, is well justified; financial markets usually require minimal oversight by regulators.

Early in its development, EMT most usefully made clear how

hard it is, even for professional money managers, to beat the market—that is, to pick stocks or other securities to earn a return higher than you would by simply buying a representative range of them. The competition among many informed investors, it was understood, led to an efficient market—that is, a market in which all new information about stocks and the economy was publicly available and was quickly, even almost instantaneously, incorporated into the price of securities. EMT therefore emphasized the advantages of holding a diversified portfolio of investments (ultimately index funds, mutual funds that track the returns of market indexes like the S&P 500) and encouraged investors to pay minimal professional management fees.

But the development of EMT is another example of how faith in the rationality of free markets was pushed too far. The journalist Justin Fox has written what may well become the standard history of the development of EMT. The theory, he says, "was a powerful idea, helping to inspire the first index funds, the investment approach called modern portfolio theory, the risk-adjusted performance measures that shape the money management business, the corporate creed of shareholder value, the rise of derivatives, and the hands-off approach to financial regulation that prevailed in the United States from the 1970s on."

But Fox is wrong, I think, when he claims EMT was free of political influence. "In some aspects the story of the rational market hypothesis parallels and is intertwined with the widely chronicled rebirth of pro-freemarket ideology after World War II," he writes. "But rational market finance was not at heart a political movement. It was a scientific one, an imposing of the midcentury fervor for rational, mathematical, statistical decision making upon financial markets."

In fact, EMT became as ideological as the other theories, and arguably more so. Of all the major economic ideas we have discussed, EMT is the most dependent on assumptions that free markets are perfect—the general equilibrium assumptions of a self-correcting economy of near-perfect markets. "What I added to the story," said Eugene Fama, a leading proponent of EMT who won a Nobel Prize for his work in 2013, "was just pointing out that you need a model of market equilibrium in order to carry out the tests of market efficiency." At first, EMT amounted to a hard-edged criticism of Wall Street financiers and money managers. Later, it became aligned with the interests of Wall Street financiers to a disturbing degree.

When I studied financial markets in graduate school, I fully bought into EMT. I was convinced that no one could beat the market averages. For *BusinessWeek*, I regularly wrote about how absurd some of these much-touted market-beating Wall Street techniques were. My education in statistics taught me that you can always find some kind of pattern in historical data if you look hard enough. But that does not mean the future will repeat the past. Stock touters on Wall Street—chartists—are forever finding trends they claim will continue. I criticized one of the chartists' favorite contentions, the so-called January effect, which holds that stock prices usually go up more in that month than in any other. I calculated that, in fact, there is a similar tendency in June. I firmly believed that the January effect was just a coincidence in the data. If enough investors knew stocks went up in January, they would simply buy in December, sending stocks up then and reducing the January rise.

Years later, however, sophisticated statistical techniques showed that there is indeed a kind of January effect. And researchers found proof of other persistent trends once scorned by academia, such as the momentum phenomenon—if stocks go up, they usually persist in going up for a few days and longer—and vice versa. A highly influential book by the economist Burton Malkiel published in 1973, *A Random Walk Down Wall Street,* converted thousands to EMT. But Malkiel had to keep revising his best seller in later printings because of new research that showed there were predictable tendencies in the market that did not conform to the purer version of EMT he'd earlier espoused. Malkiel began to allow for serious *inefficiencies* in the efficient markets story.

For the typical investor, trying to beat the market took too much time and required constant research. If you did not invest in large volume, your trading commissions could eat away all your profits. This warning was the beneficial legacy of EMT. But increasingly pure interpretations of EMT would prove to have a serious downside.

EMT begins with a theory about the value of stocks that was established at the turn of the nineteenth century and still holds. The intrinsic value of a publicly traded stock is the sum of all future dividends (or earnings). Future dividends must be discounted for the time value of money. For example, if someone offered you a contract to pay you $1,000 in ten years, you would not pay $1,000 today for that contract; you would pay something less because you could earn money on the initial investment over those ten years— even if just the minimal interest paid by a Treasury bill. Also, because their prices can fluctuate around their true value, stocks are risky. You may well be buying at a price that is higher than the intrinsic value or selling at a price that is lower.

A first step in the new thinking was taken in 1952 by Harry Markowitz of the University of Chicago, a future Nobel Prize winner. Markowitz showed that the risk of holding stocks—volatility—

could be sharply reduced by buying a wide variety of them. Stock prices move differently in varying economic conditions. Some stocks might do well in certain booming conditions; others might be affected by local recessions. A diversified portfolio would offset the price fluctuations of individual stocks and result in, on average, positive gains with less variation in the portfolio. If you chose to sell, odds were you wouldn't have to worry about bad timing. You would typically earn returns, it was later hypothesized, according to the intrinsic values of the stocks.

This conclusion contrasted with much of the advice on Wall Street at the time, which was to put a few well-chosen eggs in one basket and watch them very closely. The legendary investor Warren Buffett practiced just this approach on his path to becoming a multibillionaire. But Buffett is the exception that proves the rule. Few can duplicate his achievement. (Buffett also helped manage some of the companies whose stock he owned, so the example is far from pure.) Far better to minimize risk by diversifying your portfolio and then watch your stocks grow on average from 7 to 9 percent—the historical return for the stock market.

Markowitz more or less invented the field of financial economics and what became known as portfolio management theory. He and other economists took the idea further. Paul Samuelson, the MIT economist and future Nobel laureate who had pushed for America's adoption of modest Keynesian policies, argued in the mid-1960s that the price variations around the intrinsic value of a stock were statistically random. With intelligent, informed investors bidding, all the information known about a company was reflected in the price of its stock already. Except for the random, unpredictable fluctuations, the stock price fairly accurately reflected the long-term value of the company. It was useless to try to predict volatility, but you could try to calculate the intrinsic value of a stock.

Like Markowitz, Samuelson believed in diversification to reduce risk. Samuelson's somewhat leftist MIT became a hotbed of efficient markets theorizing, along with the conservative University of Chicago.

The basic precept of the new theory was now clear: all new analyses of and information about companies and the economy were almost immediately incorporated into stock prices by the many active, rational investors trading the securities. It was very difficult to get a jump on your competitors. Well-trained professionals were scouring the nation—it would soon be the world—for any information that might give them an edge on the future of a stock price.

The assertion that stock prices fluctuate randomly made it unlikely that one could pick winners—that is, individual stocks that would rise much more rapidly than the rest of the market. Randomness by its very definition is impossible to predict. The trend you think you see may well evaporate. In a coin toss, sometimes heads will come up five times in a row, but that doesn't mean you should bet on it to happen a sixth time. The Wall Street chartists who claimed they could predict the future by extending the trends of the past had little ground to stand on if the efficient markets theorists were right.

A student of Milton Friedman's, Eugene Fama was an especially early advocate of efficient markets theory—he is often credited with coining the term—and eventually became one of its most extreme advocates. In his breakthrough 1965 article, he wrote:

> An "efficient" market is defined as a market where there are large numbers of rational, profit-maximizers actively competing, with each trying to predict future market values of individual securities, and where important current information is almost freely available to all participants.

In an efficient market, competition among the many intelligent participants leads to a situation where, at any point in time, actual prices of individual securities already reflect the effects of information based both on events that have already occurred and on events which, as of now, the market expects to take place in the future. In other words, in an efficient market at any point in time the actual price of a security will be a good estimate of its intrinsic value.

Fama was now claiming that markets were *very* efficient and that the price of a company's stock was at almost any point in time a true reflection of the value of the company.

To help prove the point, Fama and others undertook "event studies." When, for example, reports of a good new product at a company were made public, they measured how quickly the company's stock adjusted upward. If a new product was disappointing, they again studied the stock market's reaction. They did countless such event studies and indeed showed that stocks adjusted very rapidly to changes in information. In some cases, prices reacted so quickly it seemed likely that researchers were uncovering instances of insider trading.

But this proved only that new information was incorporated into the price, not that stock prices were close estimates of the intrinsic value of companies at most times. So EMT advocates turned their attention to the performance record of investment managers. Could they beat the market on any consistent basis? If they could not, it would provide strong evidence that stock prices too quickly reflected the true future value of companies for even professionals to get an edge.

The main problem to solve was how to adjust for the risk that managers took. Some would produce returns above the market average by buying high fliers—unusually risky stocks, typically those of young companies with exciting new products. But others would lose money doing the same thing. How could investors separate the lucky money managers from those truly talented at assessing the prospects of these companies?

Adjusting for risk—measuring it somehow—was difficult, but several economists came up with a creative way to do so. William Sharpe, another future Nobelist, devised a measure he called beta, which compared the volatility of a stock to the volatility of an average of all stocks. (John Lintner of Harvard developed a similar model.) If you bought stocks with a beta of 1.0, you were taking no more risk than you would by investing in the market as a whole. The value of your portfolio should follow the market both up and down. Sharpe's theory, derived from Markowitz, suggested, technically speaking, that you shouldn't beat the market unless you took more risk than could be diversified away. If you bought stocks with a high or low beta, you were taking either above-average risk or below-average risk. A low beta was the least risky—you'd make less when the market went up and lose less when it went down. Over time, a portfolio with such groups of stocks should either outperform or underperform the market. Advocates of EMT and the related portfolio management theory argued that money managers who beat the market did so not because they had a special talent for picking stocks but because they took more risk. In other words, their portfolios had a beta above 1.0.

Exhaustive research showed what these economists had expected: once risk adjustments were made, all but a statistically insignificant handful of investment managers outperformed the market once their performance was adjusted for risk. That is, they did no better than what the beta suggested they should do. These empirical results were arresting. Investing even in mutual funds, with large numbers of expertly chosen stocks in their portfolios, did not make sense for a typical investor. The market was too efficient to beat. Very few did better than their beta suggested.

In his enthusiasm, Fama made a couple of very strong claims. First, he assumed these studies showed that stock prices reflected the future value of companies with a *very* high degree of accuracy; many of his peers did not think of them as accurate. Second, he argued that because stock prices were mostly right, reflecting all available information, serious speculative bubbles couldn't truly exist; prices just couldn't get that far out of alignment with reality—a bubble—for more than a brief period of time. Big shifts in prices mainly reflected sharp changes in circumstances, such as major technological advances or a sudden economic recovery from recession. "The word 'bubble' drives me nuts," he said in a 2007 interview. In 2013, even with the devastation of the 2008 crash fresh in mind, he told *The New York Times,* "I don't even know what a speculative bubble means."

Milton Friedman, a market purist, of course, had earlier claimed that the financial markets worked nearly perfectly. Financial markets not only encouraged speculation but also depended on it. Fama was saying much the same thing. Buyers and sellers would of course arrive at the appropriate price for a stock, and that price would not gyrate out of control.

Friedman made his statement about the efficiency of financial markets with regard to currencies. At the Bretton Woods Conference in 1944, John Maynard Keynes had recommended setting up a world trading system where currencies would be fixed to the dollar, which would in turn be fixed to gold. Keynes largely mistrusted currency speculation and believed that fixing the value of currencies within a narrow range would enhance trade by reducing uncertainty. Friedman claimed just the opposite. Currencies should be traded like securities in a free market, he said, which would result in a value being established for them that would equalize imports and exports—a rational price for the currency. The higher the currency, the more expensive the exports—and vice versa. If a nation's exports were less competitive, its currency might fall in value, providing a stimulus to economic growth by increasing exports.

There was criticism that speculation in currencies would drive their values to irrational highs and lows. Friedman reasserted the Invisible Hand. If a currency was overvalued, he contended, some smart seller would take advantage and drive the price down; if it was undervalued, some smart buyer would take advantage and drive the price up. Currency prices would therefore not get out of hand. "It just seemed to me sensible that the only way you make money was by buying low and selling high," said Friedman, "and not the other way around. And if that's the case, then people who destabilize the market [buy high and sell low] lose their shirt, and so they aren't going to be around for long."

Friedman thus denied the possibility of herd behavior. But people do sometimes buy high, the price keeps going up, and so many more buy still higher. Similarly, many follow the lead of sellers and sell still more. Markets can move rapidly to extremes. Financial markets have been subject to fashions and fads for hundreds of years. Friedman's view was dependent on faith that market participants were always intelligent and rational—or at least that enough of them were at every point in time—and were rarely caught up in fads.

In fact, growing evidence would show how irrational investors could be—but it was ignored. What most would call excessive speculation was said by EMT purists to be merely market activity in search of a right price. Some economists concluded that traders could not really manipulate prices. If they pushed them too high, someone would sell and they'd eventually lose money. The theory gained adherents among economic centrists and became the conventional wisdom. Many economists argued that the escalation of oil prices in the summer of 2007 was not the result of Wall Street speculation but simply reflected the expected oil shortage in China. When the price dropped precipitously not long after, many changed their minds. The head of the Commodity Futures Trading Commission, Gary Gensler, a former Goldman Sachs trader, knew better. He later proposed that the volume of oil trading be limited, just one of his attempts to limit speculation.

In 2007, the business writer Michael Lewis scornfully castigated those who criticized the exploding market for derivatives. The prices of derivatives were unregulated, and even hidden from customers, but Lewis was not concerned about rising levels of buying and selling. In a piece for Bloomberg News, he said, "None of [the critics] seemed to understand that when you create a derivative you don't add to the sum total of risk in the financial world; you merely create a means for redistributing that risk. They have no evidence that financial risk is being redistributed in ways we should all worry about."

In other words, there are no real bubbles of more than fleeting significance. Lewis later learned his lesson. He wound up writing the finest book on the crash, *The Big Short*, in which he described better than anyone how inefficient the financial markets in derivatives had become. In an economy under the thrall of efficient markets thinking, derivatives went unregulated, and that was a major cause of the 2008 crash.

As for currencies, the U.S. attorney general in 2013 at last announced a criminal investigation of Citigroup and several major banks for manipulation of currency markets. If derivatives markets were truly efficient, such manipulation would have been minimized as smart buyers found competitive sellers who didn't distort prices in their favor. It was about time.

The theoretical tide had begun to turn around well before this. Studies by various economists using sophisticated techniques showed that there were repeating patterns in financial markets. A handful of investment managers did beat the market. Warren Buffett and the hedge fund manager George Soros, active investors since the 1950s, were everyone's favorite examples. But two lesser-known investors had earlier made a fortune in the options market—the over-the-counter market of puts and calls that allowed investors to put up very little money to buy or sell a stock at a certain price by a future date. A mathematician, Edward Thorp, and a statistical economist, Sheen Kassouf, developed models showing that the prices of options were significantly out of line with the prices of their underlying stocks. The two made a killing, and in 1967 they wrote a book called *Beat the Market.* Over the next decade, many others adopted the techniques they offered in it, reducing the profitable opportunities. Their example demonstrated that markets with little trading could be unusually inefficient—providing more profitable opportunities. Options were now being traded on exchanges.

Academics in the growing field of behavioral finance undertook experiments to show that investors were not rational. The classic experiments were those in which participants were offered money or the option to gamble for more with a high probability of winning. Most of the time, participants took the certain money. People are not purely rational, these experiments strongly suggested, thus challenging a prime assumption of the Invisible Hand. They are generally risk averse. They irrationally avoid possible losses. A smart investor weighing the odds more objectively could take advantage of the risk aversion and find good buys in the securities investors shied way from. Clearly, markets now seemed less efficient.

Fama at last admitted that there were "superior intrinsic-value" analysts. "There will always be new information which causes intrinsic values to change," he wrote. Such gifted or hardworking analysts could, as he put it, predict the "appearance of new information."

Fama also eventually conceded that there were some persistent trends in stocks that seemed to defy EMT. Stocks with low price-to-earnings ratios and those whose assets (book values) were low compared to their prices usually outperformed the market. Fama, ever the skeptic, argued that stocks with low prices compared to earnings were probably inherently riskier than those with higher prices, so on average they should rise more quickly. Stock performance had to be adjusted for the risk taken. The anomaly Fama had a harder time dismissing was the persistence of a stock's momentum. A stock that rose often continued to rise, and one that fell often continued to fall. Fama could not rationalize this empirical finding, and he acknowledged that the market couldn't be entirely efficient.

But even if inefficiencies existed, it remained unlikely that easy profits could be made on stocks thought to be undervalued. This was Fama's last defense. The profits that could be made buying mispriced stocks were not great enough on average to offset the commissions paid on the transactions. This was particularly true for smaller investors, who enjoyed no commission discounts.

As more research was conducted challenging Fama's purist version of EMT, several conflicting forms of the theory emerged. Proponents of the weak form, as Justin Fox nicely summarized, argued that stock prices could not be predicted from their past movements. This was the antichartist position.

The semistrong version became the most popular, and the one eventually promoted by Burton Malkiel in *A Random Walk Down Wall Street*. There were departures from the intrinsic value of a stock, which a good analyst could find, but transaction costs, as Fama noted, would prevent the typical investor from benefiting from them. It was better to buy index funds, which usually had low management fees.

The third form of EMT was the strongest. It maintained that the market was so clairvoyant it even incorporated nonpublic information into prices. Fama used this form to say that financial markets not only reflected all information but were right about the future.

The strong form of EMT attracted an increasing number of critics, but it retained its influence, and the stronger view of EMT served as the foundation for the financial deregulation of the 1990s and 2000s. In 2002, for example, Alan Greenspan explained his views on regulation and disclosure in the derivatives market this way: "By design, this market, presumed to involve dealings among sophisticated professionals, has been largely exempt from government regulation. In part, this exemption reflects the view that professionals do not require the investor protections commonly afforded to markets in which retail investors participate. But regulation is not only unnecessary in these markets, it is potentially damaging, because regulation presupposes disclosure and forced disclosure of proprietary information can undercut innovations in financial markets just as it would in real estate markets."

In the 1970s, a decade of economic tumult and confusion, government as noted became an easy scapegoat for high inflation and unemployment. As antigovernment ideology grew, the early and stronger versions of EMT lent an academic justification to the first stages of financial deregulation. Jimmy Carter led an attack on regulations that had limited the interest rates banks could pay.

American businesses were also losing a lot of market share to Japanese and European companies. Americans were buying Sonys, Nikons, Toyotas, Volkswagens, and BMWs. European clothing and appliance manufacturers supplanted American stalwarts. America's trade deficit began to rise inexorably. Corporate profits in general sagged, and inflation was adding new uncertainties to decision making.

Many business leaders blamed unions for driving wages too high and thus keeping American prices uncompetitive, and auto companies in particular claimed that cheap labor was the main advantage of Japanese manufacturers. But it turned out that the Japanese were making higher-quality cars far more efficiently. Wall Street took notice of the heavy cash positions of some American companies. They seemed lazy.

Some economists believed the main problem was that the managers of these behemoths were not acting like owners; they did not have the entrepreneurial spirit. And they believed EMT provided the answer as to how to motivate them. Never mind that these companies—General Electric, General Motors, Standard Oil, U.S. Steel, Johnson & Johnson, Merck, Kmart, and Safeway, to name a few—had performed well in the 1950s and 1960s and, in many cases, for several generations before that. As the historian Alfred Chandler showed in *The Visible Hand* (1977), they were all run well by managers, not owners. To Chandler, entrepreneurs founded great companies, and managers built them.

But history is rarely a cherished discipline among economists, and case studies are too often neglected. The fashionable new idea was that managers had to be turned into entrepreneurs with ownership stakes and that shareholders had to transform fat and lenient companies that worked cooperatively with labor unions into lean and mean companies fit for a global economy.

In the wake of the 1929 market crash, these big companies were challenged on similar grounds by two liberal thinkers. Adolf Berle and Gardiner Means analyzed two hundred companies and concluded that corporate managers—agents of the owners or the shareholders, as they called them—did not have the entrepreneurial drive necessary to run them well.

Disregarding the work of Chandler, many thought this same analysis was applicable to the 1980s. The Chicago-trained Michael Jensen was a star scholar who contributed to early EMT. After teaching at the University of Rochester, he moved to Harvard Business School. Jensen, who had done several important event studies and made valuable innovations to Sharpe's beta theory, believed he had the tools to make American business vigorous again. He became the foremost academic champion of the unfriendly takeover movement led on Wall Street by Morgan Stanley's investment bankers and the brilliant lawyer Joseph Flom. Low stock prices encouraged corporations to enter bidding wars for valuable companies, often against the wishes of the boards of those companies. Lured by the enormous profits to be made, old-line investment banks created a wave of the unfriendly acquisitions they had initially frowned upon.

While many criticized the takeover wars that resulted, Jensen said it was just a case of the free market at work for the good of all. In a seminal 1986 piece, "The Takeover Controversy," he argued that the bear market that began in the early 1970s correctly kept stock prices low because executives were mismanaging corporations. After all, according to EMT, the stock price reflected the real value of a company. Prices were not incorrectly low, they were rationally set.

The Japanese incursion was juxtaposed with American failure. Competition would not raise the level of the work of these "agents," Jensen said, referencing Berle and Means. Many executives were not merely lazy but had also built uncompetitive empires for their own benefit, maintaining businesses that were going stale to preserve their jobs. Through the advent of hostile takeovers, financial markets would make America competitive again. The acquiring companies would target inefficient ones and either improve them or discard them.

Hostile takeovers and, later, leveraged buyouts usually involved acquirers taking on massive amounts of debt. To Jensen, this was beneficial because it forced companies to spend their excess cash on tax-deductible debt service—an enormous government subsidy for these takeovers—and to cut costs and peel away failing businesses. As evidence, Jensen noted how well shareholders of companies that were taken over did.

Of course they did; the prices of their companies were bid up in the increasingly aggressive competition among buyers. By dropping unprofitable businesses and cutting jobs, an acquired company often improved its profit margins. But that was not necessarily good for America. No doubt, some of the weak subsidiaries should have been closed, but many others were allowed to disappear from the American business scene without attempts at revitalizing them. And lazy corporate managers weren't necessarily replaced by vigorous, smart newcomers, as promised.

Jensen had a harder time claiming that takeovers were good for the acquiring companies. Because these companies typically overpaid in bidding contests, their stock usually then fell or at best rose slowly. In 1997, Mark Sirower of the Boston Consulting Group did a thorough analysis of the benefits to the acquiring companies that remains conclusive. "It is more likely than not that any given acquisition will fail," he concluded in *The Synergy Trap*. The economists Eileen Appelbaum of the Center for Economic and Policy Research and Rosemary Batt of Cornell University researched the rise of leveraged buyouts and privatizations (basically, acquisitions made by financial partnerships) and showed that on balance these companies reduced employment and failed to raise productivity.

A core principle of efficient markets theory is that there are enough players to offset bad decisions with good ones. In takeovers, a relative few—investment bankers and lawyers; takeover artists like Carl Icahn, T. Boone Pickens, and the leveraged buyout specialists Henry Kravis and George Roberts; and privatizers like Pete Peterson and Stephen Schwarzman of Blackstone—made giant decisions on their own. This was closer to a monopoly than a competitive free market. Compensation for the dealmakers was also far too generous; fees, based on the size of the acquisitions, ranged into the hundreds of millions. The high bidding was largely made possible, as Appelbaum and Batt documented, by the tax deductibility of the interest on debt. The top takeover practitioners became billionaires, many of them, including Icahn and Kravis, climbing the *Forbes* list of the 400 richest Americans.

CEOs were also given enormous incentives to participate in takeovers. Typically, the upper management of the target of a leveraged buyout got a big piece of the action, profiting significantly as stock prices soared when bids were made. They were thus wooed with unprecedented compensation packages to remain atop the target, and CEOs were enticed away from other companies to run the new acquisitions. By cutting costs—not least labor costs—CEOs managed to raise short-term profits in order to pay back the debt incurred in the takeover and to stimulate higher stock prices. Short-termism was not so much born but strongly reinforced by EMT.

Jensen, the champion of takeovers, advocated sizable stock options as an efficient means of compensation for all top management. Such options enabled managers to buy stock at a price that would make them fortunes if the stock rose. Jensen thought it obvious that giving them equity positions was the key to making them act like owners, not managers. And most important, the stock price, under the strong version of EMT which argued they represented the true long-term value of the company, would reflect how good a job they did managing their companies. If it went up, they got rich by making the companies healthier—that is, if EMT truly held.

Stock options were not reported as a compensation expense (except as a footnote), an exception allowed by the accounting profession and not challenged by Congress or the SEC. They were not seen as a direct outlay of cash, like salaries or bonuses, but they would take their toll by diluting earnings. As executives cashed in their stock options, the sudden increase in shares outstanding reduced the profits allocable to shareholders.

In the 1990s, with stock prices hitting new highs in the roaring high-technology bull market, the value of these options soared. By some studies, the average CEO compensation reached three hundred times and more what the average worker made. Bill Clinton took no action to force stock options to be expensed, so total profits were not affected. To the contrary, on the advice of his future Treasury secretary Robert Rubin, he had put a $1 million cap on the tax deductibility of salaries early in his administration. This made stock options all the more valuable.

Michael Jensen's tone was often contemptuous of those who did not "understand" the theory of how stock options would transform business. It was soon clear, however, that high compensation for CEOs did not lead to better performance. It merely contributed to a bubble reinforced by short-term profit objectives, from which the executives benefited enormously. Once the stock market started to tumble in 2000, Jensen changed his tune. He now said he was no longer a proponent of a strong version of EMT. The integrity of business managers also mattered, he began to argue, probably surprising all of his former colleagues. It was Milton Friedman who argued that the only obligation of business was to make a profit. And it was EMT that provided the theoretical justification that the stock price told investors all they needed to know about how well managed a company was.

By the 1990s, many of the purer and more strident claims of the efficient markets theorists had foundered. But the damage had been done. Deregulation was in full flower, and high compensation to executives encouraged not long-term corporate health but short-term profit manipulation, often at the expense of workers. The outsize speculation in high-technology stocks found direct justification among those economists who were skeptical of the existence of bubbles.

At the height of the bull market in the mid-1990s, Jeremy Siegel of the University of Pennsylvania wrote a book, *Stocks for the Long Run,* that added fuel to the fire. Despite soaring stock prices, the academic community, still under the spell of EMT, rarely warned people off the market. Maybe stock prices at unusually high levels compared to earnings were anticipating a set of optimistic events not experienced before. Alan Greenspan was the nation's leading advocate of this "new economy" of high-technology companies linked to the Internet, which he concluded was another full-fledged industrial revolution. As Fed chairman, he refused even to lean against the wind by raising interest rates or capital requirements for financial firms. Burned by warnings of irrational exuberance once before, Greenspan kept silent.

Siegel, an intrepid empiricist, comprehensively tracked stock and bond prices since 1802. In his book, he revealed that a $1 investment in stocks in 1802 would have been worth about $7.5 million by 1997. As surprising, he found that the same investment in bonds would have earned only $10,700. Siegel's main point was that over the long run stocks were a far better investment than bonds, no matter when they were bought, even at the height of a high-technology boom.

Still more provocative, Siegel found that stocks *usually* outperformed bonds over shorter periods. Over any ten-year period, for example, an investment in stocks would have done better than an investment in bonds 80 percent of the time. The message was that investors should almost only buy a diversified portfolio of stocks to minimize risk and should make sure their annual management fees were low. With the advent of index funds—pioneered for smaller investors by Vanguard in Pennsylvania—this was now possible. Siegel's empirical work offered further incentive to buy stocks even when prices seemed high, especially as EMT made clear that these prices reflected the future value of companies.

The scholar who toppled this theoretical house of cards was Robert Shiller. His 2000 book, *Irrational Exuberance,* made unmistakable that it would be hard to ever again take seriously the contention that stock prices were somehow "right." A Yale professor, Shiller had been working since the early 1980s on showing the inefficiencies in the stock market. If stock prices were really the equivalent of the sum of dividends, discounted for the time value of money, then why did they fluctuate so much while dividends did not?

When stock prices were looked at through the long lens of history, the assertion that they reflected future dividends (or earnings) seemed absurd. From about 1871 to 2005, stock prices rose seven to eight times as fast as earnings, and they were far more volatile. The stock market rose three and a half to four times between 1994 and the top of the bull market in 2000. But in this period, corporate earnings rose by less than 60 percent. EMT suggested that earnings should have risen much faster to justify the rise in stock prices.

When Shiller looked at individual stocks, not just stock averages, the case was even stronger. He found that over time individual stocks often rose much faster and with more volatility than did their dividends. If stock prices were actually "right," how could this be?

Shiller showed clearly, except to diehards like Fama, that speculative bubbles existed and were damaging. "I define a speculative bubble as a situation in which news of price increases spurs investor enthusiasm," he wrote, "which spreads by psychological contagion from person to person, in the process amplifying stories that might justify the price increases and bringing in a larger and larger class of investors, who, despite doubts about the real value of an investment, are drawn to it partly through envy of others' successes and partly through a gambler's excitement." This is just what Friedman and Fama said couldn't happen.

As the housing bubble formed in the 2000s, the Friedmanite argument was similar. The financially sophisticated community had learned how to package risky mortgages in ways that were far less risky for investors, it was said. Bankers ultimately got carried away, packaging still more risky mortgages into highly complex securities. The appetite of pension fund and other money managers for them grew. Greenspan and Bernanke, still adherents of EMT, resisted any claim that this was a bubble and did nothing about it.

Speculation and outright manipulation also often pushed the prices of key commodities to unsupportable levels. They no longer reflected real-world shifts in supply and demand. But EMT, which argued that even soaring prices generally reflected actual demand, kept economists on the sidelines. In the summer of 2007, as noted, the price of oil reached extreme heights. Many economists argued it was not speculation but a radical shift in demand for oil as China grew. Reality quickly sank in, and the dollar price of oil fell to less than half its summer high. But by raising fuel prices that summer—gasoline hit record levels—the economy was damaged.

Similarly, in the spring of 2013, the skyrocketing price of gold suddenly collapsed, bringing other commodity prices down with it. The price of ethanol, which refiners were forced to use by the government to produce more environmentally friendly fuel, was another example, rising by twentyfold over six months in 2013. There was less and less doubt that businesses and traders had manipulated markets.

The head of the Commodity Futures Trading Commission, a former Goldman Sachs executive, it is worth repeating, had said forthrightly that speculation affected commodity prices, often increasing them substantially. Denial of such market realities was at the heart of the decision by the Clinton administration, with support from Greenspan, to prohibit regulation of financial derivatives. An intervention in the commodity markets was virtually unthinkable, given prevailing economic fashion.

The tendency toward herd behavior in financial markets was documented by historical economists like Charles Kindleberger of MIT and the Keynesian scholar Hyman Minsky of Washington University—only to be denied by EMT advocates. Besides the aforementioned experiments showing that people could not assess risk clearly, other psychological studies found that they were often open to suggestion, typically went along with the crowd, and could be highly influenced by a good narrative, like the story of an unprecedented "new economy," thus making them susceptible to fashions and fads.

One study of the subprime crisis is especially instructive. Well-informed investors should make more-rational decisions than uninformed investors. But researchers at Princeton, Dartmouth, and the University of Michigan found that the supposedly well-informed bankers they studied had little sense about whether housing prices were highly inflated, and they actually took bigger losses in their investments than the uninformed investors. There were biases and herd behavior at work, even among the experts. Such psychological traits explained a lot of the patterns in stock prices that researchers were beginning to uncover—patterns of stock behavior that efficient markets theorists once said could not exist.

EMT foundered on a central question: Are market fluctuations random because investors are irrational? Fashionable trading and speculative bubbles, however unsensible, do exist. Shiller made a strong case for this, and he won a Nobel Prize in tandem with Fama—an odd, even disturbing, juxtaposition. Fama believed in little more than investor rationality. Has the Nobel in another field ever gone to two practitioners with views more diametrically opposed?

There is another lesson to be learned. What we consider the long term is only one sample of history. Drawing universal conclusions from even a few hundred years of history is dangerous. Siegel's analysis covered a period in which interest rates tended to rise or remain stable, which meant bonds generally did poorly and stocks did well. Since the publication of his book, interest rates have largely fallen, making bonds a particularly good investment. The gap in returns between stocks and bonds has narrowed.

The trail of damage left by EMT includes blind deregulation, a failure to address asset bubbles, dominance of short-term profit objectives to allow CEOs to maximize the value of their shares, and a wasteful takeover movement. All these in turn have harmed the economy and most Americans by leading to lower wages, recession, market crashes, misdirected investment of the nation's savings, and rising inequality. Business managers and financial executives account for most of the famed "one percent."

One final bit of evidence to undermine the claims of EMT advocates was put forth by Lucian Bebchuk of Harvard Law School. He found that over time there was no relationship between how much CEOs and other managers earned and how their companies fared. Apparently, making CEOs rich owners rather than merely well-paid managers was just another romantic, incorrect hypothesis of EMT ideologues.

EMT contributed significantly to the crash of 2008. A fairly strong form of it was still widely accepted then by many economists, and it gave credibility to the self-serving politics of a Wall Street community determined to keep regulations minimal. Shiller's early work was held suspect by the profession, and it took the Yale professor courage to persist in his point of view against the market utopians. MIT and Harvard Business School, to take two prestigious examples, were beacons of EMT preaching, not to mention the University of Chicago. Unsurprisingly, Fama said the Dodd-Frank financial reform legislation had gone too far. EMT has left quite a sad legacy.

A world of financial reforms with a more realistic view of speculative excess and conflicts of interest on Wall Street—a world freed from extreme EMT ideas—would serve the United States and Europe well. The principles are clear. Excessive speculation has to be limited by requirements for more capital and less borrowing. Securities have to be traded in the open light of day (under Clinton, legislation was passed to forbid this). Financial firms cannot speculate with federally insured savings. Fraud has to be closely regulated; free-market competition won't get the job done. Clear-cut conflicts of interest, such as those that exist with ratings agencies, must be eliminated; again, competition is not enough. Incentives must be righted; bankers cannot be allowed to make money when they are right and lose little when they are wrong. Tax advantages for leveraged investments, such as leveraged buyouts, should be reduced or ended. Potential monopolistic price setting of fees and commissions by the financial community should be investigated.

These may not be all the steps that should be taken, but they were all neglected in the run-up to the 2008 crisis, partly if not largely because of undue faith in EMT. Lobbying power had its part as well, of course, but the Wall Street lobbyists used financial theory to justify the deregulatory request. Misapplied ideas again resulted in great damage.

Chapter Six

Globalization: Friedman's
Folly Writ Large

The central policies of today's globalization advocates are to eliminate tariffs, minimize government intrusion (mostly industry subsidies and regulations), and allow the value of currencies to be determined by floating them in the financial markets. International trade and reduced market intervention will result in widely distributed prosperity, it is said.

Though you would not know it from the way journalistic pundits and most sophisticated economists have talked about globalization in recent decades, the economic development of today's rich world since the 1800s was mostly accompanied by just the opposite: high tariffs, government investment in industry, financial regulations, and fixed values for currencies.

The globalization advocates are not only determined to make one world of free trade in goods and services. They are also determined to make the world into one efficient financial marketplace by removing controls on bank loans, bonds, and other flows of capital. Industrial policies to subsidize industries should be minimized. Ideally, according to many of these advocates, governments should be ever smaller and their budgets should be balanced (over the course of a business cycle) to minimize inflation. Once again, then, high inflation is seen as a primary nemesis. Today's globalization also calls for deregulating labor—letting wages be set freely in a market, not unduly influenced by unions or protected by government through limitations on firing or minimum wage laws. The U.S. government under Democrats and Republicans alike has been the leading advocate of this set of policies, which is generally known as the Washington consensus.

As we shall see, the Washington consensus has failed. A World Bank paper, in admitting to the errors of its own former allegiance to that point of view, put it this way: "The principles of . . . 'macroeconomic stability, domestic liberalization, and openness' have been interpreted narrowly to mean 'minimize fiscal deficits, minimize inflation, minimize tariffs, maximize privatization, maximize liberalization of finance,' with the assumption that the more of these changes the better, at all times and in all places—overlooking the fact that these expedients are just *some* of the ways in which these principles can be implemented."

The World Bank's emphasis on domestic liberalization (liberalization generally means freeing markets, including labor and finance, from government restrictions) and openness still overstated the economic case for globalization based on the uncritical acceptance of the general equilibrium model we have been discussing. The bank could not be shaken from its fundamentalist ideology completely. Opening markets to world trade can and should be beneficial. That is not the problem; it has worked in the past. But after the first stages of free trade in the 1950s and 1960s, post–World War II globalization was unleashed with an ideological intensity mostly blind to compromise, nuance, and history. Its unstated central assumption was that laissez-faire, spread everywhere, is almost all the governance the world needs. If it sounds familiar, it is Friedman's Folly writ large, a crude one-size-fits-all strategy that would, many economists maintained, result in global general equilibrium and maximum prosperity.

My goal here is to make clear how a single, oversimplified idea won over so many international economists. This ideology has had a huge and often damaging role in global policymaking, including notably at the World Bank and the International Monetary Fund.

Once presented with the economists' simplified set of theories about globalization, some media pundits became enthusiastic converts. There was a crusade against the supposedly economically uneducated, in both the rich world and developing countries, who saw globalization as a threat to their jobs and their cultures. In particular, the influential *New York Times* columnist Thomas L. Friedman insisted globalization was undiluted common sense. Free trade and government restraint were the ideal paths to social and economic progress for rich and poor alike, he wrote in his 1999 book, *The Lexus and the Olive Tree.* Cut tariffs to create as free a market worldwide as existed among the fifty individual states within the United States. Let competition flourish without government interference to drive all producers to maximum efficiency. Allow capital to flow without limitations so that entrepreneurs could develop as quickly as possible opportunities that were sadly unexploited. Free markets would force nations to toe the line on inflation and overspending on social programs. If as many obstacles to private profit as practicable were removed, including wage regulations and overpowerful unions, the standard of living for almost all would soon rise.

By 2005, even as the advocates of the Washington consensus were retreating in the face of many failures, Friedman, in his best-selling *The World Is Flat,* applauded how many countries were adapting their policies to the world of rapid electronic communication, which would expand the power and competitive efficiencies of the free market. Friedman was the phrasemaker of the movement, but these views were supported by most economists, even as they modified their earlier claims. Martin Wolf, the influential *Financial Times* columnist, a mostly orthodox economist, was almost as influential and persistent a crusader as Friedman. Anti-globalization arguments were the "big lie," he wrote, conjuring up images of George Orwell's *1984.* Lawrence Summers had already signed on to a one-size-fits-all policy. "The laws of economics are like the laws of engineering," he said to a reporter in 1991. "One set of laws works everywhere." A widely read 1998 book, Daniel Yergin and Joseph Stanislaw's *The Commanding Heights,* declared that free markets had now proved themselves victorious. Francis Fukuyama was one of the first to champion market liberalization as the ideal state of a nation, which he did in his 1992 book, *The End of History and the Last Man.* With a few exceptions, the media and economists were all in.

The wide-eyed optimism about globalization was part and parcel of the orthodox shift toward utopian equilibrium theory. Disciplined by competition with each other, all nations, including developing ones, would make what they manufactured best. Trade would soar, information would spread at the speed of light, wages would rise, and poverty would decline dramatically. Rich nations would benefit along with the poor. If inequality of incomes was rising in the United States, economists at first argued, it had little to do with globalized trade and almost everything to do with inadequate education and changing technologies.

One cannot entirely blame Thomas Friedman for adopting this

view. Trade theory was widely advocated by scholars and increased trade among nations had often been beneficial. But the reality was not as simple as advocates claimed it was. Proper trade theory holds that there are inevitable losers, too. Economic growth has often been subpar for developing nations that adopted the Washington consensus, including almost all of South America. In most regions, observed Joseph Stiglitz, the rate of unemployment was higher in 2002 than in 1990, when market liberalization spread in earnest. Or it worked for a while but soon led to a financial crisis, as in East Asia. Russia, which privatized in one fell swoop, was much wealthier than China two decades ago and is now significantly poorer. There are better ways to adopt economic knowledge to specific nations' problems, but the ideological sweep of globalization overwhelmed thoughtfulness.

Much of the media and many economists seemed to overlook deliberately the basic hard and disappointing facts.

- There was no economic precedent for the kind of globalization being advocated. The Industrial Revolution was not impeded by the high tariffs and fixed currencies that were maintained then. Only Britain, the world's richest nation and largest manufacturer, consistently promoted a version of free trade in the 1800s. But self-interest ruled the country's decisions. If there were lower tariffs elsewhere, it meant Britain could export goods more easily, and few could compete with the quality of its products.

- A central tenet of free-trade theory is that not all benefit: some, often many, workers lose jobs to foreign nations when trade is expanded. The United States and others have frequently been unable to maintain full employment and high-paying jobs, and promises of adequate social programs to offset losses or reduced wages resulting from free trade have rarely been kept.

- The first emerging economies after World War II—Japan, Korea, Taiwan, Malaysia—did not immediately open their financial or goods markets to foreign competition. They adopted protectionist policies to shield infant industries from trade, subsidized import substitution industries, invested significantly in broad-based education, and manipulated currencies to stimulate exports.

- Most of these nations with emerging economies emphasized, and often generously subsidized, exports to stimulate growth. These exports, not the liberalization of trade, were the drivers of their economic successes. Not every country could maintain export surpluses, however. Someone had to buy the goods.

- India and China, the emerging giants, opened their markets to international trade and capital only slowly. It is often claimed that India grew rapidly as barriers to free trade were reduced in the early 1990s, but in fact the nation began growing rapidly in the early 1980s, when its economy was still relatively closed. China introduced foreign competition into its country cautiously, maintaining severe controls on capital and investment and subsidizing key industries. After China joined the World Trade Organization, it reduced its subsidies of local industries according to WTO dictates but turned to manipulating its currency to stimulate exports.

- Latin America's import substitution policies of the 1970s were not the unambiguous failure of protectionist policies that globalization advocates widely claimed. Tariffs had been raised so that domestic industries could develop unhindered by international competition. But economic growth was stronger there in the 1970s than it was in the following decades, when, under the influence of the Washington consensus, Latin America adopted globalization policies that opened its markets to foreign trade and investment.

- World levels of poverty fell as many nations benefited from economic growth. But lower poverty rates, according to the World Bank, were largely due to poverty reductions in China and to a lesser degree India, neither of which adopted the market liberalization policies prescribed. The poverty threshold is also painfully low: the equivalent of $1.25 a day in the United States. It is really a measure of minimum tolerable penury in the poorest nations. In the meantime, incomes became more unequal within many nations—including in most of the rich nations.

- Between World War II and the late 1970s, the golden age of rich nations, the globalization regime was much more "shallow," to use economist Dani Rodrik's term, involving flexible trade rules and regulations, fixed currencies, and more capital controls. It was not the rules-based, floating-currency model followed later, though its success was used to support these purer free-trade rules. In the second era of post–World War II globalization, when the increasingly market-oriented policies of the WTO, IMF, and World Bank led to market liberalization being enforced more strictly, economic growth was slower in many regions.

- Once capital restrictions were eliminated, the free flow of investments, often short term in nature, contributed to major crises in East Asia, Russia, Argentina, and Turkey in the mid-1990s and to the demise of the Long-Term Capital Management hedge fund in the United States. Floating currencies were major factors in the financial crisis of 2008, as U.S. financial institutions channeled capital flows from China to make risky, often deceitful loans to homebuyers at low interest rates.

- The huge trade surpluses that arose in export-oriented nations, particularly Germany and China, were offset by trade deficits in the United States and much of Europe, undermining growth in these latter nations. These imbalances are not indefinitely sustainable, an issue major nations haven't yet come to terms with.

The nineteenth-century experience of rich nations is widely ignored by economists. In a time of substantial tariffs, fixed currencies, and robust government interventions, there was vigorous globalization, nevertheless. Trade expanded and capital flowed among nations. Labor moved across borders, in particular to North America.

In the early 1800s, American exports of cheap tobacco and cotton were critical to the Industrial Revolution, and trade was brisk despite the tariffs on manufactured goods the United States had adopted under President James Madison. International trade in the late 1800s, increasingly among America, Europe, and Britain, was also critical to the so-called second industrial revolution of oil, steel, machinery, and more complex mass-produced goods, eventually including automobiles. America's main exports were still agricultural products, with cotton leading the way. But especially high tariffs protected the young manufacturing sector from competitive imports; on balance, the protections more than offset the increased prices on domestic manufactures that Americans had to pay.

Major nations mostly fixed their currencies to gold in this era; there were no major floating currencies. The fixed currencies sometimes required higher interest rates than were ideal, but they also made it possible for goods to be priced internationally with certainty and for capital to flow across boundaries to build railroads, pipelines, steel mills, and much else because there was less fear of falling currency values.

After World War II, the advocacy for free trade spread, and tariffs were cut by roughly 30 percent. The new trade and currency arrangements were made at the 1944 conference in Bretton Woods, New Hampshire, where Keynes represented Britain. The higher tariffs imposed early in the Great Depression were fresh in mind and were correctly thought to have contributed to the severe downturn.

Trade grew rapidly after World War II among Europe, the United States, and Japan—more rapidly than GDP. This strongly reinforced economists' faith in free-trade theory. The movement to reduce tariffs, capital controls, industry subsidies, and other trade restrictions became intense. But little attention has been paid to how different the first twenty-five to thirty years of the post–World War II era, ruled by the Bretton Woods agreement, was from the second, when much of the agreement was abandoned or seriously modified. As noted, the first era had relatively loose and flexible trade regulations, even as tariffs were cut. It was fairly easy to cheat.

Moreover, the flow of capital remained tightly regulated. Currencies were pegged to the dollar—or, to be precise, there was a managed peg with limited room to devalue or revalue. The dollar in turn was pegged to gold; ultimately only central banks could cash in their dollars—thirty-five dollars per ounce of gold. Without fixed currencies, prices were uncertain, and because currencies were traded like any security, they were subject to speculative excesses. Fixing currencies to the strong dollar, and fixing the dollar to gold, had worked well for two decades.

The decidedly more liberalized era started in the 1970s with the floating of currencies. As America's trade deficits started to rise, the dollar became clearly overvalued and could no longer be maintained as an official anchor. (A highly valued currency makes exports more expensive to buyers from other nations.) The dollars that accumulated overseas when Americans bought foreign goods were being cashed in for gold. Under President Nixon, the tie to gold was dropped, and the major currencies were set to float in the financial markets without government constraints—long a recommendation of Milton Friedman's.

In the 1980s and 1990s, further tariff reductions were agreed upon, but now protectionist measures, such as subsidizing industries, were tightly restricted. These policies were formalized in 1995 with the creation of the World Trade Organization, which policed trade regulations more closely than was the case under Bretton Woods.

Among the more important changes, capital controls were mostly abandoned. The United States started eliminating them in the 1970s, as did Europe generally in the 1980s. Emerging economies were encouraged—or, in reality, often required—to end controls in the 1990s. The new era of comprehensive market liberalization—the Washington consensus—had begun. It was far different from the Bretton Woods era, which had done so much to generate confidence in free trade and capital flows and on which confidence in globalization was built.

The period of Washington consensus–style globalization was mostly a failure, but advocates were reluctant to admit it. Latin America found it difficult to compete, and growth slowed. With no constraints on fast-moving capital or currency trading, financial crises were frequent. The strongest emerging nations like China liberalized only gradually, to repeat, renouncing allegiance to the Washington consensus.

Income inequality in rich nations, economists eventually began to concede, was partly a consequence of the offshoring of jobs and outsourcing of production. There were, as free-trade theory predicted, many losers. The proportion of low-wage jobs created during the economic recovery from the Great Recession, which technically ended in 2009, was unusually high, some of it having to do with globalization. Free capital flows did not just hurt poor nations. In the Eurozone, there were enormous property bubbles as, for example, German and French banks lent liberally to developers in Spain and Greece. Capital flows from China enabled mortgage brokers to charge low interest rates on mortgages, which were often sold to people who could not afford them. America's currency remained strong largely because it was the single trustworthy reserve currency in the world, but this kept prices of its exports high. The world still put its money in U.S. dollar debt.

If we define globalization as the expansion of the world into one economy, as many do, we begin to see how complex and immense such an ambition really is and how inadequate an economic orthodoxy dedicated to the Invisible Hand can be. It was hard enough to unite domestic economies like the United States to build commercial trade and establish a single currency. But the world is not one nation with long-standing traditions and rules of law. It is also not one huge economy with roughly similar economic conditions. Rather, it is composed of national economies at many different stages of evolution, some very poor and lacking resources or financial institutions. It is not ruled by one set of technologies but by many dissimilar and competing ones, efficiency often related to a nation's size. Its citizens have different cultures and ideas about what constitutes a full life.

Free trade and financial liberalization, which included the reduction or elimination of regulations on interest rates and cross-border investment, were so attractive to economists partly because free trade is indeed a good and even powerful idea—in the abstract.

If someone in a neighboring town sells excellent shoes at a price much lower than in your town, you should have the right to buy them. Similarly, if the United States grew corn more efficiently than Britain did, the British should have been allowed to buy it free of tariffs. This was one of Adam Smith's principal arguments. "If a foreign country can supply us with a commodity cheaper than we ourselves can make it," he wrote in *The Wealth of Nations*, "better buy it of them with some part of the produce of our own industry employed in a way in which we have some advantage."

This was known as absolute advantage. Smith had talked about an absolute advantage in manufacturing some goods. About forty years later, David Ricardo pointed out that there were "comparative" advantages that further reinforced the benefits of free trade. N. Gregory Mankiw made a nice analogy to the golfer Tiger Woods. Even if Tiger Woods can mow his own lawn faster than his gardener, he can use his time much more lucratively by practicing his swing or doing a commercial. Woods has an absolute advantage in both cases, but the principle of comparative advantage holds that he would be better off hiring his slower gardener than doing the work himself because he makes much more devoting his time to what he is especially good at.

The same is true for countries. In Ricardo's famous example, Portugal could produce both wine and cloth more cheaply than Britain, but it could produce wine so much more cheaply that it made sense for it to sell its wine for Britain's cloth. Portugal had an absolute advantage in both, but its comparative advantage in wine made free trade with Britain advantageous for both nations. Portugal could buy more cloth, and Britain more wine.

Paul Samuelson helped to exalt the Ricardian idea of comparative advantage when he said that it was the one undisputed and nontrivial idea in economics. But once again, a beautiful idea in economics had extreme assumptions as its foundation. If free trade led Portugal to make less cloth, what would happen to all those textile workers who lost their jobs? The assumption was that they would almost all find new jobs, but many probably would not. Free trade can work well if full employment can be maintained—which is usually an unrealistic assumption.

Free trade is also supposed to make all nations more efficient through competition. But there are difficulties with such a theory. A lot of America's productivity growth was due to economies of scale—the more produced, the lower the unit cost of steel or automobiles, for example. If rich nations have such huge industries, a start-up company in a developing country cannot compete easily if that country is open to free trade. Shouldn't there be room for protection of infant industries? It would seem there should also be room for government investment in industries where risk is too high to encourage large investment. But free-trade enthusiasts frown on this because it amounts to government interference with Ricardian principles.

Returning to social programs, government should be allowed to develop a substantial safety net and training programs for workers who lose jobs as markets are opened. The United States has such a program today, but it is trivial in size and provides only temporary help. The demand of the Washington consensus to suppress budget deficits while simultaneously opening up markets limits such needed social programs.

A counterexample highlights the point. Norway has one of the most open trade policies but also one of the biggest governments (as a proportion of the size of its economy) in the world. Its support for those who lose their jobs because of free trade is significant. Its people strongly favor both free trade and big government. As Dani Rodrik has noted, no economist who fully understands trade theory should propose reducing tariffs and other protections without also proposing an increased social safety net of unemployment insurance and job training.

Economic growth was so rapid in the first two decades of tariff reductions after World War II that economists romanticized and exaggerated the role played by free trade. By the late 1960s, unemployment had fallen to around 3 percent. To economists, it looked as if free trade were a win-win. In the United States, wages rose and income inequality was reduced, even as trade increased.

But much else contributed to this rapid growth, including repressed demand during World War II, the Marshall Plan, which created demand for U.S. exports, and new technologies and highly profitable investment opportunities. High defense spending even after the war provided ongoing Keynesian demand, and falling world oil prices reduced manufacturing and transportation costs dramatically.

Ironically, in the early 1940s, Paul Samuelson and the economist Wolfgang Stolper, at Harvard at the time and later at the University of Michigan, made clear that there had to be some losers in free trade. Their theorem has been elaborated and expanded, but any claim that free trade benefits all is simply wrong. As Paul Krugman observed, "Now we're talking about broad swaths of the population hurt by trade. It's a good bet that almost all US workers with a high school degree or less are hurt by Chinese manufactured exports, at least slightly."

One critical point remains: the beneficial role of a single strong currency. The two most prosperous periods of international trade, the late 1800s and the Bretton Woods era, were dependent on a

sound, reliable currency to serve as a basis for trade—what economists refer to as a hegemon. In the earlier period, it was Britain's
pound sterling, which was fixed to gold. Gold has such a long tradition of value that fixing a currency to it is thought to provide a stable, unchanging foundation. Trade and capital flows were secured.
After World War II, it was the dollar. The peg created at the Bretton Woods Conference allowed room for modest changes in currency values and occasional devaluations. But countries basically
anchored themselves to the dollar, making both trade and investment more stable.

Over time, however, the gold standard became difficult to maintain. In the United States, trade surpluses turned to deficits in the
1970s as the country began to import more goods than it exported,
especially with inflation of its goods prices increasing. The economist Robert Triffin had long anticipated that the peg established at
Bretton Woods could not last. The dollars paid for foreign goods
mounted overseas, and the United States had to keep interest rates
up to attract foreign investors to buy its bonds. With foreign countries starting to demand gold rather than just bonds for their dollar
holdings, President Nixon abandoned the gold standard in 1971.
This began the era mentioned earlier of currencies unfixed to gold
or any major currency, even the dollar. These floating currencies
enabled nations to avoid crises that required dramatic devaluations, but they also affected the prices of goods being exported and
imported. For example, the floating U.S. dollar was usually uncom-
petitively high in value, harming American exports, because even
without a gold peg it remained the one currency that the world's
nations and investors trusted and in which it kept its funds. A single dollar price was supposed to be the equilibrium point for two
different sets of buyers and sellers—those who traded goods with

the United States and those who invested in U.S. securities. But that could not work; you usually needed different dollar prices for each market. Few talked about the inherent conflict.

Concerns about free trade grew in the 1980s. On the whole, the General Agreement on Tariffs and Trade, which attempted to reduce trade barriers, favored wealthy and powerful nations. In particular, rich nations kept subsidizing domestic agriculture at the expense of the many poorer nations trying to export agricultural commodities. As a result, so-called market liberalization led to slow growth in many regions.

The World Trade Organization, the successor to GATT, cut tariffs still more, with poor nations often bearing the brunt. The WTO also developed a mechanism by which countries could challenge practices such as dumping, the selling of products below cost overseas. It was the WTO that generally demanded that nations stop subsidizing local industries and protecting infant ones. In the meantime, rich nations sought tighter control over the use of intellectual property, alleging that developing nations were "stealing" new technologies. Never mind that Americans had stolen technologies from Europe throughout the 1800s. Unlike in the modern era, there was no one to stop them.

In 1999, the WTO meeting in Seattle was adjourned amid street demonstrations over intellectual property rights, environmental issues, and the plight of newly developing nations. Orthodox economists had seemed oblivious to the growing anger, even among their own nations' workers. The support for the North American Free Trade Agreement, which opened borders between Mexico, the United States, and Canada, was another example of economists' remaining insensitive to lost jobs. They argued that America's trade surplus with Mexico would rise, undoubtedly creating new jobs.

But it did not. A strong case can be made that the direct impact was a loss of jobs. Krugman, whose primary academic research was in trade theory, said that he still believed in NAFTA (because new jobs would be created elsewhere in the domestic economy, I presume) but nevertheless criticized the oversimplified claims in its behalf made by many economists. They were ideologues, not scholars.

Economists also carelessly encouraged the premature end of capital controls for developing nations. In the 1990s, Stanley Fischer, an official at the IMF and a former economics professor at MIT (he's now vice chairman of the Federal Reserve), urged that developing nations open their financial markets to overseas investment without restrictions like transactions taxes and limits on investments with short-term debt. The pressure on developing nations to open their markets was not based on serious research or empirical studies, just theory. According to Rodrik, Fischer later acknowledged how little evidence there was that capital mobility was a key to growth.

The highly regarded MIT economist Rudi Dornbusch, who had written a textbook with Fischer, turned on a dime. In 1996, he strongly recommended a tax on international financial transactions—a restraint on capital flows. By 1998, he reversed his position completely, claiming that capital flows should be free. "The correct answer to the question of capital mobility is that it ought to be unrestricted," wrote Dornbusch. To Rodrik, this was an undisguised and sudden ideological shift on Dornbusch's part, not one based on evidence.

In the late 1980s and early 1990s, the rapid growth of Korea, Malaysia, Indonesia, Taiwan, and Singapore, among other Asian nations, was partly dependent on the flow of Western capital into long-term investments like plant and equipment. This success made the benefits of capital flows seem obvious. But the new gold rush would not last for long, as Western investment shifted, often to "hot" short-term investments.

Thailand provided as clear and tragic an example of the dangers of this willy-nilly market liberalization as there was. Thailand had pegged its currency to the U.S. dollar in 1984. (It had pegged it to a lower level years earlier.) By reducing the possibility that the value of the Thai baht would fall, such a peg attracted foreign investors. In 1985, the United States, with cooperation from European and Japanese central banks, suddenly lowered the value of the dollar against its competitors to promote its exports. This was stipu-lated in an agreement known as the Plaza Accord, named after the New York hotel where negotiations took place. Thailand directly benefited because its exports were suddenly much cheaper, as its currency fell with the dollar. The currencies of Japan, Taiwan, and Korea rose against the dollar and the baht, making their exports relatively expensive. These countries moved their manufacturing to places like Thailand, where labor was cheaper and they would have the advantage of the lower currency. This was the source of Thailand's miraculous boom in manufacturing: manufactured goods rose from about 25 percent of exports in the 1980s to 63 percent in 1990.

The West attributed the Thai boom mostly to liberalized trade and financial policies. International banks and pension funds started lending to and investing in Thailand, trusting that its gov-ernment would keep the value of the baht fixed to the dollar. But investment, including from hedge funds, soon flowed to real estate and other speculative activities, and inflation began to rise.

Thailand's currency advantage was about to end. The Japanese yen fell against the dollar in the mid-1990s, so Japanese companies moved manufacturing back home. With the price of its exports increasing, Thailand soon ran a huge trade deficit, and the investors who once loved putting their money into the country became wary that it would not be able to maintain the value of the baht. In 1996, Thailand was caught in a vicious circle: as inflation and the trade deficit continued to rise, capital fled and the baht fell (undermining exports and stimulating inflation at the same time).

The Washington consensus then made matters worse. In return for funds to bail the nation out—it could not pay its debt—the IMF demanded draconian cuts in social spending and a sharp hike in interest rates to stop the fall of the baht, provoking severe recession, bankruptcies, and unemployment. No medicine could have been worse. Western economists and policymakers blamed Thailand for bad policies that led to real estate and other speculation, but they should have blamed the elimination of controls on Wall Street and Western money heedlessly flowing into the country. Thailand's collapse spread to Korea, Taiwan, Malaysia, and other Asian nations. Painful recessions followed. "When countries on the periphery of the global system such as Thailand and Indonesia are overcome by crisis," noted Rodrik, "we blame them for their failures and their inability to adjust to the system's rigors." Above all, Western critics argued, these economies were not transparent. In fact, as Joseph Stiglitz pointed out, the World Bank and the IMF were among the least transparent of institutions. Finally, the IMF somewhat softened its demands, and the Seattle disruptions forced the WTO to rethink its strict terms. Thomas Friedman and Martin Wolf, however, continued to write mostly unqualified endorsements of sweeping globalization.

Given the failures of the Washington consensus, it proponents started to concede the need for revamping. By 2002, the economist most responsible for the Washington consensus, John Williamson, agreed it was a "damaged brand." In his defense, he insisted that his ideas had been oversimplified by others. Williamson acknowledged the damaging crises in Asia and the poor economic performance of many nations that had liberalized, especially those in South America. He argued for a more nuanced approach. As he said in a speech titled "Did the Washington Consensus Fail?":

> I draw two conclusions.... (1) Countries ought not to have adopted the Washington Consensus as an ideology. As Moisés Naím ... said, an ideology is a thought-economizing device. There will always be other things that matter besides those included in any attempt to lay out a general set of policy guidelines, and for a policymaker to imagine that s/he can stop thinking and simply follow a set of policies that someone else has concocted is irresponsible. (2) Anyone offering a new set of policy guidelines as of 2002 has a duty to include a set of suggestions as to how crises can be avoided.

These are constructive points—especially his contention that there are "other things that matter." An intelligent globalization means not the Invisible Hand writ large but rather specific policies for each nation at a given point in time. Williamson came to believe that *a one-size-fits-all set of policies was inappropriate.* Individualized economics—dirty economics, as I'd put it—are good economics.

Among the undeniable ironies is the fact that the sharp cuts in worldwide poverty rates about which globalization proponents profusely boasted cannot be simply attributed to market liberalization. As noted, most of the poverty reduction has occurred in China and, to a lesser degree, India, where liberalization policies were deliberately restrained. Excluding China, poverty rates are down only about 10 percent. The $1.25-a-day poverty line is disgraceful, however. If we move the poverty line up the income scale to, say, $2.50 a day, there is almost no fall in poverty levels. This suggests that an enormous number of people live just above the World Bank's poverty line as globalization marches on. What is more, improvements in poverty and inequality occurred in Latin America in the 2000s when the IMF and the World Bank lowered their hold in those nations.

Some scholars have thrown up their hands in despair over the spotty success of free-trade theory and of aid to developing nations from the World Bank and advanced nations. They cite global aid projects that have failed time and again. But the errors of globalization have more to do with the attachment to an ideology than with the failure of good intentions, as some have implied.

Recent experience offers a handful of lessons that can lead to more constructive trade, capital, and currency policies. These lessons all point to pragmatic compromises rather than sweeping proposals, to a focus on the details and particularities of a case rather than a search for a universal formula.

The first is that gradual reform is more effective than a sudden turn to free markets, deregulation, and privatization. Shock therapy in Russia was a glaring failure. Nations like Thailand and Argentina reformed too quickly and eventually paid the price.

The historical models of sustained growth are clear. They include the gradual development of core industries and diversification to avoid dependency on one or two of them; improvements in literacy and education, with emphasis on women; the building of a system of finance; the slow and deliberate opening of capital markets; and, usually, the protection of labor from abusive low wages and working conditions. The last of these items has often been missing in developing nations such as China, which is now trying to reform labor markets, and Vietnam, which is not.

A strong domestic market based on decent wages and conditions for workers can be a key to growth. We have yet to see whether China will evolve into a higher-wage nation with strong consumer demand. Much of Germany's export success has also been dependent on low wages for a rich nation, a fact not widely recognized in the United States.

A second lesson is that each nation typically requires different policies and should be left room for experimentation. Some spend too much on social programs, others too little; some need transportation infrastructure, others improved banking; some require literacy programs, others advanced education or programs targeted to educate women and protect them from abuse; some need to protect infant industries, others to privatize bloated state industries; some require higher wages, others a reduction in inflated labor costs; some need worker protections like unemployment insurance, others labor mobility. One-size-fits-all liberalization is an enemy of this approach. The trade agreements the United States enters into should place a priority on workers' rights and minimum wages, but each policy has to be fitted to a nation's particular needs.

The particulars matter. One inherent difficulty poor nations have in trying to catch up is that rich nations enjoy the advantages of economies of scale mentioned earlier. The political scientist Robert Wade of the London School of Economics points out how economies of scale lead to a virtuous circle of growth for large nations. Big markets enable that. Smaller, poorer nations often cannot reach the scale needed to take advantage of such benefits unless their companies are protected by tariffs on competing imports. As a result, we see that a majority of manufactured goods are sold by one rich nation to another, not by the poor to the rich as simple economic theory has asserted because labor costs are lower. The advantages of plant size, adequate transportation infrastructure, and large domestic markets where consumers made good wages were neglected by the theorists. Industry protectionism may well be justified under these circumstances.

A third lesson is that models of growth that depend indefinitely on exports are not sustainable. The large imbalances in trade between China and much of the world, notably the United States, distort economies. Trade deficits, due in part to an undervalued Chinese currency, reduce GDP for the United States and increase it for China. But the resulting high dollar—made even higher by serving as the world's reserve currency—attracts investment, especially from China, and must be invested in U.S. assets. This results in lower interest rates in the United States (and, in the 2000s, it led to a mortgage bubble) but a growing risk for Chinese investments because the dollar may not remain strong forever.

A similar set of circumstances exists in Europe. Germany runs huge trade surpluses based on the fixed euro and restrained wages, and other European nations usually run deficits. One of Keynes's objectives at Bretton Woods was to level these imbalances. His proposal, never adopted, was to create a mechanism that would force surplus nations to reduce their exports.

The imbalances are the consequence of purist free-trade theory and the failure of floating currencies to adjust markets as Friedman and others had predicted they would. Contrary to what Friedman said, these currencies are neither well priced by market forces nor even generally stable. They can remain inefficiently high, such as the U.S. dollar, or can be manipulated to stay low, such as the Chinese renminbi. Again, simplistic market solutions failed. We don't need to fix currencies to each other narrowly, but we can fix them loosely, leaving room for fluctuations in the market and for devaluations and revaluations.

Ideally, more global governance of currencies could help balance trade and reduce currency fluctuations. But the world is not moving in that direction. Today, regional trade agreements are in vogue and are used for political reasons. America's Asian trade pact, known as the Trans-Pacific Partnership, seems, at this writing, designed as a weapon to isolate China. Moreover, if it is adopted, it will likely be signed by Vietnam and other nations with extremely poor records on workers' rights.

Trade theory has much to offer. But turning it into a faith-based formula for world governance has failed poor nations and workers in the rich world alike. Most economists are advocates of free trade, but they cannot neglect the other side of the case—businesses and workers will be sacrificed. Government policies are needed to address these issues. Businesses require small-business loans and other adjustment policies, and workers require a significantly stronger safety net of unemployment and health insurance and job training.

In *The Lexus and the Olive Tree,* Thomas Friedman admired the "golden straitjacket" that economists were fitting on the world. All would have to abide by free-market principles. But were the economists right in their strongly held arguments? The economist Robert Driskill comprehensively reviewed their writings about free trade and found their analyses devoid of "critical thinking." They were not "balanced," their recommendations "more like a zealous prosecutor's advocacy."

Earlier in the 2000s, Joseph Stiglitz wrote, "There is no theoretical underpinning to believe that in early stages of development, markets by themselves will lead to efficient outcomes." But under the Washington consensus, markets were raised to preeminence and government was increasingly given a backseat. Ironically, noted Stiglitz, the creation of the World Bank, to make development work, "reflected a recognition of the importance of market failures. If the neoclassical model *were* correct, the shortage of capital would be reflected in higher returns to capital, and private markets would ensure the flow of capital from the capital rich advanced industrial countries to the capital poor developing world."

Globalization has not merely been unable to meet expectations. The ideological implementation of free-trade policies hurt many countries. We should shake off the attractiveness of these single big ideas and take off the golden straitjacket that, as most straitjackets do, restricts us. Intelligent global governance, freed of ideology, can be designed to exploit in individual countries the benefits of free trade while avoiding its pitfalls.

Chapter Seven

Economics Is a Science

The pretense that economics is a science is harmful in that it gives economic ideas more credibility than they often deserve. Policymakers—and U.S. citizens—are unaware of the questionable underpinning of much of the advice offered by economists, which has time and again led to gravely incorrect policy decisions.

But evidence often does not seem to matter. Only in recent years have most economists softened their antagonism to a higher minimum wage, despite the persuasive analyses undertaken by some since the 1990s that it can be beneficial. Similarly, most in the profession have only lately broadened their thinking about the adverse effects of offshoring jobs. A renewed interest in financial regulation, including higher capital requirements, was provoked only by the devastating 2008 financial crisis, which revealed gaping holes in efficient markets theory. The position of some economists from prestigious universities on the benefits of austerity economics was a mockery of good research, as updated scholarship has clearly shown. Despite this intellectual flexibility, policymakers seem to think that most economists know what they are talking about when they agree with them, or they cynically use them to promote their own political agendas in areas such as financial regulation, free trade, and workers' rights.

Also, there has been a de facto censorship of needed ideas that don't fit today's ideological preferences. For example, until the slow recovery after 2009, economists generally did not even enter into a discussion about the role of consumer demand and high wages as sources of economic growth. The orthodox conversation instead focused on low inflation and the dangers of rising wages.

I don't mean to say that economists have not made admirable contributions. They have added a great deal to our knowledge of the *failures* of markets due to financial inefficiencies, behavioral irrationalities, unequal information between buyers and sellers, prices that are not transparent, and persistent poverty traps in developing nations.

There have also been constructive efforts to incorporate new statistical tools and behavioral analyses. To take a couple of examples, economists found a method to price some kinds of derivatives, and they developed ways to incentivize workers to participate in private pension plans. Labor economists in particular do empirical work that produces useful conclusions, often corrections of free-market theory. This has been true of minimum wage research and the debunking of economists' claims that labor regulations in Europe have stymied growth.

But the latter research has not pushed aside the dominant and damaging loyalty to the Invisible Hand, and certain valuable research, as noted, has been entirely neglected. The Australian economist Steve Keen, for example, predicted the full extent of the credit crisis, warning that free markets are not necessarily stable. Though he won top prize in a contest sponsored by nonorthodox economists to determine who anticipated the crisis, orthodox economists essentially ignored his warnings.

Eric Maskin, a Nobelist who believes that economics is closer to a science than critics like myself do, has pointed out a handful of excellent, if more general, research efforts that also warned of potential instabilities in finance and the wide-ranging collapses that could occur. Maskin asserts that economics parallels science because it can explain factors such as growth and recession, even if it can't predict them. He showed that some economists did forecast, however vaguely, a market crash. Too bad they were neglected, he said.

If economics was truly a science, such efforts of reputable economists at good schools would not have been ignored. Major findings in medical research or physics are not simply swept aside because most scientists have different views. Science builds on earlier work. As for the after-the-fact explanatory capacities of economics, consider the disagreements about the causes of the 2008 financial crisis or the recent controversies addressed earlier over austerity economics and how to revive growth.

Experimentation and empirical proof in economics rarely rise to the standards of true science; if they did, they could not be cast aside. Partly this is because so much of economics is about establishing econometric relationships that find strong coincidences of change—among the most famous is the link between the growth of money and GDP—but don't prove one variable causes another. As often as not, the next group of statisticians finds a contradictory result (or works hard to do so). New statistical techniques can refine the causal relationship, but they are still blunt tools. Similarly, simulations by economists are typically oversimplified. The real world, dependent on human behavior, is too complex.

The basis of much of economics is a set of value judgments, a claim as widely denied as it is generally true. The Invisible Hand cannot be divorced from a bias in favor of laissez-faire solutions.

Economists opposed to active government involvement find adherence to the Invisible Hand comfortable as they do a belief in self-adjusting economies. Given the predominance today of such views, judgments are often skewed because the path to professional success requires conformity, not scientific objectivity.

Although a young, provocative Lawrence Summers wrote a 1991 treatise casting doubt on the scientific pretenses of economic empiricism, many economists are proud to think of their field as akin to physics. It is a "positive" discipline, they say, based on empirical demonstration and proof. Economists feel most secure when speaking with the authority of numbers. "Positive economists," the economist Walter Nicholson wrote, "believe that one reason for the success of economics as a discipline is that it has been able to emulate successfully the positive approach taken by the physical sciences rather than becoming involved in the value-laden normative approach taken by some of the other social sciences."

The objective of most sciences is to seek universal rules. Physics can rely on complex experiments or mathematical proofs, sophisticated versions of what most of us learned in high school subjects like plane geometry and elementary calculus. Economics emulates science in its sheer ambition, which is also to seek universal rules. But compared to the physical sciences, its ability to make sound predictions is weak and to devise unambiguous proofs even weaker.

A central obstacle in economic testing is that there is leeway in forgiving real-world outcomes that are the opposite of what was predicted. You simply can't claim that an economic proposition is truly wrong. For example, the failure of the Washington consensus policies in South America was evident. Yet the conservative American economist Anne Krueger, who promoted them when she was at the World Bank, insisted that the policies were simply not extreme enough and had been abandoned too early. The philosopher Karl Popper argued that if social scientists can't clearly demonstrate that something is false, there is no way to determine that it is true, a criticism often leveled at economics.

Nevertheless, most economists would likely claim that their profession is a study of what is, not what ought to be, thus distinguishing it from philosophy or politics. John Maynard Keynes's father, John Neville Keynes, wrote in the 1800s that economics should be as free of value judgments as possible—every assertion should be proved. John Neville Keynes realized there were other ways of practicing economics, including normative economics—prescriptions for what ought to be—but he separated true economics from those.

Milton Friedman was one of the leading positivists of contemporary economics, a champion of economics as science. In his 1953 essay "The Methodology of Positive Economics," he cited Neville Keynes at length. To Friedman, as long as a model of economic outcomes has predictive abilities, it is adequate. As he wrote of positive economics, "Its task is to provide a system of generalizations that can be used to make correct predictions about the consequences of any change in circumstances. Its performance is to be judged by the precision, scope, and conformity with experience of the predictions it yields. In short, positive economics is, or can be, an 'objective' science in precisely the same sense as any of the physical sciences."

Friedman claimed that the assumptions underlying an economic model—for example, of how GDP can be affected by the money supply, his most-cited contribution—need not be proved or even sensible. In other words, we don't really have to know *how* money affects GDP; we only have to show that the ups and downs of the money supply are closely related to the ups and downs of GDP and that one predicts the other.

The leading mathematician in macroeconomics was not a political conservative, however. Paul Samuelson, a Keynesian, pioneered the use of math in contemporary economics. Robert Lucas said he learned his math by carefully reading Samuelson's doctoral thesis. But Samuelson strongly objected to Friedman's view. Predictiveness, he believed, was not all that mattered when devising a model of how economic outcomes are affected; relationships had to make sense, too.

When Friedman wrote about predictability in the early 1950s, he was understandably optimistic that empirical evidence would eventually support economic theories; research on the subject at that point was limited. His tome with Anna Schwartz, *A Monetary History of the United States, 1867–1960,* a monumental empirical work, did show a relationship in the broadest sense between GDP and the growth of money, which economists had not seen illustrated in such detail before. But it did not prove a *causal, predictable* relationship between money and GDP. The data showed that the money supply could grow without raising GDP. In fact, the relationship between GDP and the growth of money changed markedly in different periods of history. As an early critic of the work, James Tobin, summed it up: "To me it seems strange to rely on a trend which regards the 1930s and 1940s as normal, and the 1920s and the 1950s as abnormal."

From this sketchy empirical relationship, Friedman devised his policy rules, saying that the Fed should allow the money supply to grow by a certain unchanging percentage each year, no matter how volatile interest rates were as a result. This neglect of the level of interest rates just to target the growth of money served as Paul Volcker's smoke screen when he caused the deep recession of 1982 to stop inflation.

Volcker said he was in fact surprised by the jump in interest rates, another testament to the fragility of economic predictiveness. But he did not believe that a more gradual approach would have worked. It is hardly clear why. His claim is evidence of his seat-of-the-pants approach, not of the science of economics.

Friedman's failure to predict the harshness of the 1982 recession is a stark example—one of many—of the failure of his theory. As long as the Fed did not reduce the money supply in early 1982, he said, the recession would be over quickly. In fact the money supply rose rapidly in 1982, as he advocated, but America entered its deepest recession since World War II. Robert Lucas's assumption that the recession would be moderate was as wrong as Friedman's, based as it was on his supposedly mathematically rigorous theory that consumers would almost immediately regain their confidence and start spending when they realized that inflation was defeated. Thomas Sargent, who along with Lucas and others created rational expectations theory, strongly argued that inflation could be stopped with "virtually no cost in real output."

If economics is a science, why do Democratic and Republican economists so often differ in their policy suggestions? N. Gregory Mankiw asked this question in a *New York Times* column. He tried to explain why he, once head of George W. Bush's Council of Economic Advisers, had different views from Jason Furman, his former student at Harvard who had recently been appointed Obama's chief economist.

Mankiw claimed that by learning the discipline of economics, he and Furman shared a special knowledge. "It forever sets you apart—for better or worse—from mere muggles," he wrote. (A Muggle, for those who haven't read the Harry Potter books, is a person with no magical abilities.) Even though they were under the same scientific tent—or, as Mankiw put it, "intellectual tradition"—they could differ on policies like taxes, income inequality, and government intervention. Observed Mankiw: "Democrats tend to want to expand the scope of the federal government to improve the lives of the citizenry, while Republicans are more fearful that centralized power leads to abuse and lack of accountability."

In fact, many Democratic economists don't just want to expand government to help the unemployed, the poor, and the sick. They also think government policy is needed to maximize economic growth by raising consumption, creating healthier workers, and enabling people to invest in their own education. It is not misplaced sentiment but a theory about how to optimize growth. They argue it can be a win-win—doing good for people while doing good for the economy. Some believe that inequality itself can reduce growth because high-income individuals don't spend enough of their incomes. Mankiw is not concerned about that. Jason Furman probably is.

Mankiw said on balance he favors "efficiency" over government policies that redistribute money. The economic argument for efficiency is that it will produce greater wealth over time and that wealth will be widely shared, but this has not been the case historically. Over the last generation, productivity has risen faster than the wages of most Americans. If Mankiw were right, wages and productivity would have risen at roughly the same rate. A place, then, must be made for government policies that are not merely an amelioration of the unevenly distributed pain of free-market economic growth but a correction of a basic failure of capitalism to maximize wealth.

Ironically, Milton Friedman would have vehemently disagreed with Mankiw's conclusion that economists with the same education could disagree on major policy issues. He argued that if economists knew all the facts, they would agree on almost all policy matters. His wife, however, believed economists were swayed by value judgments. "I have always been impressed by the ability to predict an economist's positive [economically scientific] views from my knowledge of his political orientation," Rose wrote in their memoirs, *Two Lucky People,* "and I have never been able to persuade myself that the political orientation was the consequence of the positive views. My husband continues to resist this conclusion, no doubt because of his unwillingness to believe that his own positive views can be so explained."

Likely nothing has pleased some economists more than giving the impression that they rely almost solely on mathematics to explain economic relationships. Math is the language of universality, of enduring ideas that are appropriate in all contexts. Physics, after all, is essentially math, so why not economics? We know that theses in physics change and are rebutted with experimentation and mathematical analysis. That is not always so in economics. The leader of the rational expectations school, which fundamentally argues that government policy can have only a deleterious effect on the economy, rested his thesis on as pure an abstraction as he could muster. "I internalized . . . [the] view that if I couldn't formulate a problem in economic theory mathematically," Robert Lucas recalled in a speech that serves as a sort of autobiography, "I didn't know what I was doing. I came to the position that mathematical analysis is not one of many ways of doing economic theory: It is the only way. Economic theory is mathematical analysis. Everything else is just pictures and talk." Naturally, this belief led Lucas to belittle those who say they "are in possession of a body of scientifically tested knowledge enabling them to determine, at any time, what . . .

responses [to economic problems] should be." He proposed instead the strongest form of one-size-fits-all policymaking, and his adherence to this big idea has made him the most influential economist of the post–Milton Friedman era.

We don't have to get into a prolonged argument about positivism, however, to wonder about the trustworthiness of economic science. Its failures are plain. Yet so strong is the ideologically based methodological hold that the errors of Lucas and his colleagues about the 1980s recession or the risks of the mid-2000s have not undone Lucas's reputation.

A good example is how small a role finance played in the more traditional models of most centrist economists. For example, only in retrospect did the work of Hyman Minsky gain respect. Minsky was decidedly nonmathematical in his approach, but he emphasized by historical example how financial speculation could eventually lead to economic fragility and breakdowns. Such thinking dated back to John Stuart Mill; later adherents included the Nobelist Gunnar Myrdal, John Kenneth Galbraith, and Charles Kindleberger. But these views were pushed aside partly because they were not conducive to easy mathematization. More important, the possibility of financial instability violated the main contentions of the Invisible Hand.

The uncritical trust in economics as a science can be illustrated by some examples we have already discussed. None is more telling than the broad acceptance of the incorrect 2010 claim by Harvard's Carmen Reinhart and Kenneth Rogoff that a national debt reaching 90 percent of GDP has historically led to a sharp drop in the rate of growth of GDP. The view fit the conservative political discourse of the time, which focused on cutting government spending after the 2008 crash.

You'd think the reaction to such an error would be an international change of heart. No such thing occurred. The budget deficit became enemy number one, and cutting social programs was seen as a high priority. Here is what Erskine Bowles, who headed President Obama's balanced budget commission with Alan Simpson, had to say: "I know [Reinhart and Rogoff] had a worksheet error in the report and my understanding is that does make a difference. But what it doesn't change is the common sense and my own personal experience in both the public and private sector that when any organization has too much debt that is an enormous risk factor and your risks go up then people lending you money will want more money for their money."

The difficulty of dealing with cause and effect in the statistical work supporting economic findings is a major concern. The hard sciences grapple with this issue well and rarely elide it. Not so in economics. The Reinhart-Rogoff paper is a classic example of such neglect.

Many economists prefer the world to work in a straight line: an action leads directly to a consequence. But economies rarely work that way. There are mathematical techniques that can distinguish some causal relationships, but they are limited. Economists have a very hard time, in short, determining which came first, the chicken or the egg—though they often assume they know and draw conclusions based on those assumptions.

When the austerity economics advocated by Harvard's Alberto Alesina and his colleagues were discredited, it did not change policymakers' minds. Alesina argued that government spending cuts could lead to growth. Those challenging his work, among them the IMF's chief economist, Olivier Blanchard, noted in devastating analyses how the research failed to account for the conditions under which austerity policies were adopted in the past. If an economy was already strengthening or could benefit from a falling currency to stimulate exports, austerity would not necessarily work. If economies were weakening, austerity made matters worse.

"So will toppling Reinhart-Rogoff from its pedestal change anything?" asked Paul Krugman in *The New York Times.* "I'd like to think so. But I predict that the usual suspects will just find another dubious piece of economic analysis to canonize, and the depression will go on and on." Jared Bernstein, a former chief economist to Vice President Joe Biden, put it in terms all too familiar: "Why wouldn't we expect a reaction from policymakers? Because they're using research findings the way a drunk uses a lamppost: for support, not for illumination. If the R&R lamppost turns out to be wobbly, the austerions (or climate-change deniers, or supply-siders) will find another one. In this town [Washington, D.C.], I'm sorry to say, you can pretty much go think-tank shopping to buy the result you seek."

After the Reinhart-Rogoff comeuppance, Adam Posen, an American economist who served on the Bank of England's monetary policy committee before becoming president of the Peterson Institute for International Economics, noted that public debt had reached 90 percent of GDP in Japan, Italy, and Belgium in the last twenty years and "nothing much happened." He went on: "Let us celebrate rather than mourn what this re-evaluation of the evidence demonstrates, even though most already should have known it: too much public debt has its costs for growth, but the extent of those costs depends on the reasons the debt accumulated and the trajectory of the economy. And it is not worth provoking a crisis [in Europe] to forestall a crisis that is unlikely to come."

Posen's good sense is not widely practiced in economics. He himself was a strong advocate of inflation targeting at one point in his career, writing the major book on the subject with Ben Bernanke and others. In this instance, however, he called for policy recommendations based not on a universal law but on particular circumstances. Sometimes debt is bad, sometimes it's useful. This is good economics, not established science.

There has been a modest backlash against some economic conventions since the 2008 crash, but it hasn't deeply reformed the profession. In his 2011 book, *The Economist's Oath,* George DeMartino argued that economists should acknowledge uncertainties as a matter of ethics before they propose policy recommendations. Like doctors, they should take an oath first to do no harm. But most policy suggestions will be a trade-off between potential harm done and good done. Can you say or do anything useful in economics without taking some risks? On the other hand, the risks should be explicated and made clear. DeMartino also encouraged a more diverse dialogue among economists to offset the gravitational pull of single-minded othodoxy. But others assert that such pluralism is not enough. Mainstream conclusions are often simply wrong, driven by false mathematical precision and shaky assumptions. Wrong should be called wrong, critics say, and ideological determination of ideas should be seen as that.

Examples of central ambiguities in economics abound. Those self-declared positivists who abjure normative approaches to economics are usually *really* normative—their values show all the time. "There is a sense in which the distinction between positive and normative is completely confused," notes the economist Lawrence Boland. "Positive policy advisors are in effect always recommending that their policy is the *best* way to achieve the given ends."

Policymaking after the 2008 crash was a real-world laboratory in which some of the failures of economic thinking could no longer be denied. American economists seemed to move momentarily to the left, with conservatives like Martin Feldstein calling for more government spending in the Keynesian tradition. To be sure, John Taylor and other conservatives remained opposed to such measures.

But across Europe, anti-Keynesian policies, demanded mostly by Germany in return for bailout funds, were intense and led directly to recession. After three or four years of painful sacrifice, small shoots of growth prompted the "austerions" to proclaim victory. The Spanish prime minister declared that the tough policies had been justified. The British Conservative Party similarly hailed the new strong recovery—one it had been forecasting would occur years earlier.

It was an absurdist drama and a masterpiece of forgetting; that people suffered and would continue to do so was somehow seen as a necessary catharsis for a better future. When the Spanish prime minister made his claim, his country's unemployment rate was around 25 percent and total income still some 20 percent below its 2007 high. When the British finance minister made his claim, his country's GDP was more than 3 percent lower than its former high. The U.S. economy, which benefited from outright Keynesian stimulus under Obama and aggressive monetary loosening under Bernanke, had regained its former high by 2010.

Obama did not ask for a second stimulus in part because Keynesianism did not have as many devout followers as some may have thought. But on balance the empirical evidence was clear: a rise in a budget deficit due to Keynesian stimulus usually resulted in a more than equivalent increase in growth. Christina Romer had gathered substantial evidence to show this, which we have already reviewed. If economics was a science, there would surely have been more agreement, but the profession could look empirical evidence in the face and casually ignore it—or devise a statistical method that showed another result. The Harvard economist Edward Glaeser had completely dismissed Keynesianism in an otherwise flattering obituary of Paul Samuelson as late as 2009. "Many people associate Samuelson with Keynesianism," he wrote. "He did, after all, make Keynes popular in the United States by writing and then selling millions of copies of a textbook that helped explain Keynes's work. But among academic economists, Keynesianism came and went."

One way to think of modern economics is as a persistent search for Archimedes's fulcrum. "Give me a lever long enough and a fulcrum on which to place it, and I shall move the world," supposedly said the great Greek mathematician. Bad economists look for the unchanging variable upon which they can build a model.

Many claim that big government and high taxes deter growth, for example. So common are such statements that it's surprising to learn there are no accepted statistical demonstrations of the automatic dampening of growth by big government. Higher tax rates are not proven disincentives to work or investment, the best studies show. Big government does not deter growth, the best studies show.

Daron Acemoglu and James Robinson have, as we have seen, made a statistical case that strong institutions are the prerequisite for economic growth—the fulcrum. But the institutions they cite are highly biased in favor of those that promote and protect free markets. Their thesis is also flawed in that it does not convincingly show whether institutions give rise to economic development or vice versa. The beginning of the causal chain remains a mystery, a very shaky fulcrum on which to base claims. If economics cannot determine this causality, how can it be a science?

The economist Ha-Joon Chang of Cambridge University points out that one must measure these institutional effects not at any single point in time but over the long period it takes a nation to develop. Of Acemoglu and Robinson's work, Chang wrote: "Not only do the theories ignore the influence of economic development on institutional changes, but they are also biased (towards 'liberalized' solutions), simplistic, linear, and pay insufficient attention to the fact that the relationship may differ across time and space." He supports the view that it is the particulars that matter:

> Institutional economists need to pay more attention to the real world, both of the present and historical—not the fairy-tale retelling of the history of the world that has come to characterize mainstream institutional economics today (from the Glorious Revolution to Botswanan political culture) but capitalism as it really has been. Very often, institutional economic theories, including many non-neoclassical kinds, have been developed on the basis of rather stylized understanding of reality. However . . . reality is often stranger than fiction and therefore our theories need to be more richly informed by real-world experiences—both history and modern-day events.

Let me give one other example of a persistent and flawed way of thinking and a misuse of methodology that is nonetheless widely accepted among economists. It involves the rising inequality of incomes in America.

The top 10 percent of earners started pulling away from the pack in the late 1970s. Today, the top 1 percent of earners take in more than 20 percent of pretax income; in 1980, they took in only 10 percent. At the same time, the taxes paid as a proportion of income by the top 1 percent have fallen. The climb in the number of billionaires is astonishing. The rising compensation of CEOs and Wall Street bankers is unfathomable. One of the more solid assumptions of economics, well supported by hard evidence, is that individuals are influenced by financial incentives and penalties. But do CEOs and investment professionals require so much remuneration to do what they do? It often incentivizes them in destructive ways and, more important, does not adequately penalize them when they make wrong decisions.

In the meantime, wages for typical male workers, discounted for inflation, have gone sideways or fallen since the late 1960s. Those who earn more than 95 percent of all other men now make about three times what those who are right in the middle of the pack make; in the early 1970s, they made two times the median. Health care and education costs have soared all the while, as more people lose coverage and the reputation of the college attended, not merely the attending of college itself, increasingly determines whether people will earn a middle-class living.

What's the biggest cause of America's rising income inequality? Ask nine out of ten economists of almost any political stripe and they will say that Americans aren't educated enough. But we should understand that this position is not firmly based on hard facts and has been upended by events since the 1990s. The education advocates boil their claim down to what they call skill-biased technology. As technology has gotten more complex, newer and greater skills are needed by workers to keep up and earn good wages.

The piece of evidence economists depend on to make this claim is that higher levels of education are closely correlated to higher incomes. From the late 1970s to the early 1990s, this was true. The gap in pay between those who had college degrees and those with only high school diplomas increased significantly. By the mid-1990s, the average woman with a college degree made about 50 percent again what a woman with only a high school diploma made in the late 1970s. For men, the increase was more dramatic, the wage gap roughly doubling.

But was this all due to college attendance? Consider a critical assumption that economists make. They assume that educational attainment is an accurate measure of job skills. Educational attainment is also, however, a measure of class. Did your parents go to college? How much money did they earn? Did you grow up in a neighborhood with a good school system? Did you and your parents have a wide circle of successful friends who could help you get a job? Did you learn important social skills from your family and others? Were you read to as a child? Did you get a sense of optimism from family members and peers who made good incomes and lived interesting lives?

All these a priori circumstances matter. They are the conditions for getting into the colleges with better reputations, doing well there, and graduating. They are also the conditions for getting goods jobs, because networking and social status count, especially in times of high unemployment. Economists' assumption notwithstanding, educational attainment may be more a reflection of social and personal characteristics than of job skills. Attending college may be less about what is learned than about the weeding process, the seals of approval, the social skills.

But college attendance is easy to measure and makes modeling cause (college) and effect (inequality) much simpler. The claim that educational attainment measures job skills allows economists to draw a straight line and avoid the ambiguities of the circle.

There are many other factors that affect wages besides college attendance. The minimum wage, adjusted for inflation, has fallen significantly since the 1970s; this has especially affected women's wages and may have particularly dampened the growth of income at the lower end of the spectrum. Indeed, as Lane Kenworthy points out, earnings for the bottom 25 percent in the United States have grown more slowly than in almost all rich nations since 1970. Most of the income for this group comes from government social programs.

That the unemployment rate was unusually high over this period is among the more important factors contributing to inequality. With many looking for work, wages could not be bargained up. At the same time, union power had decreased. And the spread of globalization saw jobs being increasingly offshored.

Economists differ on how to weight the importance of these factors. Solid economic research shows that these were important influences on wages. But until fairly recently, educational inequality almost automatically got the nod. "To my mind, the evidence is most persuasive that the growing inequality I think the most worrisome . . . stems primarily from the gap between the demand for the highly educated and their supply," Raghuram G. Rajan wrote in his lauded 2010 book, *Fault Lines.* Rajan, who later became president of the Central Bank of India, at least doffed his cap to other possible explanations of inequality that might require new government policies, like the low minimum wage or the crushing of unions by business. Two of the leading proponents of the educational explanation of inequality and stagnating wages, Claudia

Goldin and Lawrence Katz of Harvard, didn't even do that. "The rise and decline of unions plays a supporting role in the story," they wrote in *The Milken Institute Review*, "as do immigration and outsourcing. But not much of a role. Stripped to essentials, the ebb and flow of wage inequality is all about education and technology."

But some orthodox economists have had strong doubts about this explanation for some time. In 2002, David Card of the University of California, Berkeley, and John DiNardo of the University of Michigan published a stinging paper showing that income inequality rose fastest between 1980 and 1986, yet the rapid advance of technology, as measured by computer use, did not occur until the 1990s, just as inequality stopped widening. Economists at the Economic Policy Institute and the New School had been making similar arguments since the late 1990s. The academic orthodoxy sloughed it off, even the paper by the highly admired Card.

Data about wages since the mid-1990s have also undermined the education argument. The gap in earnings between college and high school graduates, though one still exists, fell sharply in recent years. Postgraduate degrees continued to pay off, but this probably had to do mostly with the growing number of MBAs, who benefited from the rapid growth and increasing profitability of finance. The soaring opportunities in finance since the 1990s probably also lifted the wages of lawyers and accountants with advanced degrees, who increasingly worked in or for financial industries. People with four-year degrees who did not go on to graduate studies experienced no increase in average earnings in the 2000s.

Inequality of income also rose among college graduates. And the number of college graduates who now take work once done by high school graduates has increased from about 30 percent to 40 percent since 2000. This "bumping down" helped keep the unemployment rate of college graduates from rising, but it lowered their wages. Hourly wages declined in the 2000s for most college graduates and grew only slowly even for those in the top 10 percent. If America had actually produced all the college graduates the economists wanted, their average wages would have been *lower* in 2013 than they already were.

Some 95 percent of income gains went to the top 1 percent of workers between 2009 (when the recession officially ended) and 2012. It just couldn't be that the top 1 percent were so much better educated than others. Moreover, the top 0.1 percent made by far the most, and they were clearly not simply better educated than the rest of the 1 percent.

In truth, inadequate education is the easy answer. The deeper socioeconomic issues that place the poor at a disadvantage are harder to contend with. Legislation to raise the minimum wage or enable workers to more easily organize into unions was not at all widely discussed until 2013. Though reforming education would be expensive, it is more politically acceptable than many other social reforms, such as outright cash grants to the poor, especially those with children. It is also consistent with free-market theories. If we just improve educational standards, the markets will do the rest. Economists mostly took the easy road.

Research carried out by New York City's Center for Economic Opportunity examined the relationship between ethnicity, education, and employment in the city. As one would expect, the more educated a demographic group, the lower its rates of unemployment over time. This was true of whites and blacks, but it was decidedly not true of Hispanics, who, regardless of education, had a high employment rate. The employment levels of Hispanics, even those without a college degree, were higher than for whites who went to college. The reason, said Mark Levitan, who managed the study, was the strong social networks of Latinos, especially immigrants. They trusted each other, got each other jobs, and demanded high work standards.

Surveys like these begin to suggest how to practice economics better. Economics should allow for ambiguities, uncertainties, unknowns, and multiple explanations. On-the-ground surveys, empirical research, and experiments should trump reliance on pure theory and massive macro-oriented research. And there has been movement in that direction. Minimum wage research is a good example. As far back as 1992, Alan Krueger of Princeton, formerly President Obama's chief economist, and David Card had conducted empirical research to see whether an increase in the minimum wage in a New Jersey locality had reduced employment in fast-food establishments. They found it had not. On balance—and in conflict with simple Invisible Hand thinking—the many case studies undertaken since then have shown no significant job loss due to an increase in the minimum wage. In fact, it sometimes raised demand in localities, fostering growth.

Psychologists led by Daniel Kahneman have done many experiments on irrationality and risk aversion in decision making. Yale's Robert Shiller has interviewed investors to find out how they made decisions.

The Invisible Hand depends on consumers knowing their material preferences, what they really want. But do they? Amitai Etzioni, a self-described communitarian from George Washington University, notes that preferences are always changing, often influenced by advertising, culture, economic circumstances, and simple human idiosyncrasies. One of the more telling positions of many economists had been that advertising had no psychological influence on consumers and was merely a way to attract attention in order to provide product information. But reliable studies have destroyed this claim. Ads do have subtle influences on consumer preferences and do far more than merely impart information. Preferences do in fact change. This speed bump in the free market is getting more attention. The efficient Invisible Hand gets very dirty.

But a comprehensive theory of how consumers determine their preferences, says Etzioni, would be too complex to be developed. Simply assuming that preferences are known to consumers and that they are stable is far easier for economists. On such assumptions are built grand but dubious economic complexes.

Economists almost always have a pat answer when asked how to make mature economies grow. It is taken as a given that more savings, human capital (education), and technological advances make economies grow. These are worthy goals, but they do not really tell us much about how economies have actually grown in the past. They are simply too abstract. The accepted growth model of Robert Solow and Trevor Swan plugged in changes in labor supply and savings to see what growth they accounted for. What was left over—the "residual"—was casually called technology. Others added educational attainment to labor, savings, and technology. The economic historian Moses Abramovitz correctly called the residual not technology but a measure of "our ignorance." Years later, he added: "It's not what we don't know that bothers me, it's all the things we do know that ain't so."

Economies of scale, the growth of trade, the availability of natural resources, educational attainment, the quality of financial institutions, military spending, the rise of wages, the establishment of unions, welfare programs, the optimism of a people, varieties of attitudes toward materialism, the sense of community, marriage and families, the broadening of freedom—these are all major factors contributing to growth, and it is hard to separate one from another. I list them here to emphasize that there are no adequate, universal theories of growth because the nature of growth on a country-by-country basis and over time is too individual and involves too many factors. This does not stop economists from insisting on a scientific-like one-note explanation of growth.

Economics offers us a helpful abstraction of growth, but it misleads us about the sources of growth in the here and now—or in the past, for that matter. Economic growth is as much the domicile of the historian, the psychologist, the philosopher, the theologian, and the sociologist as it is of the economist. Economics should move in the direction of a more inclusive discipline. The strong bias to make it a science—to presume it is a science—is self-defeating. The bias is in fact anti-intellectual.

The best critics of orthodox economics are often economists themselves; they can be independent thinkers, even when orthodox. The inequality specialist, Thomas Piketty, largely an orthodox economist, wrote in a book published in 2014, "To put it bluntly, the discipline of economics has yet to get over its childish passion for mathematics and for purely theoretical and often highly ideological speculation at the expense of historical research and collaboration with other social sciences." Yet Piketty falls prey to many of the mainstream assumptions about general equilibrium theory as well. This book, *Seven Bad Ideas,* is by no means a wholesale condemnation of orthodox economics. Markets, after all, can work to distribute goods efficiently, education does matter, people are influenced by financial incentives, technological advances are the building blocks of economic growth, and finance facilitates such growth. And some orthodox economists have done excellent work.

But does the central claim of orthodox economics hold? Does the Invisible Hand alone—without a strong government of rules and prohibitions and a society with traditions of decency and community responsibility—lead to beneficial harmony? Does the Invisible Hand assure adequate investment in education, research, and transportation, sufficient regulation of business, and the fair distribution of income? Can we describe these unfulfilled needs as simple market failures that can be fixed, or does the idea of the market itself have fundamental weaknesses that must be constantly, not merely occasionally, addressed?

In actuality, some markets are always failing; it is just a matter of how much. Society is the center of the economy, not the other way around. The path to the financial collapse of 2008 and the Great Recession that followed started with an ideological turn in the 1970s that sought to denigrate government rather than reform it. Economists centrally participated in that shift, emphasizing the laissez-faire philosophies of their discipline over more pragmatic and nonideological ones. Many of them are profoundly responsible for what has happened to America and the world. Value judgments overwhelmed objectivity, fashion overwhelmed serious thought, and opportunity overwhelmed honest methodology.

The early classical economist John Stuart Mill thought economics was by nature "hypothetical." In his magnum opus, *Principles of Political Economy,* he wrote that economists believe competition is the great regulator, the driving force of Adam Smith's Invisible Hand. But Mill insisted custom may be a great regulator as well, foreshadowing by a couple of centuries the criticisms I've offered here. Economists can only make their claims hypothetically, he argued. "It would be a great misconception of the actual course of human affairs, to suppose that competition exercises in fact this unlimited sway," he stated in defiance of the Invisible Hand. The benefits of competition were mere hypotheses. Observation of life suggests strongly that customs matter probably as much.

This great economist of the early 1800s was dedicated to empirical investigation. He remains the best guide to what economics can and should be.

Acknowledgments

I must thank Jon Segal, my editor, several times over for his indispensable and elegant editing and many pertinent suggestions and questions. I also thank Sonny Mehta for his persistent faith in me and, similarly, my agent, Charlotte Sheedy, for her constant, enthusiastic support and good ideas. I also heartily thank my main researcher, Ellis Scharfenaker, for his intelligent insights and lightning-quick acquisition of relevant sources. And also thanks to Jon Segal's highly competent assistant Meghan Houser and the publicity, marketing, and copyediting staff of Knopf.

My deeply insightful wife, Kim Baker, is the backbone of my writing life. This book would be far less than what it is without her.

Notes

Introduction: Damage

4 "central problem of depression prevention": Robert Lucas, "Macroeconomic Priorities," *American Economic Review* 93, no. 1. pp. 1–14, American Economic Association, 2003), http://pages.stern.nyu.edu/~dbackus/Taxes/Lucas%20priorities%20AER%2003.

4 "the state of [macroeconomics] is good": Olivier J. Blanchard, "The State of Macro" (working paper 14259, August 2008), 1, http://www.nber.org/papers/w14259.

5 called the period from the early 1980s to around 2005: Ben S. Bernanke, "The Great Moderation" (remarks at the meeting of the Eastern Economics Association, Washington, D.C., February 20, 2004).

5 "The stability of the economy is greater": Charlie Rose, PBS, December 26, 2005.

5 During the period in which Friedman: Wage and employment data are from Bureau of Labor Statistics releases. Inequality data are from Thomas Piketty and Emmanual Saez, http://elsa.berkeley.edu/~saez/TabFig2012prel.xls.

6 In some states, prison costs: Adam Skolnick, "Runaway Prison Costs Thrash State Budgets," *Fiscal Times,* February 9, 2011, http://www.thefiscaltimes.com/Articles/2011/02/09/Runaway-Prison-Costs-Thrash-State-Budgets.

6 Economic mobility had stalled: Raj Chetty, Nathaniel Hendren, Patrick Kline, Emmanuel Saez, Nicholas Turner, "The Equality of Opportunity Project" (Harvard University, University of California, Berkeley, 2013), http://www.equality-of-opportunity.org/.

6 The employment of teens: Adrienne L. Fernandes-Alcantara, "Youth and the Labor Force: Background and Trends" (Congressional Research Service, May 10, 2012), http://www.fas.org/sgp/crs/misc/R42519.pdf.

6 And most tragically, the richest nation: Max Fisher, "How 35 Countries Compare on Child Poverty (the U.S. Is Ranked 34th)," *Washington Post,*

April 15, 2013. Based on United Nations Children's Fund data measuring poverty relative to the median income. U.S. measures of childhood poverty, based on an actual poverty line, show roughly similar levels of poverty—about 22 percent.

7 In sum, the growth of GDP: Deaton, *The Great Escape,* 167–218.

8 "It is important to start by stating the obvious": Olivier Blanchard, Giovanni Dell'Ariccia, and Paolo Mauro, "Rethinking Macroeconomic Policy" (International Monetary Fund, February 12, 2010), 10.

9 "The political debates take place": Summers, "Commanding Heights."

10 "We thought of monetary policy": Blanchard, Dell'Ariccia, and Mauro, "Rethinking Macroeconomic Policy," 3.

10 the level of federal public investment: Madrick, *Age of Greed,* 235–43. For details, see federal budget tables at http://www.whitehouse.gov/sites/default /files/omb/budget/fy2013/assets/hist.pdf.

12 "We thought of financial regulation": Blanchard, Dell'Ariccia, and Mauro, "Rethinking Macroeconomic Policy," 6.

14 The U.S. housing crash: Such estimates are rough and depend on timing, but $8 trillion is a decent ballpark number. Chris Isidore, http://money.cnn .com/2011/06/09/news/economy/household_wealth/.

14 More than ten million people: Armijo, "The Political Geography."

15 Unemployment tripled in Korea and quadrupled in Thailand: "Costing the Casino: A Survey of the Economic and Social Impact of Currency Crises on Developing Countries," 7, http://www.google.com/url?sa=t&rct=j&q=& esrc=s&source=web&cd=1&ved=0CCYQFjAA&url=http%3A%2F%2Fwww .waronwant.org%2Fabout-us%2Fpublications%2Fdoc_download%2F59 -costing-the-casino&ei=_cTrUuGTAdHKsQS4k4GADA&usg=AFQjCNGP 77Z3-a1mvau4LIX48RyWpkHDgA&bvm=bv.60444564,d.cWc.

15 Many orthodox economists noted: Chen and Ravallion, "More Relatively-Poor People."

17 "I want to point out a bias": Nelson, *Technology,* 232.

18 "Any point of view is interesting": Dickstein, "The Moment of the Novel," 89.

Chapter 1: The Beautiful Idea: The Invisible Hand

20 Since then, the incomes of the major rich nations: Angus Maddison remains the principal source of historical growth data. A good summary can be found at http://www.ggdc.net/maddison/oriindex.htm. See also Angus Maddison, *The World Economy* (Paris: OECD Publishing, 2003).

21 The slow expansion of prosperity: Fernand Braudel, *Civilization and Capitalism* (New York: Harper & Row, 1999), 54. The Stanford economic historian Nathan Rosenberg argues that both a large market and technological

"opportunity" are "each necessary, but not sufficient" (*Inside the Black Box* [Cambridge: Cambridge University Press, 1982], 231–32). For a more contemporary argument, see also Madrick, *Why Economies Grow.*

23 This was the cornerstone: Smith, *Wealth of Nations,* bk. 1, chap. 1.

24 Thomas Jefferson enthusiastically cited: Joyce Appleby, *Thomas Jefferson* (New York: Times Books, 2003), 97.

25 In his book on Ronald Reagan: Wilentz, *Age of Reagan.*

25 But the proposal, known as Proposition 1: Cannon, *Governor Reagan,* 378.

27 Yet a detailed report by the Rand Corporation: Christopher G. Pernin et al., *Unfolding the Future of the Long War: Motivations, Prospects, and Implications for the U.S. Army* (Santa Monica, Calif.: Rand Corporation, 2008).

31 The historian Emma Rothschild: Rothschild, *Economic Sentiments,* 192.

31 "Man has almost constant occasion": Smith, *Wealth of Nations,* 22.

32 Emma Rothschild, appropriately skeptical: Rothschild, *Economic Sentiments,* 122.

32 A rare readable rebuttal: Foley, *Adam's Fallacy.*

32 Foley is part of this tradition: Taylor, *Maynard's Revenge.*

34 "one man draws out": Smith, *Wealth of Nations,* 22.

35 When Ford started out: See generally Chandler, *Visible Hand.* See also Madrick, *Why Economies Grow.*

36 Smith knew this: Smith, *Wealth of Nations,* 26.

36 "By directing that industry": Ibid., 292.

36 The fact that Smith used the term: Ibid., 53.

37 "When the quantity of any commodity": Ibid., 54.

39 Léon Walras, the influential French economist: Léon Walras, *Elements of Pure Economics,* trans. William Jaffe (London: Allen and Unwin, 1954). Original publication 1878.

41 At the turn of the nineteenth century: Thomas C. Leonard, "'A Certain Rude Honesty': John Bates Clark as a Pioneering Neoclassical Economist," *History of Political Economy* 35, no. 3 (2003).

43 This conclusion, arrived at by economists: Schlefer, *Assumptions Economists Make,* 191.

Chapter 2: Say's Law and Austerity Economics

46 "If demand proves insufficient": Blaug, *Economic Theory in Retrospect,* 149.

46 "in the aggregate": Foley, *Adam's Fallacy,* 37.

47 As long as prices and wages: Blaug, *Economic Theory in Retrospect,* 151.

47 "Could the capitalist system": Ibid.

47 As Keynes put it: Keynes, *The End of Laissez-Faire,* 36.

47 "Liquidate labor, liquidate stocks": Herbert Hoover, *The Memoirs of Herbert Hoover*, vol. 3, *The Great Depression, 1929–1941* (New York: Macmillan, 1952).

48 "The implicit view behind standard models": For a general scathing critique of textbook economics, see David Colander et al., "Financial Crisis."

48 "It turns out that John McCain": Mulligan, "Economy," quoted in Schlefer, *Assumptions Economists Make*, 158.

49 "Products are paid for by products": quoted in Blaug, *Economic Theory in Retrospect*, 29.

50 An elaborate mathematical theory: See John Geanakoplos, "Arrow-Debreu Model of General Equilibrium," in *The New Palgrave: A Dictionary of Economics*, eds. John Eatwell, Murray Milgate, and Peter Newman (London: Macmillan, 1987), 116–24.

50 "Arrow devised his model": Conversation with the author, December 2013.

51 Duncan Foley called this general equilibrium model: Foley, *Adam's Fallacy*, 166.

51 The MIT-trained economics commentator: Schlefer, *Assumptions Economists Make*, 8–12, 192.

52 "Depressions cannot be permanent": Blaug, *Economic Theory in Retrospect*, 29.

54 The economist Stephen Marglin: Stephen A. Marglin, "Introduction: Resurrecting Keynes; The General Theory As It Might Have Been" (unpublished paper, 2011).

55 "It is important to say": Brad DeLong, "Macroeconomics in the Public Square," *Grasping Reality with Every Possible Tentacle* (blog), October 16, 2013, https://www.google.com/search?q=brad+de+long%2C+%E2%80%9CIt +is+important+to+say%2C+loudly%2C+that+Say%E2%80%99s +Law+is+not+true%2C&ie=utf-8&oe=utf-8&aq=t&rls=org.mozilla: en-US:official&client=firefox-a&channel=fflb. Blaug has a more extensive analysis of Say's own ambiguity on the matter (Blaug, *Economic Theory in Retrospect*).

57 "What I resisted in Keynes": quoted in David C. Colander and Harry Landreth, *History of Economic Thought* (Cheltenham, U.K.: Edward Elgar, 1996), 159–60.

58 Milton Friedman's rebellion against Keynes: For the most accessible analysis of his monetarism, defense of free markets, and causes of the Great Depression, see Friedman, *Capitalism and Freedom*.

60 Of course, the result was: Thomas J. Sargent, another Nobelist and rational expectationist, underestimated the depth of the 1981 recession. See how wrong he was in his "Stopping Moderate Inflation: The Methods of Poincaré and Thatcher" (working paper, Federal Reserve Bank of Minneapolis, 1981).

61 According to one economist: Schlefer, *Assumptions Economists Make,* 20.

62 These economists habitually ignored: A pioneer in exploring these ideas is Avner Offer of Oxford. See Offer, "Facing Future Adversity."

63 "On the right is the classical view": Mankiw, "Reincarnation of Keynesian Economics."

63 But to reemphasize, as Jonathan Schlefer observed: Schlefer, *Assumptions Economists Make,* 69.

63 Almost all textbooks: Mankiw, *Principles of Economics,* 276, quoted in Bofinger, "Teaching Macroeconomics," 24. For a thorough criticism of the plausibility of downward-sloping aggregate demand curves, see Colander, "Stories We Tell."

64 In March 2009, the supposedly nonpartisan: The author participated in this one-sided event; only a handful of Keynesian or even traditional economists were pitted against a couple of dozen economists of a new classical bent.

64 "Well I guess everyone is a Keynesian": Fox, "Bob Lucas."

65 "Keynesian fiscal stimulus advocates": See Cochrane, "Fiscal Stimulus."

66 There were lots of outspoken anti-Keynesians: Mankiw, "Stimulus Spending Skeptics"; http://www.bloomberg.com/apps/news?pid=newsarchive&sid=ajz1hV_afuSQ&refer=home; http://faculty.chicagobooth.edu/john.cochrane/research/papers/fiscal2.htm.

66 In a 2011 paper: Romer, "What Do We Know?"

68 A notable exception was: Blinder, *After the Music Stopped,* 345–47.

69 "So if we confront this crisis without": Remarks by the president and vice president at Opening of the Fiscal Responsibility Summit, February 23, 2009, http://www.whitehouse.gov/the-press-office/remarks-president-and-vice-president-opening-fiscal-responsibility-summit-2-23-09.

71 "This is Alesina's hour": Coy, "Keynes vs. Alesina."

72 In the fall of 2010, economists: "Will It Hurt? Macroeconomic Effects of Fiscal Consolidation," in International Monetary Fund, *World Economic Outlook* (October 2010). For a journalistic review, see *The Economist,* September 30, 2010. February 2012 analysis by VoxEU is fairly definitive; see Chowdhury, "Revisiting the Evidence."

73 The 90 percent threshold: "Debt Reduction Hawks and Doves," *Washington Post,* January 26, 2013, http://www.washingtonpost.com/opinions/debt-reduction-hawks-and-doves/2013/01/26/3089bd52-665a-11e2-93e1-475791032daf_story.html; John Nichols, "Paul Ryan's Austerity Agenda Relies on Bad Math, Coding Errors and a 'Significant Mistake,'" *Nation,* April 17, 2013, http://www.thenation.com/blog/173920/paul-ryans-austerity-agenda-relies-bad-math-coding-errors-and-significant-mistake#; Lyons, "George Osborne's."

73 No one could duplicate: Herndon, Ash, and Pollin, "Does High Public Debt?"

74 As the Fed cut its target interest rate: Gauti B. Eggertsson, "What Fiscal Policy Is Effective at Zero Interest Rates?" in *NBER Macroeconomics Annual 2010,* eds. Daron Acemoglu and Michael Woodford (Cambridge, Mass.: MIT Press, 2011), 59–112, http://www.nber.org/chapters/c1202.7.

74 Britain provided one of the clearest examples: For a good summary, see Altman, "Cameron's Leap."

75 None of this occurred: Milliken and Fincher, "UK Budget Deficit."

75 The *New Statesman* found: Eaton, "Exclusive."

76 "economics is a branch": Martin Wolf told New England National Public Radio; see http://www.nepr.net/news/eus-financial-crisis-doesnt-end-nations-borders.

77 In July 2013, the president finally told: Edsall, "On Second Thoughts."

78 "There has always been a purist streak": Solow, "State of Macroeconomics."

Chapter 3: Government's Limited Social Role: Friedman's Folly

81 Since the 1970s: Lane Kenworthy, "America's Struggling Lower Half" (Roosevelt Institute's Bernard L. Schwartz Rediscovering Government Initiative paper, June 21, 2012).

82 Leading new thinkers: Acemoglu and Robinson, *Why Nations Fail.*

82 "Economic institutions": Ibid., 74–75.

83 "Inclusive economic institutions": Ibid., 75–76.

85 "It is widely believed": Friedman, *Capitalism and Freedom,* 7.

85 "The kind of economic organization": Ibid., 9.

85 "The possibility of co-ordination": Ibid., 13.

86 "The great advances of civilization": Ibid., 3–4.

87 Almost all the science: Mazzucato, *Entrepreneurial State,* 64–66, 95–109.

89 In a 1995 interview: Doherty, "Best of Both Worlds."

89 "The closest approach that the United States": Burgin, *Great Persuasion,* 177.

90 Wages grew at about 1 percent: Williamson and Lindert, *American Inequality.*

91 There is a clear-cut natural example: Nancy L. Stokey and Sergio Rebelo, "Growth Effects of Flat-Rate Taxes," *Journal of Political Economy* 103, no. 3 (June 1993).

92 In one of his best-known short pieces: Milton Friedman, "The Methodology of Positive Economics," in Friedman, *Essays in Positive Economics.*

93 "Which if any of the great": Friedman, *Capitalism and Freedom,* 197.

93 "exceptions": Ibid., 199.

94 "Insofar as minimum wage laws": Ibid., 180.

94 "Derived from the assumption": Biewen and Weiser, "New Approach," 1.

95 In a piece she wrote: Romer, "Business of the Minimum Wage."

95 Recently, economists have been using: John Schmitt, "Why Does the Minimum Wage Have No Discernible Effect on Employment?" (Center for Economic and Policy Research, 2013), http://www.cepr.net/documents/publications/min-wage-2013-02.pdf.

96 "The appropriate recourse": Friedman, *Capitalism and Freedom,* 109–11.

96 Simply stated, there was no: See in general Bourgin, *Great Challenge.*

97 Scholars estimate that almost two-thirds: Allan Kulikoff, *The Agrarian Origins of American Capitalism* (Charlottesville: University of Virginia Press, 1992), 45.

98 By the 1820s, America was committing itself: Lindert, *Growing Public,* 1:88–89.

99 Even those skeptical of tariffs: Douglas A. Irwin, "Historical Aspects of U.S. Trade Policy," *NBER Reporter* (Summer 2006).

106 "In many ways Milton Friedman": Summers, "Commanding Heights."

107 "When government was smaller": *Economist,* "Great Innovation Debate," 24.

108 "Not only has government funded": Mazzucato, *Entrepreneurial State,* 62.

108 Seventy-seven of the eighty-eight: Ibid., 63.

108 An e-mail Lawrence Summers wrote: Roberta Rampton and Mark Hosenball, "In Solyndra Note, Summers Said Feds 'Crappy' Investor," Reuters, October 3, 2011, http://www.reuters.com/article/2011/10/03/us-solyndra-idUSTRE7925C520111003.

109 As Friedman wrote: Friedman, "What Every American Wants."

110 Frank Knight was the preeminent economist: Burgin, *Great Persuasion,* 190.

110 The conservative economist: Tyler Cowen, *The Great Stagnation: How America Ate All the Low-Hanging Fruit of Modern History, Got Sick, and Will (Eventually) Feel Better* (New York: Dutton, 2011).

113 "The fiercest contests": Keynes, *End of Laissez-Faire,* sec. 5.

113 "conceives of men": Friedman, *Capitalism and Freedom,* 12.

113 In the philosopher Isaiah Berlin's: Isaiah Berlin, "Two Concepts of Liberty" (lecture at Oxford, 1958). See Isaiah Berlin, *Liberty* (Oxford: Clarendon Press, 2004).

114 In the words of the philosopher: The book I found most influential: Amartya Sen, *Inequality Reexamined* (Cambridge, Mass.: Harvard University Press, 1992). Sen's occasional coauthor, Martha Nussbaum, should also be credited with contributing to these ideas.

Chapter 4: Low Inflation Is All That Matters

117 "Inflation targeting is the new orthodoxy": Epstein and Yeldan, *Beyond Inflation Targeting,* 3.

117 One of the leading advocates: Bernanke et al., *Inflation Targeting,* 3.

117 "[A] reason for setting price stability": Ibid., 16.

118 More than a little ironically: Ibid., 18.

118 Moderate levels of inflation: Ibid., 14.

118 Some economists make a strong case: George A. Akerlof, William T. Dickens, and George L. Perry, "The Macroeconomics of Low Inflation," *Brookings Papers on Economic Activity,* 1 (1996): 1–76.

118 As far back as 1988: Testimony before the Committee on Banking, Finance and Urban Affairs, U.S. House of Representatives, February 13, 1988.

118 In 1996, he told: Transcript of the Federal Open Market Committee meeting, July 2–3, 1996, http://www.stlouisfed.org/publications/cb /articles/?id=823#3.

119 In a late 2013 piece: Ben. S Bernanke, "A Century of U.S. Central Banking: Goals, Frameworks, Accountability," *Journal of Economic Perspectives* 27, no. 4 (Fall 2013): 3–16.

121 But as the economist John Schmitt: John Schmitt, "The Indispensability of Full Employment for Shared Prosperity," in *Restoring Shared Prosperity: A Policy Agenda from Leading Keynesian Economists,* eds. Thomas I. Palley and Gustav A. Horn (CreateSpace Independent Publishing Platform, 2013), 135–45.

121 "The rate of pay increase": Testimony of Chairman Alan Greenspan, the Federal Reserve's semiannual monetary policy report before the Committee on Banking, Housing, and Urban Affairs, U.S. Senate, February 26, 1997.

121 In a speech two years later: William Greider, *The Soul of Capitalism: Opening Paths to a Moral Economy* (New York: Simon & Schuster, 2003), 12.

123 But by the mid-1970s: Federal Reserve Bank of Boston, *The Impact of Inflation,* 1997.

124 "How do we know when": Alan Greenspan, "The Challenge of Central Banking in a Democratic Society," speech to the American Enterprise Institute for Public Policy Research, Washington, D.C., December 5, 1996.

125 Noting that, on balance, the rate: Glyn, *Capitalism Unleashed,* 149.

127 The economist Alan Blinder: Blinder, *Economic Policy.*

127 Volcker, unsympathetic to those: Martin Feldstein, "An Interview with Paul Volcker," *Journal of Economic Perspectives* 27, no. 4 (Fall 2013): 105–20.

129 "We don't have inflation": William Greider, *Secrets of the Temple: How the Federal Reserve Runs the Country* (New York: Simon & Schuster, 1987), 140.

130 Moreover, war spending deprived: Conversation with the author, November 2013.

130 Many progressives believe people: See, for example, Hacker and Pierson, *Winner-Take-All Politics.*

131 By 1983, even the French Socialist: Glyn, *Capitalism Unleashed,* 28.

132 One of Margaret Thatcher's actions: Ibid., 27–28.

133 "Milton Friedman revived the economics of liberty": George Jones, "Thatcher Praises Friedman, Her Freedom Fighter," *Telegraph,* Novem-

ber 17, 2006, http://www.telegraph.co.uk/news/uknews/1534387/Thatcher
-praises-Friedman-her-freedom-fighter.html.

136 "Contrary to what was believed": Bernanke et al., *Inflation Targeting*, 14.

136 The Nobelist George Akerlof: "The New Case for Keynesianism: Interview
with George Akerlof," *Challenge* 50, no. 4 (July–August 2007): 5–16.

137 Two Dutch economists: Storm and Naastepad, *Macroeconomics Beyond the
NAIRU*.

Chapter 5: There Are No Speculative Bubbles

139 "was a powerful idea": Justin Fox, *The Myth of the Rational Market: A History
of Risk, Reward, and Delusion on Wall Street* (New York: Harper Business,
2009), 4.

140 "What I added to the story": "Interview with Eugene Fama," Federal Reserve
Bank of Minneapolis, November 2, 2007, http://www.minneapolisfed.org
/publications_papers/pub_display.cfm?id=1134.

141 A highly influential book: Malkiel, *Random Walk*.

141 A first step in the new thinking: Markowitz, *Portfolio Selection*.

142 Paul Samuelson, the MIT economist: Ibid., 192.

143 "An 'efficient' market is defined": Eugene F. Fama, "Random Walks in Stock
Market Prices," *Financial Analysts Journal* 21, no. 5 (September–October
1965).

143 Adjusting for risk: It became known as the capital asset pricing model. William F. Sharpe, "Capital Asset Prices: A Theory of Market Equilibrium Under
Conditions of Risk," *Journal of Finance* 19, no. 3 (September 1964): 425–42.

146 "The word 'bubble'": "Interview with Eugene Fama."

146 "I don't even know": Binyamin Appelbaum, "Economists Clash on Theory,
but Will Still Share the Nobel," *New York Times*, October 14, 2013.

146 Friedman made his statement: Friedman, *Essays in Positive Economics*, 175.

148 The head of the Commodity Futures Trading Commission: Gensler was
careful to say he wanted not to eliminate speculation but to curb potential
excesses. Zachary A. Goldfarb, "Oil Speculation Limits Weighed," *Washington Post*, July 20, 2009.

148 "None of [the critics] seemed": Michael Lewis, "Davos Is for Wimps, Nin-
nies, Pointless Skeptics: Michael Lewis," Bloomberg News, January 30, 2007.

148 He wound up writing: Lewis, *Big Short*.

149 they wrote a book called: Thorp and Kassouf, *Beat the Market*.

149 The classic experiments: Daniel Kahneman, Jack L. Knetsch, and Richard H.
Thaler, "Anomalies: The Endowment Effect, Loss Aversion, and Status Quo
Bias," *Journal of Economic Perspectives* 5, no. 1 (Winter 1991): 193–206.

150 "There will always be new information": Justin Fox is generally excellent on
these issues. See Fox, *Myth*, chap. 6; Fama, "Random Walks," 76.

151 "By design, this market": Alan Greenspan, "Regulation, Innovation, and Wealth Creation" (speech to the Society of Business Economists, London, September 25, 2002).

153 In a seminal 1986 piece: Michael Jensen, "The Takeover Controversy: Analysis and Evidence," in *Knights, Raiders and Targets: The Impact of the Hostile Takeover,* ed. John Coffee and Susan Rose-Ackerman (New York: Oxford University Press, 1988).

155 "It is more likely than not": Sirower, *Synergy Trap;* Eileen Appelbaum and Rosemary Batt, "A Primer on Private Equity at Work," *Challenge* (September–October 2012): 5–38.

157 At the height of the bull market: Siegel, *Stocks.*

158 The scholar who toppled this theoretical house of cards: Shiller, *Irrational Exuberance.*

159 "I define a speculative bubble": Ibid., 2.

160 Reality quickly sank in: Morgenson and Gebeloff, "Wall St. Exploits."

160 Similarly, in the spring of 2013: Popper, "Price of Gold."

160 There was less and less doubt: Chilton, "Speculators."

161 One study of the subprime crisis: Ing-Haw Cheng, Sahil Raina, and Wei Xiong, "Wall Street and the Housing Bubble" (September 2013), http://www.google.com/url?sa=t&rct=j&q=&esrc=s&source=web&cd=2&ved=0CC4QFjAB&url=http%3A%2F%2Fwww.aeaweb.org%2Faea%2F2014conference%2Fprogram%2Fretrieve.php%3Fpdfid%3D586&ei=rNTnUozZNefPsASN2YGwAg&usg=AFQjCNH7tGUlFNSbkEIhdS7IN1-_lYQbvA&bvm=bv.59930103,d.cWc.

162 One final bit of evidence: Lucian Bebchuk and Jesse Fried, *Pay Without Performance: The Unfulfilled Promise of Executive Compensation* (Cambridge, Mass.: Harvard University Press, 2004).

Chapter 6: Globalization: Friedman's Folly Writ Large

165 "The principles of . . . 'macroeconomic stability, domestic liberalization, and openness'": *Annual Report 2005,* The World Bank, Washington, D.C., 11.

166 his 1999 book: Friedman, *Lexus.*

166 Friedman, in his best-selling: Friedman, *World Is Flat.*

167 Antiglobalization arguments were: Cited in Robert Hunter Wade, "Is Globalization Reducing Poverty and Inequality?" *World Development* 32, no. 4 (2004): 567–89.

167 "The laws of economics": Cited in Naomi Klein, *The Shock Doctrine: The Rise of Disaster Capitalism* (New York: Henry Holt, 2007), 275.

167 A widely read 1998 book: Yergin and Stanislaw, *Commanding Heights.*

167 Francis Fukuyama was one of the first: Francis Fukuyama, *The End of History and the Last Man* (New York: Free Press, 1992).

168 In most regions: Stiglitz, *Making Globalization Work,* 8.

172 But little attention has been paid: This is a major theme of chapter 4 of Rodrik, *Globalization Paradox.*

173 Income inequality in rich nations: David H. Autor, David Dorn, Gordon Hanson, and Jae Song, "Trade Adjustment: Worker Level Evidence" (June 2013), http://economics.mit.edu/files/8897.

175 "If a foreign country can supply": Smith, *Wealth of Nations,* 193.

175 About forty years later: Ricardo and Kolthammer, *Principles.*

175 N. Gregory Mankiw made a nice analogy: Mankiw, *Principles of Economics,* 54–55.

176 A lot of America's productivity growth: Wade, "Globalization, Poverty, and Inequality," 309–13.

177 Their theorem has been elaborated: Rodrik, "Stolper-Samuelson."

177 As Paul Krugman observed: See http://economistsview.typepad.com/econ omistsview/2007/04/on_the_other_ha.html.

180 Krugman, whose primary academic research: Ibid.

180 Economists also carelessly encouraged: Rodrik, *Globalization Paradox,* 296.

181 Thailand provided as clear and tragic: Ravenhill, *Global Political Economy,* 4–6.

182 "When countries on the periphery": Rodrik, *Globalization Paradox,* 5.

182 In fact, as Joseph Stiglitz pointed out: Joseph Stiglitz, "The Post Washington Consensus Consensus" (Initiative for Policy Dialogue, 2004), http://policydialogue.org/files/events/Stiglitz_Post_Washington_Consensus_Paper.pdf.

183 As he said in a speech: Williamson, "Washington Consensus."

184 Most of the poverty reduction: Chen and Ravallion, "Developing World."

184 Some scholars have thrown up their hands: William Easterly, *The Elusive Quest for Growth: Economists' Adventures and Misadventures in the Tropics* (Cambridge, Mass.: MIT Press, 2001). See also his later works.

187 The economist Robert Driskill comprehensively reviewed: Cited in Rodrik, *Globalization Paradox,* 52.

188 "There is no theoretical underpinning": Stiglitz, "Post Washington Consensus Consensus."

Chapter 7: Economics Is a Science

190 certain valuable research, as noted, has been entirely neglected: See http://www.debtdeflation.com/blogs/2010/05/14/revere-award-for-economics/.

191 He showed that some economists: See http://fivebooks.com/interviews/eric -maskin-on-economic-theory-and-financial-crisis.

191 Partly this is because: A very good set of examples about how seemingly good research is easily shown to be wrong can be found in chapter 10 of Lindert, *Growing Public.*

192 Although a young, provocative: Lawrence Summers, "The Scientific Illusion in Empirical Macroeconomics," *Scandinavian Journal of Economics* 93, no. 2 (June 1991): 129–48.

192 "Positive economists": Nicholson, *Microeconomic Theory*, 6, quoted in Schlefer, *Assumptions Economists Make*, 24.

192 Yet the conservative American economist: Anne O. Krueger, "Macroeconomic Situation and External Debt in Latin America" (remarks, February 1, 2006), https://www.imf.org/external/np/speeches/2006/020106.htm.

193 The philosopher Karl Popper: See Blaug's difficult, insightful, and controversial book *The Methodology of Economics; or, How Economists Explain* (Cambridge, U.K.: Cambridge University Press, 1980).

193 As he wrote of positive economics: Friedman, *Essays in Positive Economics*, 4.

194 His tome with Anna Schwartz: Milton Friedman and Anna Jacobson Schwartz, *A Monetary History of the United States, 1867–1960* (Princeton, N.J.: Princeton University Press, 1963).

194 "To me it seems strange": James Tobin, "The Monetary Interpretation of History," *American Economic Review* 55, no. 3 (June 1965): 464–85.

195 But he did not believe: Feldstein, "Interview with Paul Volcker."

195 In fact, the money supply rose rapidly: Milton Friedman, "The Yo-Yo Economy," *Newsweek*, February 15, 1982, http://0055d26.netsolhost.com /friedman/pdfs/newsweek/NW.02.15.1982.pdf. On the behavior of the money supply, see Robert L. Hetzel, "Monetary Policy in the Early 1980s" (working paper 84-1, Federal Reserve Bank of Richmond, May 1984), http:// www.richmondfed.org/publications/research/working_papers/1984/pdf /wp84-1.pdf.

195 Robert Lucas's assumption: For a summary of the predictive failures of Lucas's rational expectations theory, see http://www.huppi.com/kangaroo /L-chilucas.htm.

195 Thomas Sargent, who along with: Sargent, "Stopping Moderate Inflations."

195 "It forever sets you apart": Mankiw, "Politics Aside."

197 "I have always been impressed": Friedman and Friedman, *Two Lucky People*, 217–18.

197 "I internalized . . . [the] view": Lucas, Lecture at Trinity University Dublin. For a strong critique of economists' infatuation with and emulation of physics, see Mirowski, *More Heat Than Light*.

198 Minsky was decidedly nonmathematical: Minsky, *Stabilizing an Unstable Economy*.

199 "I know [Reinhart and Rogoff]": Erik Wasson, "Bowles Dismisses 'Flaws' in Favorite Debt Study," *On the Money* (blog), *Hill*, April 19, 2013, http:// thehill.com/blogs/on-the-money/budget/295017-bowles-dismisses-flaws-in -favorite-debt-study.

200 "So will toppling Reinhart-Rogoff": Paul Krugman, "The Excel Depression," *New York Times*, April 18, 2013.

200 "Why wouldn't we expect": Jared Bernstein, "The Reinhart/Rogoff Mistake and Economic Epistemology," *On the Economy: Jared Bernstein Blog,* April 18, 2013, http://jaredbernsteinblog.com/the-reinhartrogoff-mistake -and-economic-epistemology/.

200 "Let us celebrate rather than mourn": Adam Posen, "A Dose of Reality for the Dismal Science," *Financial Times,* April 19, 2013.

201 In his 2011 book: DeMartino, *The Economist's Oath.*

201 "There is a sense in which": Lawrence Boland, "Current Views on Economic Positivism," in *Companion to Contemporary Economic Thought* ed. Michael Bleaney et al. (New York: Taylor and Francis, 1992).

203 "Many people associate Samuelson": Edward L. Glaeser, "Remembering Samuelson, Who Forever Fused Economics with Math," *Economix* (blog), *New York Times,* December 14, 2009, http://economix.blogs.nytimes .com/2009/12/14/remembering-samuelson-who-fused-economics-with -math/.

203 there are no accepted statistical demonstrations: Lindert, *Growing Public;* Slemrod and Bakija, *Taxing Ourselves.*

204 "Not only do the theories ignore": Chang, "Institutions and Economic Development." *Why Nations Fail* had not yet been published. Chang partly based his comments on Daron Acemoglu, Simon Johnson, and James A. Robinson, "Institutions as the Fundamental Cause of Long-Run Growth," in *Handbook of Economic Growth,* vol. 1A eds. Philippe Aghion and Steven N. Durlauf (Amsterdam: Elsevier, 2005), 385–472.

207 "To my mind, the evidence": Raghuram G. Rajan, *Fault Lines* (Princeton, N.J.: Princeton University Press, 2010), 29.

208 "The rise and decline of unions": Goldin and Katz, "Future of Inequality."

208 But some orthodox economists: Card and DiNardo, "Skill-Biased Technological Change."

208 The gap in earnings between college and high school: https://chronicle.com /article/Earnings-Gap-Narrows-but/142175/

208 Economists at the Economic Policy Institute: Mishel et al., *State of Working America,* 211, 302; Howell and Wieler, "Skill-Biased Demand Shifts."

208 This "bumping down": Mishel et al., *State of Working America,* 303–5; Catherine Rampell, "It Takes a B.A. to Find a Job as a File Clerk," *New York Times,* February 19, 2013, http://www.nytimes.com/2013/02/20/business /college-degree-required-by-increasing-number-of-companies.html ?pagewanted=1&smid=tw-share.

209 Moreover, the top 0.1 percent: Piketty, *Capital in the Twenty-First Century,* 314.

209 Research carried out by: Mark Levitan, "The CEO Poverty Measure, 2005– 2011" (working paper, NYC Center for Economic Opportunity).

210 the many case studies undertaken: John Schmitt and David Rosnick, "The Wage and Employment Impact of Minimum-Wage Laws in Three Cities"

(CEPR Reports and Issue Briefs 2011–07, Center for Economic and Policy Research).

210 Amitai Etzioni, a self-described communitarian: Amitai Etzioni, "Crossing the Rubicon," *Challenge* 57, no. 2 (March–April 2013).

211 The accepted growth model: On Solow, Swan, and Abramovitz, see Francesco Caselli, "Palgrave Entry on 'Growth Accounting,'" http://personal.lse .ac.uk/casellif/papers/growthaccounting.pdf.

212 "To put it bluntly": Piketty, *Capital in the Twenty-First Century*, 32.

213 In his magnum opus: John Stuart Mill, *Principles of Political Economy* (Toronto: University of Toronto Press; London: Routledge and Kegan Paul, 1965), 232.

Bibliography

Acemoglu, Daron, Simon Johnson, and James A. Robinson. 2005. "The Rise of Europe: Atlantic Trade, Institutional Change, and Economic Growth." *American Economic Review* 95 (3): 546–79.

Acemoglu, Daron, and James A. Robinson. 2012. *Why Nations Fail: The Origins of Power, Prosperity, and Poverty.* New York: Crown Publishers.

Aghion, Philippe, and Steven N. Durlauf, eds. 2005. *Handbook of Economic Growth.* Amsterdam: Elsevier.

Akerlof, George A., and Paul M. Romer. 1993. "Looting: The Economic Underworld of Bankruptcy for Profit." *Brookings Papers on Economic Activity* 24 (2): 1–74.

Altman, Daniel. 2012. "Cameron's Leap Off the Fiscal Cliff." *Foreign Policy,* December 3. http://www.foreignpolicy.com/articles/2012/12/03/camerons_leap_off_the_fiscal_cliff.

Armijo, Leslie E. 2001. "The Political Geography of World Financial Reform: Who Wants What and Why?" *Global Governance* 7 (4): 379–96.

Bernanke, Ben S. 2007. "Global Imbalances: Recent Developments and Prospects." Board of Governors of the Federal Reserve System.

Bernanke, Ben S., and Mark Gertler. 1999. "Monetary Policy and Asset Price Volatility." Federal Reserve Bank of Kansas City, *Proceedings:* 77–128.

Bernanke, Ben S., Mark Gertler, and Simon Gilchrist. 1998. "The Financial Accelerator in a Quantitative Business Cycle Framework." C.V. Starr Center for Applied Economics, New York University.

Bernanke, Ben S., Thomas Laubach, Frederic S. Mishkin, and Adam S. Posen. 2001. *Inflation Targeting: Lessons from the International Experience.* Princeton, N.J.: Princeton University Press.

Besley, Tim. 2009. Letter to the Queen, July 22.

Biewen, Martin, and Constantin Weiser. 2011. "A New Approach to Testing Marginal Productivity Theory." IZA Discussion Paper 6113, Institute for the Study of Labor.

Bivens, Josh. 2013. "A Slight Bit of Substance on the Reinhart and Rogoff 90 Percent Debt Threshold." *Economic Policy Institute Blog*, April 17. http://www.epi.org/blog/slight-bit-substance-reinhart-rogoff-90/.

Bivens, Josh, and John Irons. 2010. "Government Debt and Economic Growth." Economic Policy Institute.

Blanchard, Olivier. 2009. "The State of Macro." *Annual Review of Economics* 1 (1): 209–28.

Blanchard, Olivier Jean, and Peter A. Diamond. 1991. "The Aggregate Matching Function." National Bureau of Economic Research.

Blaug, Mark. 1996. *Economic Theory in Retrospect*. 5th ed. Cambridge, U.K.: Cambridge University Press.

Blinder, Alan S. 1979. *Economic Policy and the Great Stagflation*. New York: Academic Press.

———. 2013. *After the Music Stopped: The Financial Crisis, the Response, and the Work Ahead*. New York: Penguin Press.

Blinder, Alan S., and Janet L. Yellen. 2001. *The Fabulous Decade: Macroeconomic Lessons from the 1990s*. New York: Century Foundation Press.

Bofinger, Peter. 2011. "Teaching Macroeconomics After the Crisis." Würzburg Economic Papers 86, University of Würzburg, Chair for Monetary Policy and International Economics.

Bourgin, Frank. 1989. *The Great Challenge: The Myth of Laissez-Faire in the Early Republic*. New York: G. Braziller.

Bowles, Samuel. 1973. "Hardly a Surprise," *Harvard Crimson,* February 27. http://www.thecrimson.com/article/1973/2/27/hardly-a-surprise-pbtbhe-decision-by/.

Brannon, Ike, and Chris Edwards. 2009. "Barak Obama's Keynesian Mistake." Cato Institute.

Buiter, Willem. 2009. "The Unfortunate Uselessness of Most 'State of the Art' Academic Monetary Economics." *Willem Buiter's Maverecon* (blog), *Financial Times,* March 3. http://blogs.ft.com/maverecon/2009/03/the-unfortunate-uselessness-of-most-state-of-the-art-academic-monetary-economics/#axzz2ukBmfcLQ.

Burgin, Angus. 2012. *The Great Persuasion: Reinventing Free Markets Since the Depression*. Cambridge, Mass.: Harvard University Press.

Cannon, Lou. 2003. *Governor Reagan: His Rise to Power*. New York: PublicAffairs.

Card, David, and John E. DiNardo. 2002. "Skill-Biased Technological Change and Rising Wage Inequality: Some Problems and Puzzles." *Journal of Labor Economics* 20 (4).

Carvalho, Laura de, Christian Proaño, and Lance Taylor. 2010. "Government Debt, Deficits, and Economic Growth: Lessons from Fiscal Arithmetic." Policy Note, Schwartz Center for Economic Policy Analysis, New School.

Chandler, Alfred D., Jr. 1977. *The Visible Hand: The Managerial Revolution in American Business*. Cambridge, Mass.: Belknap Press.

Chang, Ha-Joon. 2002. *Kicking Away the Ladder: Development Strategy in Historical Perspective*. London: Anthem.

———. 2011. "Institutions and Economic Development: Theory, Policy and History." *Journal of Institutional Economics* 7 (4): 473–98.

Chatelain, Jean-Bernard, and Kirsten Ralf. 1996. "The Failure of Financial Macroeconomics and What to Do About It." University Library of Munich, Germany.

Chen, Shaohua, and Martin Ravallion. 2008. "The Developing World Is Poorer Than We Thought, but No Less Successful in the Fight Against Poverty." Policy Research Working Paper 4703, World Bank Development Research Group, August 2008.

———. 2012. "More Relatively-Poor People in a Less Absolutely-Poor World." *Review of Income and Wealth* 59 (1): 1–28.

Chilton, Bart. 2012. "Speculators and Commodity Prices—Redux." U.S. Commodity Futures Trading Commission. http://www.cftc.gov/PressRoom /SpeechesTestimony/chiltonstatement022412.

Chowdhury, Anis. 2012. "Revisiting the Evidence on Expansionary Fiscal Austerity: Alesina's Hour?" VoxEU. http://www.voxeu.org/debates/commentaries /revisiting-evidence-expansionary-fiscal-austerity-alesina-s-hour.

Cipolla, Carlo M. 1994. *Before the Industrial Revolution: European Society and Economy, 1000–1700*. 3rd ed. New York: Norton.

Clark, John Bates. 1894. *The Philosophy of Wealth: Economic Principles Newly Formulated*. Boston: Ginn.

———. 1899. *The Distribution of Wealth: A Theory of Wages, Interest and Profits*. New York: Macmillan.

Cochrane, John H. 2009. "Fiscal Stimulus, Fiscal Inflation, or Fiscal Fallacies?" University of Chicago Booth School of Business. http://faculty.chicagobooth .edu/john.cochrane/research/papers/fiscal2.htm.

Colander, David. 1995. "The Stories We Tell: A Reconsideration of AS/AD Analysis." *Journal of Economic Perspectives* 9 (3): 169–88.

Colander, David, Hans Föllmer, Armin Haas, Michael Goldberg, Katarina Juselius, Alan Kirman, Thomas Lux, and Brigitte Sloth. 2009. "The Financial Crisis and the Systemic Failure of Academic Economics." Department of Economics, Middlebury College.

Cottarelli, Carlo, Paolo Mauro, Lorenzo Forni, and Jan Gottschalk. 2010. "Default in Today's Advanced Economies: Unnecessary, Undesirable, and Unlikely." International Monetary Fund.

Coy, Peter. 2010. "Keynes vs. Alesina. Alesina Who?" *Bloomberg Businessweek,* June 29. http://www.businessweek.com/stories/2010-06-29/keynes-vs-dot-alesina -dot-alesina-who.

Darby, Michael R., John Haltiwanger, and Mark Plant. 1984. "Unemployment-Rate Dynamics and Persistent Unemployment Under Rational Expectations." Department of Economics, UCLA.

Angus Deaton. 2013. *The Great Escape.* Princeton, N.J.: Princeton University Press.

DeLong, J. Bradford. 2000. "The Triumph of Monetarism?" *Journal of Economic Perspectives* 14 (1): 83–94.

DeMartino, George. 2011. *The Economist's Oath: On the Need for and Content of Professional Economic Ethics.* New York: Oxford University Press.

Dickstein, Morris. 2013. "The Moment of the Novel and the Rise of Film Culture." *Raritan* 33 (1): 86–103.

Doherty, Brian. 1995. "Best of Both Worlds." *Reason,* June. http://reason.com/archives/1995/06/01/best-of-both-worlds.

Donaldson, John B., Natalia Gershun, and Marc P. Giannoni. 2013. "Some Unpleasant General Equilibrium Implications of Executive Incentive Compensation Contracts." *Journal of Economic Theory* 148 (1): 31–63.

Driskill, Robert. 2007. "Deconstructing the Argument for Free Trade." http://www.vanderbilt.edu/econ/faculty/Driskill/DeconstructingfreetradeAug27a2007.pdf.

Dube, Arindrajit. 2013. "Guest Post: Reinhart/Rogoff and Growth in a Time Before Debt." *Next New Deal: The Blog of the Roosevelt Institute,* April 17. http://www.nextnewdeal.net/rortybomb/guest-post-reinhartrogoff-and-growth-time-debt.

Eaton, George. 2012. "Exclusive: Osborne's Supporters Turn on Him." *The Staggers* (blog), *New Statesman,* August 15. http://www.newstatesman.com/blogs/politics/2012/08/exclusive-osbornes-supporters-turn-him.

Economist. 2009. "The Other-Worldly Philosophers." July 16.

———. 2010. "Cutting Edge." September 30.

———. 2013. "The Great Innovation Debate." January 12.

Edsall, Thomas B. 2013. "On Second Thoughts." *Opinionator* (blog), *New York Times,* February 13. http://opinionator.blogs.nytimes.com/2013/02/13/on-second-thoughts/.

Eichengreen, Barry. 2008. "Origins and Responses to the Current Crisis." *CESifo Forum* 9 (4): 6–11.

Epstein, Gerald A., and A. Erinç Yeldan, eds. 2009. *Beyond Inflation Targeting: Assessing the Impacts and Policy Alternatives.* Cheltenham, U.K.: Edward Elgar.

Feld, Lars P. "Towards a New Monetary Constitution in Europe: The Proposal of the German Council of Economic Experts (GCEE)." Institute for New Economic Thinking.

Feldstein, Martin. 2008. "Did Wages Reflect Growth in Productivity?" Department of Economics, Harvard University.

Foley, Duncan K. 1975. "Problems vs. Conflicts: Economic Theory and Ideology." *American Economic Review* 65 (2): 231–36.

———. 2006. *Adam's Fallacy: A Guide to Economic Theology.* Cambridge, Mass.: Harvard University Press.

Follette, Glenn R., and Louise Sheiner. 2008. "An Examination of Health-Spending Growth in the United States: Past Trends and Future Prospects." Social Science Research Network.

Fox, Justin. 2008. "Bob Lucas on the Comeback of Keynesianism." *Time,* October 28. http://business.time.com/2008/10/28/bob-lucas-on-the-comeback-of-keynesianism/#ixzz2rQbbbM00.

Friedman, Milton. 1953. *Essays in Positive Economics.* Chicago: University of Chicago Press.

———. 1982. *Capitalism and Freedom.* Edited by Rose D. Friedman. Chicago: University of Chicago Press. First edition, 1962.

———. 2003. "What Every American Wants." *Wall Street Journal,* January 15.

Friedman, Milton, and Rose D. Friedman. 1998. *Two Lucky People: Memoirs.* Chicago: University of Chicago Press.

Friedman, Thomas L. 1999. *The Lexus and the Olive Tree.* New York: Farrar, Straus and Giroux.

———. 2005. *The World Is Flat: A Brief History of the Twenty-First Century.* New York: Farrar, Straus and Giroux.

Frijters, Paul, David Johnston, and Michael Shields. 2012. "The Optimality of Tax Transfers: What Does Life Satisfaction Data Tell Us?" *Journal of Happiness Studies* 13 (5): 821–32.

Frydman, Roman, and Michael D. Goldberg. 2007. *Imperfect Knowledge Economics: Exchange Rates and Risk.* Princeton, N.J.: Princeton University Press.

Fuchs, Victor R., Alan B. Krueger, and James M. Poterba. 1998. "Economists' Views About Parameters, Values, and Policies: Survey Results in Labor and Public Economics." *Journal of Economic Literature* 36 (3): 1387–425.

Geanakoplos, John. 2009. "The Leverage Cycle." Cowles Foundation for Research in Economics, Yale University.

Ghemawat, Pankaj. 2007. "Why the World Isn't Flat." *Foreign Policy* 159 (March–April): 54–60.

Glyn, Andrew. 2006. *Capitalism Unleashed: Finance, Globalization, and Welfare.* New York: Oxford University Press.

Goldin, Claudia, and Lawrence F. Katz. 2009. "The Future of Inequality: The Other Reason Education Matters So Much." *Milken Institute Review* (3rd quarter). http://www.milkeninstitute.org/publications/review/2009_7/26-33mr43.pdf.

Graeber, David. 2011. *Debt: The First 5,000 Years.* New York: Melville House.

Greenaway, David, Michael Bleaney, and Ian Stewart, eds. 1991. *Companion to Contemporary Economic Thought.* London: Routledge.

Greenspan, Alan. 1999. "The Interaction of Education and Economic Change." 81st Annual Meeting of the American Council on Education, Washington, D.C., February 16.

Hacker, Jacob S., and Paul Pierson. 2010. *Winner-Take-All Politics: How Washing-*

ton Made the Rich Richer—and Turned Its Back on the Middle Class. New York: Simon & Schuster.

Hargreaves, Steve. 2012. "Obama's Alternative Energy Bankruptcies." *CNNMoney,* October 22. http://money.cnn.com/2012/10/22/news/economy/obama-energy -bankruptcies/index.html.

Herndon, Thomas, Michael Ash, and Robert Pollin. 2013. "Does High Public Debt Consistently Stifle Economic Growth? A Critique of Reinhart and Rogoff." Working Paper, Political Economy Research Institute, University of Massachusetts Amherst. http://www.peri.umass.edu/236/hash/31e2ff374b6377b2 ddec04deaa6388b1/publication/566/.

Hirschman, Albert O. 1982. "Rival Interpretations of Market Society: Civilizing, Destructive, or Feeble?" *Journal of Economic Literature* 20 (4): 1463–84.

Howell, David R., and Susan S. Wieler. 1998. "Skill-Biased Demand Shifts and Wage Collapse in the United States: A Critical Perspective." *Eastern Economic Journal* 24 (3): 343–66.

International Monetary Fund. 2012. *The Liberalization and Management of Capital Flows: An Institutional View.*

Jones, George. 2006. "Thatcher Praises Friedman, Her Freedom Fighter." *Telegraph,* November 17.

Kansra, Nikita, and Sabrina A. Mohamed. 2012. "Krugman to Mankiw and Ferguson, Tsk! Tsk!" *Flyby* (blog), *Harvard Crimson,* August 19. http://www .thecrimson.com/article/2012/8/19/mankiw-romney-citation-paper/.

Kay, John. 2011. "Economics: Rituals of Rigour." *Financial Times,* August 25.

Keen, Steve. 2011. *Debunking Economics: The Naked Emperor Dethroned?* Rev. ed. London: Zed Books.

Keynes, John M. 1926. *The End of Laissez-Faire.* Reprint. New York: Prometheus Books, 2004.

Kohn, Meir. 2001. "The Expansion of Trade and the Transformation of Agriculture in Pre-industrial Europe." Dartmouth College, Hanover, N.H.

Konczal, Mike. 2013a. "It's Alberto Alesina's World and We're All Just Unemployed in It." *Next New Deal: The Blog of the Roosevelt Institute,* March 5. http://www .nextnewdeal.net/rortybomb/its-alberto-alesinas-world-and-were-all-just -unemployed-it.

———. 2013b. "Researchers Finally Replicated Reinhart-Rogoff, and There Are Serious Problems." *Next New Deal: The Blog of the Roosevelt Institute,* April 16. http://www.nextnewdeal.net/rortybomb/researchers-finally-replicated- reinhart-rogoff-and-there-are-serious-problems.

Kregel, Jan. 2008. "Financial Flows and International Imbalances—the Role of Catching-up by Late Industrializing Developing Countries." Levy Economics Institute.

Krugman, Paul. 2009. "A Dark Age of Macroeconomics (Wonkish)." *New York Times,* January 27.

———. 2013a. "The Excel Depression." *New York Times,* April 18.

———. 2013b. "Rich Man's Recovery." *New York Times,* September 12.

Landes, David S. 2003. *The Unbound Prometheus: Technological Change and Industrial Development in Western Europe from 1750 to the Present.* Cambridge, U.K.: Cambridge University Press.

Landreth, Harry, and David C. Colander. 1994. *History of Economic Thought.* 3rd ed. Boston: Houghton Mifflin.

Ledwith, Sara, and Antonella Ciancio. 2012. "Special Report: Euro Zone Crisis Forces 'Dismal Science' to Get Real." Reuters, July 3.

Leijonhufvud, Axel. 1973. "Life Among the Econ." *Economic Inquiry* 11 (3): 327–37.

———. 2008. "Keynes and the Crisis." Centre for Economic Policy Research.

———. 2009. "Out of the Corridor: Keynes and the Crisis." *Cambridge Journal of Economics* 33 (4): 741–57.

Lewis, Harry. 2013. "Richwine and the FAS Hegemony over the PhD." *Bits and Pieces* (blog), May 20. http://harry-lewis.blogspot.com/2013/05/richwine -and-fas-hegemony-over-phd.html.

Lewis, Michael. 2010. *The Big Short: Inside the Doomsday Machine.* New York: Norton.

Lindert, Peter H. 2004. *Growing Public: Social Spending and Economic Growth Since the Eighteenth Century.* 2 vols. Cambridge, U.K.: Cambridge University Press.

Lindert, Peter H., and Jeffrey G. Williamson. 2001. "Does Globalization Make the World More Unequal?" NBER Working Paper 8228.

Lucas, Robert E., Jr. 1980. "Rules, Discretion, and the Role of the Economic Advisor." National Bureau of Economic Research.

———. 2002. *Lectures on Economic Growth.* Cambridge, Mass.: Harvard University Press.

———. 2011. Lecture at Trinity University, Dublin, Ireland.

Lyons, James. 2013. "George Osborne's Favourite 'Godfathers of Austerity' Economists Admit to Making Error in Research." *Mirror,* April 17. http://www.mirror.co.uk/news/uk-news/george-osbornes-favourite-economists -reinhart-1838219.

Madrick, Jeff. 2002. *Why Economies Grow: The Forces That Shape Prosperity and How to Get Them Working Again.* New York: Basic Books.

———. 2011. *Age of Greed: The Triumph of Finance and the Decline of America, 1970 to the Present.* New York: Knopf.

Malkiel, Burton Gordon. 1973. *A Random Walk Down Wall Street.* New York: Norton.

Mandel, Michael J. 1998. "The Zero Inflation Economy." *BusinessWeek,* January 19.

Mankiw, N. Gregory. 1991. "A Quick Refresher Course in Macroeconomics." National Bureau of Economic Research.

————. 1992. "The Reincarnation of Keynesian Economics." National Bureau of Economic Research.

————. 2004. *Principles of Economics.* 3rd ed. Mason, Ohio: Thomson / South-Western.

————. 2006. "The Macroeconomist as Scientist and Engineer." Cambridge, Mass.: Harvard Institute of Economic Research.

————. 2008. "Stimulus Spending Skeptics." *Greg Mankiw's Blog: Random Observations for Students of Economics,* December 18. http://gregmankiw.blogspot.com/2008/12/stimulus-spending-skeptics.html.

————. 2013. "Politics Aside, a Common Bond for Two Economists." *New York Times,* June 29.

Mankiw, N. Gregory, and Mark P. Taylor. 2010. *Economics.* Cengage Learning EMEA.

Markowitz, Harry M. 1991. *Portfolio Selection: Efficient Diversification of Investments.* 2nd ed. Cambridge, Mass.: B. Blackwell.

Mason, Will E. 1956. "The Stereotypes of Classical Transfer Theory." *Journal of Political Economy* 64.

Mayer, Thomas. 2001. "The Role of Ideology in Disagreements Among Economists: A Quantitative Analysis." *Journal of Economic Methodology* 8 (2): 253–73.

Mazzucato, Mariana. 2013. *The Entrepreneurial State: Debunking Public vs. Private Sector Myths.* London: Anthem.

McCallum, Bennett T. 1984. "Macroeconomics After a Decade of Rational Expectations: Some Critical Issues." National Bureau of Economic Research.

McKinnon, Ronald I. 2010. "Why Exchange Rate Changes Will Not Correct Global Trade Imbalances." SIEPR Policy Brief, Stanford University.

Merton, Robert C. 1977. "On the Cost of Deposit Insurance When There Are Surveillance Costs." Sloan School of Management, MIT.

Milliken, David, and Christina Fincher. 2013. "UK Budget Deficit Barely Falls in 2012/13, More Pain Ahead." Reuters, April 23. http://uk.reuters.com/article/2013/04/23/uk-britain-borrowing-idUKBRE93M09020130423.

Minsky, Hyman P. 1986. *Stabilizing an Unstable Economy.* New Haven, Conn.: Yale University Press.

Mirowski, Philip. 1989. *More Heat Than Light: Economics as Social Physics, Physics as Nature's Economics.* Cambridge, U.K.: Cambridge University Press.

Mishel, Lawrence, Josh Bivens, Elise Gould, and Heidi Shierholz. 2012. *The State of Working America.* 12th ed. Ithaca, N.Y.: Cornell University Press.

Morgenson, Gretchen, and Robert Gebeloff. 2013. "Wall St. Exploits Ethanol Credits, and Prices Spike." *New York Times,* September 14. http://www.nytimes.com/2013/09/15/business/wall-st-exploits-ethanol-credits-and-prices-spike.html.

Moss, David A. 2009. "An Ounce of Prevention: Financial Regulation, Moral Hazard, and the End of 'Too Big to Fail.'" *Harvard Magazine,* January–February.

Mulligan, Casey B. 2008. "An Economy You Can Bank On." *New York Times,* October 9.

Nelson, Richard R. 2006. *Technology, Institutions, and Economic Growth.* Cambridge, Mass.: Harvard University Press.

Nicholson, Walter. 1972. *Microeconomic Theory: Basic Principles and Extensions.* Hinsdale, Ill.: Dryden Press.

Offer, Avner. 2013. "Facing Future Adversity." *Challenge* 56 (4): 38–50. doi: 10.2753/0577-5132560404.

Orlowski, Lucjan T. 2000. "Ben S. Bernanke, Thomas Laubach, Frederic S. Mishkin, and Adam S. Posen, Inflation Targeting: Lessons from the International Experience." *Journal of Comparative Economics* 28 (2): 422–25.

Papadimitriou, Dimitri B., L. Randall Wray, and Yeva Nersisyan. 2010. "Endgame for the Euro? Without Major Restructuring, the Eurozone Is Doomed." Levy Economics Institute.

Pierce, Andrew. 2008. "The Queen Asks Why No One Saw the Credit Crunch Coming." *Telegraph,* November 5.

Piketty, Thomas. 2014. *Capital in the Twenty-First Century.* Cambridge, Mass.: Harvard University Press.

Pilkington, Philip, and Warren Mosler. 2012. "Tax-Backed Bonds—a National Solution to the European Debt Crisis." Levy Economics Institute.

Popper, Nathaniel. 2013. "Price of Gold Takes a Flashy Fall; Other Markets Follow." *DealBook* (blog), *New York Times,* April 15. http://dealbook.nytimes .com/2013/04/15/golds-plunge-shakes-confidence-in-a-haven/?_r=0.

Rampell, Catherine. 2013. "Yes, Even Young College Graduates Have Low Unemployment." *Economix* (blog), *New York Times,* March 5. http://economix .blogs.nytimes.com/2013/03/05/yes-even-young-college-graduates-have-low -unemployment/.

Ravenhill, John, ed. 2005. *Global Political Economy.* New York: Oxford University Press.

Reinert, Erik S. 2007. *Globalization, Economic Development and Inequality: An Alternative Perspective.* Cheltenham, U.K.: Edward Elgar.

Reinhart, Carmen M., and Kenneth S. Rogoff. 2008. "This Time Is Different: A Panoramic View of Eight Centuries of Financial Crises." National Bureau of Economic Research.

———. 2009. *This Time Is Different: Eight Centuries of Financial Folly.* Princeton, N.J.: Princeton University Press.

———. 2010. "Growth in a Time of Debt." NBER Working Paper 15639.

Ricardo, David, and F. W. Kolthammer. 1817. *The Principles of Political Economy and Taxation.* Reprint. Mineola, N.Y.: Dover Publications, 2004.

Ritholtz, Barry. 2013. "Did Greenspan Steal the Phrase 'Irrational Exuberance'?" *The Big Picture* (blog), January 28. http://www.ritholtz.com/blog/2013/01 /did-greenspan-steal-the-phrase-irrational-exuberance/.

Rodrik, Dani. 2008a. "Goodbye Washington Consensus, Hello Washington Confusion? A Review of the World Bank's Economic Growth in the 1990s: Learning from a Decade of Reform." *Panoeconomicus* 55 (2): 135–56.

———. 2008b. "Stolper-Samuelson for the Real World." *Dani Rodrik's Weblog: Unconventional Thoughts on Economic Development and Globalization,* June 16. http://rodrik.typepad.com/dani_rodriks_weblog/2008/06/stolper -samuelson-for-the-real-world.html.

———. 2011. *The Globalization Paradox: Democracy and the Future of the World Economy.* New York: Norton.

Romer, Christina D. 2011. "What Do We Know About the Effects of Fiscal Policy? Separating Evidence from Ideology." Speech at Hamilton College, November 7. http://elsa.berkeley.edu/~cromer/Written%20Version%20of%20Effects %20of%20Fiscal%20Policy.pdf.

———. 2013. "The Business of the Minimum Wage." *New York Times,* March 2.

Romer, David. 2000. "Keynesian Macroeconomics Without the LM Curve." National Bureau of Economic Research.

———. 2012. *Advanced Macroeconomics.* 4th ed. New York: McGraw-Hill / Irwin.

Ross, Don. 2010. "Should the Financial Crisis Inspire Normative Revision?" *Journal of Economic Methodolgy* 17 (4): 399–418.

Rothschild, Emma. 2001. *Economic Sentiments: Adam Smith, Condorcet, and the Enlightenment.* Cambridge, Mass.: Harvard University Press.

Sargent, Thomas J. 1981. "Stopping Moderate Inflations: The Methods of Poincaré and Thatcher." Federal Reserve Bank of Minneapolis.

Schadler, Susan. 2012. "Sovereign Debtors in Distress: Are Our Institutions Up to the Challenge?" CIGI Papers, Institute for New Economic Thinking.

Schlefer, Jonathan. 2012. *The Assumptions Economists Make.* Cambridge, Mass.: Belknap Press.

Schumpeter, Joseph A. 1955. "Economic Possibilities in the United States." In *Readings in Fiscal Policy,* edited by Andrew Smithies and Keith Butters. London: Richard D. Irwin.

Setser, Brad. 2010. "The Political Economy of the SDRM." In *Overcoming Developing Country Debt Crises,* edited by Barry Herman, José Antonio Ocampo, and Shari Spiegel. New York: Oxford University Press.

Shaikh, Anwar M., and Rania Antonopoulos. 1998. "Explaining Long-Term Exchange Rate Behavior in the United States and Japan." Levy Economics Institute.

Shiller, Robert J. 2005. *Irrational Exuberance.* 2nd ed. Princeton, N.J.: Princeton University Press.

Siegel, Jeremy J. 1994. *Stocks for the Long Run: A Guide to Selecting Markets for Long-Term Growth.* Burr Ridge, Ill.: Irwin.

Sirower, Mark L. 2000. *The Synergy Trap: How Companies Lose the Acquisition Game.* New York: Free Press.

Slemrod, Joel, and Jon Bakija. 2000. *Taxing Ourselves: A Citizen's Guide to the Great Debate Over Tax Reform.* 2nd ed. Cambridge, Mass.: MIT Press.

Smith, Adam. 1993. *An Inquiry into the Nature and Causes of the Wealth of Nations.* New York: Oxford University Press.

Solow, Robert. 2008. "The State of Macroeconomics." *Journal of Economic Perspectives* 22 (1): 243–46.

Staley, Oliver, and Michael McKee. 2009. "Yale's Tobin Guides Obama from Grave as Friedman Is Eclipsed." Bloomberg News, February 27.

Stevenson, Betsey, and Justin Wolfers. 2013. "Refereeing Reinhart-Rogoff Debate." Bloomberg News, April 28.

Stiglitz, Joseph E. 2007. *Making Globalization Work.* New York: Norton.

———. 2010. *The Stiglitz Report: Reforming the International Monetary and Financial Systems in the Wake of the Global Crisis.* New York: New Press.

Storm, Servaas, and C. W. M. Naastepad. 2012. *Macroeconomics Beyond the NAIRU.* Cambridge, Mass.: Harvard University Press.

Summers, Lawrence. 2001. "Commanding Heights" PBS interview, April 24. http://www.pbs.org/wgbh/commandingheights/shared/minitext/int_lawrence summers.html.

———. 2002. "Panelist: International Finance and Crises in Emerging Markets." In *American Economic Policy in the 1990s,* edited by Jeffrey Frankel and Peter Orszag. Cambridge, Mass.: MIT Press.

———. 2009. "Larry Summers on Push for Economic Stimulus Package." Interview by Stuart Varney. *Your World with Neil Cavuto,* Fox News, February 9.

Svensson, Lars E. O. 2002. "What Is Wrong with Taylor Rules? Using Judgment in Monetary Policy Through Targeting Rules." NBER Working Paper 9421.

Taylor, Lance. 2011. *Maynard's Revenge: The Collapse of Free Market Macroeconomics.* Cambridge, Mass.: Harvard University Press.

Taylor, Lance, Christian Proaño, Laura de Carvalho, and Nelson Barbosa. 2012. "Fiscal Deficits, Economic Growth and Government Debt in the USA." *Cambridge Journal of Economics* 36 (1): 189–204.

Thorp, Edward O., and Sheen T. Kassouf. 1967. *Beat the Market: A Scientific Stock Market System.* New York: Random House.

Varoufakis, Yanis, and Stuart Holland. 2011. "A Modest Proposal for Overcoming the Euro Crisis." Levy Economics Institute.

Wade, Robert Hunter. 2005. "Globalization, Poverty, and Inequality." In *Global Political Economy,* ed. John Ravenhill. New York: Oxford University Press.

Wall Street Journal. 2013. "Government Is a Good Venture Capitalist." August 27.

Wilentz, Sean. 2008. *The Age of Reagan: A History, 1974–2008.* New York: Harper.

Williamson, Jeffrey G., and Peter H. Lindert. 1980. *American Inequality: A Macroeconomic History.* New York: Academic Press.

Williamson, John. 2002. "Did the Washington Consensus Fail?" Outline of speech at the Center for Strategic and International Studies, Washington, D.C., November 6.

Wray, L. Randall. 2013. "FED Minutes Reveal FOMC Was Clueless as Economy Crashed in 2007." *EconoMonitor,* January 18.

Yergin, Daniel, and Joseph Stanislaw. 1998. *The Commanding Heights: The Battle for the World Economy.* Rev. ed. New York: Simon & Schuster, 2002.

Zettelmeyer, Jeromin, and Kenneth Rogoff. 2002. "Bankruptcy Procedures for Sovereigns: A History of Ideas, 1976–2001." International Monetary Fund.

Index